WITHOUT RESERVE

Also by Richard Harton:

UNDER THE HAMMER
AN AUCTIONEER'S LOT

Without Reserve

Richard Harton

St. Martin's Press
New York

Library of Congress Cataloging-in-Publication Data

Harton, Richard.
Without reserve / Richard Harton.
p.   cm.
ISBN 0-312-09939-8
1. Harton, Richard.   2. Antique dealers—England—Biography.   I. Title.
NK1133.26.H37A3   1993
381′.17′092—dc20
[B]   93-26914   CIP

First published in Great Britain by Little, Brown and Company.

First U.S. Edition: January 1994
10 9 8 7 6 5 4 3 2 1

*For Laura, who always enjoys
seeing her name in print.*

Chapter 1

I raised the hammer and held it there for a second or two in the hope that somebody else would make just one more bid.

'. . . All finished at five thousand, five hundred pounds . . .?' I asked, scanning the sea of faces in the packed saleroom.

It was no good – nobody spoke. There were no discreet movements of catalogues, no subtle nods, no sly winks, no noses being scratched. The room seemed to be holding its breath and everyone in it was statue-still. It was clear that the slightly-built man at the back of the room was about to become the owner of Lot 132.

'Sold, then,' I said, bringing down the hammer, 'at five thousand, five hundred pounds to . . .'

He was a regular buyer at Hampson's good furniture sales. He paid top prices for the pieces he wanted, and he settled his accounts on the dot.

'. . . er . . .'

In short, he was an ideal buyer. Or at least he would have been but for the two complications which accompanied any purchase he made. The first was that for some inexplicable reason I could never remember his name. The second was that he had a pronounced speech hesitation; an impediment which reached near-paralytic proportions whenever he was required to give his name in front of a saleroom full of people. And here I was about to put him through the ordeal yet again.

1

'. . . to Mr . . . er . . .'

My voice tapered away to nothing as I scribbled the price in the Auctioneer's Book. I looked down at my clerk, seated beside the rostrum.

'I've forgotten his name again,' I whispered.

'Whose?'

'At the back . . .' I hissed, without looking up, '. . . medium height, slim, grey hair . . .'

She craned her neck as she surveyed the phalanx of dealers at the far end of the room.

'. . . the one with the stutter,' I continued.

'Oh, Mr Bilston!' she said.

'That's it – Bilston! Well done!' I murmured gratefully, once again sitting up in the rostrum and facing the crowd. It was not a moment too soon either, for poor Mr Bilston's face was already beginning that series of contortions which normally preceded the faltering delivery of the first syllable of his surname.

'Five thousand, five hundred pounds . . .' I repeated, '. . . Bilston.'

As I announced the buyer's name, I watched for his tortured expression to melt into the look of relief I recalled from the only other occasion on which I had managed to get his name right. But it did no such thing. Instead, it became even more agonised.

'Na . . . na . . . na . . . na . . .' he struggled.

I was helpless. It was pointless trying to anticipate what he was trying to say since his initial stammerings frequently bore no resemblance to the target word.

'. . . No! . . .' He succeeded in forming the adverb quite suddenly. 'It's . . . it's . . . it's . . .'

The whole room was hushed again, the tension almost palpable.

'. . . it's . . . Wah . . . Wah . . . Wah . . . Wah . . .'

The antiques trade has the reputation of being traditionally ruthless and hard-hearted, but I don't

2

believe there was a single person in the saleroom that afternoon who was not willing Mr Bilston to articulate whatever it was he was trying to say.

'. . . Wah . . . Wah . . .' he went on, then, with what appeared to be a superhuman effort, he spat out the single word he had been striving for: 'Woodford!'

So that was it. He had been bidding on behalf of his near neighbours in the Cotswolds – Woodford Antiques.

'Thank you, Mr Bilston,' I said, correcting the entry in my book as the saleroom once again began to hum with a low murmur of conversation.

As Mr Bilston smiled pleasantly and returned to studying his catalogue, it struck me, not for the first time, that his affliction seemed to have a more debilitating effect on those around him than it did on the man himself. It certainly took me longer to recover than it appeared to take him.

Shortly after bringing down the hammer on the last lot of the sale, I clambered out of the rostrum and made my way upstairs to the Chairman's office. His secretary had delivered a note to me while I was taking the furniture auction. It had obviously been hastily scrawled by the man himself and was characteristically direct – 'Richard – See me asap – Bob.'

I knocked on his door and entered. He was busily stuffing files into an already bulging briefcase.

'Ah, Richard! Good sale?'

'Yes, it seemed to go very well,' I said. 'I'm not sure of the total but there was very little unsold.'

'Good, good,' he said, clearly preoccupied with his hurried packing. 'I'm sure it will be fine. Are you doing anything this weekend?'

'I don't think there's anything planned. Sarah and I were . . .'

'Good – I need you to go to Wales.'

'Wales? Why?'

'To make a valuation for the Honourable Diana Pickering. Do you know of her?'

'No, should I?'

'Not unless you're a student of the turf I suppose. Her father was a great bloodstock man and Diana's pretty horsey herself.'

'What's the valuation for?' I asked.

'She's trying to break her father's family trust. It's a bit complicated but you'll find it all in there,' he said, handing me a fat grey file. 'I've been messing about with it for years on and off but it looks as though the lawyers are actually going to do something about it at last.'

I opened the file and glanced at it. 'When's she expecting me?' I asked.

'Mid-afternoon on Saturday. The valuation shouldn't take you long – there's only about a dozen or so pieces.'

'So I'll be back by late Saturday night?'

'Not exactly.' He stopped struggling with the catch of his briefcase for a moment, looked up and smiled. 'You're booked in to stay at the house on Saturday. It's a social occasion as well as business. You're there for a full-blooded country weekend, old chap – best of luck!'

'Just a minute, Bob,' I said. 'How come you're not able to go? I take it it was originally in your diary.'

'Hah! Done it!' he said, eventually doing up the catch. 'Sorry, what did you say, Richard?'

'I said: how come I'm going, not you?'

'Oh, I'm afraid something's cropped up. Anyway, valuations are your field, Richard. Aren't they?'

I gave him a long, hostile look and turned to go.

'Oh, by the way, Richard. You can assure Sarah that you won't be led astray by Diana.'

'Why's that?'

'She'll be eighty next year.'

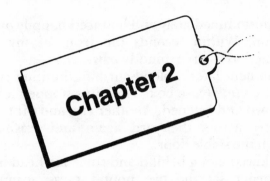

Chapter 2

The Honourable Diana Pickering's home, Hillsley House, stood in open country not far from Abergavenny. A substantial, square, stone building, it glowered down from a gently sloping hillside, with the distant Black Mountains as its backdrop. The narrow, pot-holed driveway snaked up the hill to a wide, flat area of weed-strewn gravel in front of the house.

A steady drizzle had been falling for some time, and every now and then it was turned into a fine, horizontal spray by the gusting west wind. The sky was leaden with rain yet to come and the faraway peaks were lost in a tumbling blanket of low cloud.

'Just the weather for a full-blooded country week-end,' I muttered as I dragged my overnight bag and briefcase from the car. A fresh squall swirled about me as I hurried over to the front door. I pulled vigorously at the old bell and waited. Several pulls later I was still waiting and still getting wet, so I decided to set off in search of my quarry.

Behind the house I discovered a sizable stable block which formed three sides of a courtyard. Most of the old buildings appeared to have been divided into loose boxes but there was a feeling of decay about the place. I was taking in the silent, deserted scene when, suddenly, the door of one of the boxes on the far side of the courtyard crashed open and a pair of young, gangling hound pups tumbled out onto the concrete. They saw me almost immediately and bounced happily over in my direction. Within seconds the front of my suit was imprinted with large, muddy paw-marks.

A moment later a blood-curdling hunting cry issued from the same loose box. The pups stopped leaping up and down and listened. Another cry, and off they went, plunging across the yard again and crashing back through the stable door.

I followed along behind and stuck my head inside. In one corner sat the two hound pups, grinning like lunatics, while in another, with her back to me, a figure was stooped, shaking out a bale of straw with a pitchfork.

'Excuse me – Miss Pickering?' I asked.

'Hold on – be with you in a minute,' the figure replied, without looking up. She distributed the last clinging lumps of straw, then pitchfork in hand she turned and advanced across the box.

She was a striking figure. Bedecked in an elderly blue spider's web of a sweater, old-fashioned baggy jodhpurs and elastic-sided boots, she looked like a superannuated stable lad. Her hair was pure white and hung down like a curtain, straight and thin, around her bony skull, framing a leathery, weather-beaten face. She smiled as she approached, revealing a row of rather uneven and slightly yellow teeth punctuated top and bottom by a couple of gaps. To complete the impression of dusty decrepitude she sported a pair of National Health spectacles with round, owl-like lenses held together across the bridge of the nose with a dirty piece of sticking plaster.

'You must be Mr Harton,' she said, clutching hold of my hand with an iron-hard grip as she proceeded to work it like a village pump. 'Good to meet you. Good journey?'

'Not bad at all,' I replied.

Behind the round lenses, a strangely youthful and

intense pair of blue eyes examined me in minute detail. I felt as though I was being X-rayed.

'Good, let's go inside – you could probably do with a cup of tea,' she said, leading the way out into the yard.

'Yes, I . . .'

'No! Stay!' she commanded suddenly, without looking back.

I froze in the doorway for a moment before realising the instructions were directed at the hound pups who had just made moves to follow us. Instantly cowed, they both dropped back into the straw in the corner of the box.

'Close the door, please, Mr Harton,' my client called as she strode across the wet concrete, rocking slightly on her bandy pins, 'otherwise they'll be in the kitchen before we are.'

I slid the bolt on the door and hurried to catch up with her.

'Are you walking the pups for the local hunt?' I asked, keen to demonstrate that I had some knowledge of field sports.

'No – they belong to the Flaxton, over near Gloucester – d'you know it?'

It had long been my practice to try to put clients at ease by giving the impression that I shared an interest in any pet subject or hobby they might touch on. It was just a fairly simple way of establishing a basic level of trust. Usually my input needed to be nothing more than a professional observation on a collection of pictures or porcelain, perhaps. But sometimes I ventured outside my own natural domain. Occasionally it was a comment on a garden shrub, an unusual bird on the bird table, or even, in one case, an appreciation of a large lop-eared rabbit. All I had to do was prime the conversation: 'Oh, isn't that a . . .' or, 'I say, what a wonderful . . .' and the client would do the rest. From then on I just needed to insert the occasional 'yes' and 'no' and 'mmm' at roughly

7

the right points. Over the years I had developed the ability to do that on automatic pilot. This somewhat blasé attitude was to prove near fatal with the Honourable Diana Pickering.

'Oh, I know of it,' I said, in answer to her question. 'I understand it has very good country.'

'Not bad. Certainly the best within striking distance of here.'

'Mmmm,' I replied.

'D'you hunt, Mr Harton?'

'Unfortunately not,' I said. 'The time . . . the expense . . . you know . . .'

'Yes, I know how it is. Mind you, it's a shame you couldn't have travelled down last night. Then you could have come out as my guest today – I'm sure you would have enjoyed it.'

'Yes,' I said.

'I usually go out twice a week, but I passed up today so that I'd be here to meet you.'

'Oh, what a pity – if only I'd known,' I murmured as she opened the back door into the scullery-cum-boot-room.

'Never mind. There'll be plenty of time for a good ride tomorrow morning. You can take out Dancer. He needs an airing.'

I didn't react immediately to what she had said because no sooner had she opened the door than I was engulfed in a pungent cocktail of smells. The aroma of leather, rubber boots and wet dogs rolled out of the scullery and over me in an asphyxiating miasma.

'What?' I eventually spluttered, automatic pilot off and back on manual control.

'Dancer,' she repeated. 'He's a super grey I bought for nothing last year. He's got a mind of his own but he's as sure-footed a jumper as I've ever had.'

'Really?' I replied, weakly.

'Yes – he'll give you a good run for your money, and

it'll do him good to have a man up for a change. He's inclined to be a bit of a bully with me.'

My heart sank. Cold, clammy perspiration bedewed the palms of my hands. I was in trouble – big trouble.

'Unfortunately, I fear I'll have to get away early tomorrow . . .' I began, as I followed Miss Pickering into a large, old-fashioned, but deliciously warm kitchen.

'Nonsense! You're catered for at lunch,' she said, making it clear that further resistance along those lines was pointless.

'But, I didn't bring any riding clothes,' I countered.

'That's no problem. I can fit you up,' she confirmed cheerfully, as she set about filling a large, old, aluminium kettle.

'The trouble is it's been years since I rode,' I said, desperation taking me to the very brink of the truth.

'Never mind,' she replied, putting the kettle on the Aga, 'it's like riding a bike – once learned never forgotten.'

The water on the bottom of the kettle hissed and spat as Miss Pickering collected a cake tin from the dresser and brought it over to the Formica-topped table which stood in the middle of the room. I re-assessed the situation: it was hopeless. There was no choice, I had to tell the truth.

'The fact is,' I began, 'I don't really ride at . . .'

'But if you're worried about it,' my client continued, putting out tea plates and knives, and ignoring my fresh protest, 'we'll just go for a gentle hack, and I'll take Dancer and you can have Duke. He wouldn't hurt a fly – he's too lazy.'

'Well, I'm not sure . . .'

'Yes, that's what we'll do,' she continued, heaping several spoonfuls of tea into a large brown pot which stood on the side of the Aga, 'you can take Duke – you'd be safe with him if you'd never ridden before in your life.'

'Well, I . . .'

'D'you take sugar?' she asked, 'only I don't, so I never have any out. And help yourself to cake – it's damned good though I say it myself. Now, how long's that kettle going to take to boil?'

She gave me another gappy-toothed grin as she turned away to the offending vessel on the Aga. I knew then, my fate was already sealed.

A tour of Hillsley House, immediately after tea, revealed Miss Pickering's home to be considerably cosier than its rather bleak exterior suggested. It also proved Bob Derby right: there were only a dozen pieces of pretty ordinary furniture which belonged to the trust, and that meant the valuation would take no time at all. I wondered once again if there was any way in which I could get back to London early and thereby escape the following day's promised ordeal. However, one fresh look at the keen, weather-beaten face and bright, youthful eyes of my hostess led me to banish for good any idea of a breakout.

'I'll leave you to it,' she said, when we returned to the ground floor following my initial inspection. 'I don't suppose there's anything there worth much, is there?'

'Not really,' I confirmed. 'It'll come to six or seven thousand in total, I suppose.'

'Never mind. If you do spot anything at all in the house that I could raise a few thousand on, sing out – times are hard.' She smiled brightly once more then turned and ambled away towards the kitchen.

As it happened, I had already seen something that would realise a few thousand, and since the item concerned was clearly not used, I had decided to mention its value to Miss Pickering over dinner. Rather unexpectedly, it looked as though my trip to Wales might be worthwhile after all.

Dinner turned out to be a supper of scrambled eggs and bacon beside the fire in the drawing room, but was

10

none the worse for that. Although Miss Pickering had seen no reason to change out of her old sweater or jodhpurs, I did notice that the gaps in her teeth had been miraculously filled with sparkling white replacements for the lost originals. I felt quite honoured by this sacrifice of comfort in favour of style on her part. She obviously only wore the dentures on special occasions and wasn't entirely at home with them; not least of all because they gave her a rather girlish lisp which seemed altogether out of character.

It was over our second whiskies, after the trays had been cleared away, that I broached the subject of valuables: 'You mentioned earlier you might be interested in selling the odd piece if it were of reasonable value.'

'Might!' she laughed. 'Mr Harton, I *need* to raise at least five thousand pounds in a hurry. Apart from anything else, I've got a huge solicitors' bill to pay. At this rate the legal fees are going to come to more than the trust's worth.'

I took a sip from my glass. 'Well,' I said, 'I don't think it will raise that much, but I've seen something here that would certainly make three to four thousand under the hammer.'

She looked up, head slightly inclined, eyes sparkling. 'Really? Whatever is it?' she asked.

'It's a set of chairs – up in the disused bedroom on the top floor.'

I had discovered them neatly stacked under dustsheets when Miss Pickering had gone off to deal with a telephone call in the middle of my guided tour. They were Chippendale style and probably dated from no earlier than the 1920s, but they were superb quality. What was more – there were fourteen of them, and such a large number made them eminently saleable.

'Oh, I know the ones you mean,' Diana Pickering replied. 'Are you sure they're worth anything? They're not very old you know. Father had them made between the wars and Mother loathed them so much he eventually had them put into store to placate her – Mother could be difficult when she chose.'

I did not doubt it. I was quite sure that Miss Pickering was also perfectly capable of digging in her heels if she wanted to.

'I'm absolutely certain they'll make at least three to four thousand, probably more.'

'Well, I'm damned,' she said with a chuckle. 'What a good job I stopped paying those storage charges.'

'Sorry?'

'I've only just got them out of store. My trustees have been paying storage charges on them for years and I only found out last month. I'd forgotten the things even existed. They were delivered here last week.'

'A fortunate piece of timing,' I said.

'Yes, you'll have one up on your boss too,' she went on. 'Robert thinks he's already had everything of value from this place. Don't tell him they were in store. Just pretend they've been here for years and he overlooked them.' She chuckled again.

'I may well do just that,' I said. 'It's a pity your mother didn't banish a few more things to the store.'

'As it happens, she did. There was a picture with them which she didn't like but which Father always insisted was worth a fortune – Lord knows why. It's an awful litttle thing. I didn't even think about showing it to you.'

'I may as well have a look at it while I'm here,' I said. 'You never know.'

After a little more persuasion on my part, Miss Pickering went off to track down the picture.

I leant forward and threw another log onto the crackling fire and suddenly recalled what tomorrow held for me. It sent a shudder of anticipatory embarrassment through me. I was still trying to work out if the discovery of the chairs might somehow be used to secure my early release when my client returned.

She was carrying a small, framed picture about a foot square. I stood up, took it from her and walked over to look at it under the light of the standard lamp behind her chair.

It was an oil on a wooden panel and, through the grime, appeared to be some sort of chubby little cherub brandishing a trumpet.

The frame was nineteenth century, the panel was oak, there was no signature or inscription, and the draughtsmanship was far from brilliant.

'What do you think?' Diana Pickering asked, sitting down again and picking up her glass. 'Is it worth anything?'

'Well, I certainly don't think it's worth a fortune,' I replied, still inspecting the picture under the rather dim light. 'I think it's probably early seventeenth-century Italian, but I'm not absolutely certain.'

'If it is what you think it is, what would it fetch?'

'My own gut-feeling – perhaps three to four hundred pounds,' I replied. 'But that's really only a guess. I would want Charles Morrison-Whyte, our Pictures Director, to have a look at it before I gave you a final figure.'

'But you don't think it's worth thousands?'

'No, Miss Pickering, I'm afraid not – definitely not thousands.'

'Never mind,' she said, finishing her whisky. 'Father never had much of an eye for anything but horses. Still, Hampson's would be prepared to sell it for me, wouldn't they – for whatever they can get?'

'Certainly, and you never know, the Pictures Department might get excited about it.'

'Oh, I don't think so,' she laughed. 'Though I do wonder where on earth Father got the idea it was worth a lot of money – we'll never know now I suppose.'

'No, I suppose not.'

'Right,' she said, slapping her hands down on the arms of her chair and pushing herself upright. 'I'm off to bed. You can stay here, watch the television, finish the whisky, do whatever you want. I've put some old corduroy trousers and a pair of boots in your room. They should fit you. I'll have the horses ready by eight, so we'll just have a cup of something and a slice of toast before we go – all right?'

'Er . . . yes . . . fine.'

'Good. D'you think you'll need an early morning call or will you wake up without one?'

'Oh, I'm sure I'll be awake in plenty of time,' I replied.

'All right, sleep well. See you in the morning.'

As the wiry, bandy figure of my hostess left the room, closing the door behind her, I sank back miserably into my chair and reached for the Scotch decanter.

Whether it was the slightly lumpy bed, the strange surroundings, or just the fear of what the morning held I don't know, but I was certainly right about not needing any sort of alarm call. I was awake in time to hear the dawn chorus strike up and, despite tossing and turning, that marked the end of my sleep for the night.

The rain, which had splashed steadily against the window panes through the early hours, had all but stopped by the time I hauled on the old pair of beige corduroy trousers put out for me. They creaked like sail canvas and seemed to have been specially starched for the occasion. The short brown boots were even creakier than the trousers, and as a result my progress across the old boards of the landing and down the squeaking staircase seemed to me to be a particularly noisy affair.

I received a short but hearty greeting from Miss Pickering, then a slice of toast later I was out in the yard contemplating a large bay gelding. It was built like a shire horse and was to be my mount.

14

I don't know if horses have the necessary muscle control to be able to raise one eyebrow, but I could have sworn that was precisely what Duke did as I approached him. He had been nuzzling around on the concrete when I stepped into the yard, but had looked up almost immediately. From that moment he had not taken his eyes off me. It seemed to me that, for a horse, he had a strangely expressive face, managing to convey every sense from incredulity to contempt in the time it took me to walk the dozen or so yards to where he was standing. On my arrival at his side he gave me one last lop-sided look, raised his head high, drew back his lips in a grotesque smile and gave what was unmistakably a long braying laugh. I could see just how the morning was going to be.

Following an ungainly but successful first attempt at mounting the beast, I adjusted my stirrup irons to about as long as they would go, and as Miss Pickering and Dancer made their way out of the yard, I squeezed my heels into Duke's barrel-belly.

The novelty of having an idiot on his back had obviously already worn off. His response was to just stand there, head down, sniffing at the wet ground.

'Giddy-up!' I urged, in the nearest thing I knew to horsey parlance.

Still he stood there, nose down, unimpressed, unmoved and seemingly immovable.

'Come on!' Miss Pickering bellowed as she turned in the saddle and looked back on the quietly somnolent scene in the yard. 'Move him on – I told you he's a lazy so-and-so – move him on!'

This had to be the ultimate humiliation: stuck there, helpless, six feet off the ground while my contumacious mount indulged in the equine equivalent of gum chewing.

'Giddy-up!' I demanded once again, this time digging both heels sharply into Duke's ribs – it was time he found out who was boss.

15

As it happened, I don't think Duke had even been in any doubt as to who was boss, and it certainly wasn't me. However, the spirited boot in the ribs I had just given him did bring about an instant reaction: he raised his head sharply, gave me a brief, evil look out of his left eye and took off across the yard at a brisk trot.

I believe that it is traditional to 'rise to the trot'. This entails rising rhythmically out of the saddle in time with the horse's stride. I am told it is both comfortable and easy once you know how. So it may be, but it is also very painful and difficult if you don't.

As Duke clattered across the concrete I rattled about on top of him, holding on for grim death. Every time I came down on the saddle I felt my spine compress as each vertebra in turn made contact with the next. My teeth also clashed together at will until I succeeded in clamping my jaws together with rigor-like ferocity.

This brief bout of torture was brought to an abrupt end when, on reaching Miss Pickering and Dancer on the other side of the yard, Duke slammed on the brakes and skidded to a halt. I was thrown forward in the saddle, and as my head went down, Duke's came up. Contact – which would probably have resulted in a broken nose for me – was avoided by a fraction of an inch. Duke gave me another of his wicked, one-eyed glances. He was beginning to enjoy himself.

'Right then,' Miss Pickering said, seemingly oblivious to my total lack of both co-ordination and control, 'let's go!' And with that she set off down the winding drive to the lane beyond.

To my great relief Duke followed on behind quietly without any prompting from me. Slowly, and in single file, we made our stately way along the narrow lane with nothing but the sound of the horses' hooves on the road and the background blur of birdsong to break the Sunday morning silence.

The lane was contained by high banks topped with neatly trimmed hedges. From my vantage point on Duke I could just see over these obstacles to the glistening, wet fields and woodland beyond. It was a quiet and peaceful landscape, and I could well understand why Diana Pickering chose to live on there in virtual solitude.

Without warning, my reverie was rudely interrupted by Duke. He didn't do anything violent; he just stopped dead under a tree which overhung the lane. Then he stretched up into the branches and started to nibble away at some young buds. Had he sat down, crossed his legs and lit a cigarette he couldn't have been more nonchalant about it. I was quite sure he'd forgotten I was in the saddle.

'Goooo-on!' I instructed, almost in a whisper since I had no wish to draw Miss Pickering's attention to my shameful situation. 'Goooo-on!' I repeated, this time digging my heels into his flanks.

There was a moment's hesitation then off he went at the trot once more. Again I was jarred and rattled about like a pea on a drum. But this time I decided I would at least be prepared for that sudden, skidding, emergency stop when it came. So, I leant back in the saddle as far as I could and braced myself for the inevitable cessation of forward thrust. Sensitive to my every thought, Duke countered the plan perfectly by breaking into a smart, spirited canter.

I thought I noticed a slightly bewildered expression on Miss Pickering's face as we flashed past her, but by that stage I didn't care very much. All my concentration was focused on not falling off the wretched horse. I clawed frantically at the saddle in a desperate effort to haul myself upright. No sooner had I got the most tenuous of grips than Duke performed his original party trick again, this time skidding to a halt under another overhanging branch. I was catapulted forward at high speed and, for the second time, only narrowly avoided a smashed nose as the brute arched back to reach up into the tree.

I was still draped around his neck like some threadbare old stole when Diana Pickering and Dancer plodded past us.

'Bit frisky today?' she enquired politely, with just the faintest hint of irony.

I dismissed the question as rhetorical and didn't trouble her with a reply.

Generally speaking, things got better as the morning went on, and although Duke continued to pause at will to chew the odd branch, he stopped indulging in the sudden bursts of speed which I'd found so unnerving. I suppose we had reached an unspoken agreement: he wouldn't worry me if I didn't worry him.

It was almost half past ten when we rounded an outcrop of woodland and, for the first time in two hours, Hillsley House came into view again. It lay to our left, at the bottom of the hill, and it looked extremely welcoming. Not that I wasn't enjoying the ride by that stage; on the contrary, I was enjoying it far more than I would have formerly thought possible. It was just that I had discovered two bones in my rear end that, hitherto, I had never even guessed existed. Now, after almost two and a half hours in the saddle, I was not sure whether I would ever be able to sit down, or come to that, stand up, again. How on earth it was that anyone as spare and bony as Diana Pickering wasn't completely crippled and in excruciating pain, I had no idea.

'Just carry on down alongside the bank,' she said, as she leant down from Dancer to close the gate we had just passed through. 'About halfway along there's a short cut – Duke knows where it is.'

Duke and I made our way slowy down the field as instructed, with Miss Pickering bringing up the rear. The bank she had mentioned was about ten feet high, densely covered in saplings and scrub, and had temporarily obscured the view of the house. As I craned my neck to get my bearings, a large dog-fox broke cover about thirty yards ahead and loped slowly across the field towards a small area of coppice on the other side. As I turned to watch him go, all hell broke loose.

Without any warning, Duke suddenly made a neat ninety-degree turn and charged at the bank. It was only by once again clutching wildly at the saddle that I avoided flying off sideways into the field. After that, self-preservation was the only thought in my mind. Duke must have attained the summit in two, perhaps three strides. It took me a little longer however, since he and I went our separate ways about halfway up the obstacle. Although, I suppose, I should be grateful that my fall rather than my neck was broken, I still can't recommend diving into blackthorn bushes as a worthwhile recreation. No sooner had I landed in the first than I was dragged out again and into the next. I suppose clinging onto the reins was a reflex action, it certainly wasn't calculated on my part.

Duke halted at the top of the bank and looked down critically on where I lay, at the base of a young silver birch – the last thing I collided with before he stopped. He blew gently through his nostrils and lowered his head to have a closer look at my broken body. I think he was just checking to see whether or not I was dead.

'Well done!' Miss Pickering's cry echoed up from the field. 'You kept hold of the reins! Damned good! Very important that!'

I tried to reply but no sound came out.

'Not hurt are you?' she asked without any note of concern.

'No . . .' I gasped, eventually, '. . . no . . . just a few . . . scratches . . . and bruises . . .' I clung to the silver birch and hauled myself to my feet.

'Good, good. When you're ready then, we'll go on.'

I staggered up to Duke who by then was cropping away unconcernedly at the fringe of jade-green grass which topped the bank. He took no notice at all as I clambered aboard once more.

By the time I had sorted myself out, Diana Pickering and Dancer had also ascended the bank and were alongside us.

'That's what I meant when I said he knew the short cut,' she explained. 'My fault, really – I should have warned you properly.'

'No, no, it was my fault. I wasn't paying attention.'

'Never mind,' she went on, 'we'll put some iodine on those cuts when we get back. You'll be good as new . . . well, very nearly, anyway.' She grinned her gappy-toothed grin once more, then pointed Dancer towards the welcoming edifice of Hillsley House. 'Let's go,' she said. 'It's all downhill from here.'

Clinging on hard to the roof of my car I gently lowered myself into the driving seat. It was half past three in the afternoon; raining again; I had the drive back to London before me; and I hurt all over.

'Don't forget this little horror,' Diana Pickering said, handing me the picture I had inspected the previous evening. 'You may as well take it with you. I'll get the local removal firm to deliver the chairs next time they come to London – a couple of weeks from now I expect.'

I took the picture and dumped it rather unceremoniously on the seat behind me.

'Good,' I replied, adjusting my aching bones to something approaching a comfortable driving position, 'I'm sure they'll sell very well.'

'I hope you're right,' she shouted, as I started the car. 'And do the best you can with Father's masterpiece – every penny counts you know.'

'I'll bear it in mind,' I smiled, 'and many thanks for a most enjoyable weekend.'

The wiry, stooped figure of Diana Pickering was still visible at the front door of Hillsley House as I pulled onto the narrow lane we had ridden down earlier that day. She raised her arm in a final wave then vanished inside.

'Hello,' the disembodied voice crackled out over the entryphone.

'It's me,' I said. 'Let me in – I'm dying.'

'Who's me?'

'You know perfectly well who it is,' I groaned. 'Let me in or I'll die on your doorstep, then you'll be sorry.'

There was a giggle then the buzzer sounded on the door catch. I let myself in and slowly made my way up to Sarah's flat.

She was waiting at the top of the stairs as I clawed my way up the final flight.

'Dear, oh dear!' she said. 'What on earth's happened to you?'

'A large gelding,' I replied, kissing her as I made it to the top of the staircase.

'Just a gelding, eh? Well, thank goodness it wasn't a stallion, darling – you would have been shipped home in a plastic bag. What did you do to annoy this horse – throw yourself in front of it?'

'Ho, ho, ho,' I muttered, hobbling past her into the flat.

'What's that you've got there?' she asked, following me in and closing the door.

I turned and handed her Miss Pickering's picture. She studied it for a few moments.

'Looks pretty awful to me,' she said eventually. 'Is it supposed to be incredibly valuable?'

'No, just a few hundred,' I said, easing myself into a chair, but I can't leave it in the car.'

'No,' she said, looking up from the painting. 'Not that I can imagine anybody wanting to steal it. After all, it's quite useless – it doesn't even look nice.'

'Philistine!'

'Possibly,' she agreed. 'Anyway, I suppose you'd like this particular Delilah to get you a medicinal Scotch.'

'That would be wonderful,' I replied, closing my eyes.

A short while later, Sarah returned with two drinks on a tray. I reached out to take mine, then looked at the tray.

'Sarah!' I said. 'How many times do I have to tell you? It's not the done thing to use seventeenth-century Italian oil paintings as drinks trays – even if you do only use the back of the panel to stand the glasses on.'

'And I thought you'd be pleased,' she smiled. 'After all, I have proved myself wrong – it *is* useful.'

Chapter 3

The receptionist replaced the telephone and smiled. 'Mr Beaumont will be down in a few minutes,' she said. 'Do take a seat. Can I get you some coffee?'

'Thank you,' I replied.

As she set off for the coffee I sat down and looked around.

I was in the world headquarters of McFaddon plc, but I might just as easily have been in the foyer of one of those select West End hotels. The offices were based in what must once have been an elegant private house just off Grosvenor Square. The reception area was wood-panelled, subtly lit, and comfortably furnished with a number of expensive armchairs arranged around a large, smoked-glass coffee table. In the centre of the table was a big bowl of fresh flowers, and encircling that were several neatly displayed copies of each of the morning's quality newspapers, as well as the previous day's *Wall Street Journal.*

The only noise, other than the muted snarling of London traffic outside, was the ticking of a French ormolu-cased clock on the marble mantlepiece, and a faint clicking noise which I guessed was coming from the unattended telephone switchboard behind the reception desk.

As I surveyed the calm, ordered scene, the door at the far end of the room opened.

'Mr Harton – I am so sorry to have kept you. I'm Malcolm Beaumont.'

23

He was a soft-spoken Oxbridge type. Medium height and smartly dressed in a double-breasted, blue pinstripe suit. Despite the burden of being Group Financial Director of this vast international engineering conglomerate, his appearance was youthful. I placed him at no more than forty to forty-five.

'Have you been offered coffee?' he went on.

I assured him I had.

'Good. Let's go straight up to the boardroom. I'm sure your coffee will find us up there.'

Malcolm Beaumont had telephoned me a week earlier and explained that he thought a valuation of the Head Office Boardroom and Directors' Dining Room was long overdue. Although he had only been with McFaddon's for a little over two years, his Office Manager had been *in situ* for nearly ten and he couldn't remember any special insurance cover ever having been arranged for those particular areas. I had agreed only too readily to come along and see what was required.

I followed Mr Beaumont out of the reception area, past two waiting lifts and up a set of stairs just beyond them.

'It's on the third floor,' he called back as he took the steps two at a time. 'The lifts are so slow it's quicker to come up this way – good for us, too, of course.'

The building we walked through on the way to the boardroom was considerably more high-tech than one would have guessed from the serene calm of the reception area. It became increasingly clear that the handsome nineteenth-century Mayfair façade hid a real ants' nest of hard-nosed, twentieth-century corporate activity.

'How many people do you employ here?' I asked.

'Just over a hundred and fifty – the office extends back into a lot of the buildings behind, so it's far bigger than it appears.'

No sooner had I got used to the high-tech, ultra

modern surroundings than we passed through a pair of swing doors straight back into the nineteenth century. It was a wide corridor, panelled in mahogany and hung with portraits of past chairmen of McFaddon's. Malcolm Beaumont gestured to a door directly ahead of us.

'That's the boardroom in there,' he said. 'The dining room is next to it.'

McFaddon's boardroom was an impressive place. It had a timeless quality which not only suggested the company had been in existence for centuries past, but also that it would be around for centuries to come – presumably, precisely the effect intended.

It was large with four windows overlooking the street below. Furnished exclusively with English pieces dating from the last half of the eighteenth century, the room had the look and feel of an enlightened, Georgian gentleman's library. There were three large, break-front bookcases, each laden with a considerable number of leather-bound volumes. Looking quickly over the titles, I found most of them to be early works on engineering – many of them rare.

'When was this library put together?' I asked.

'I understand about two thirds of it had always belonged to the company. The other third was collected between the wars by the then Chairman – Sir William Standish. He was a bit of an enthusiast, I believe. Are there any valuable copies amongst it?'

'Yes,' I replied. 'I think it amounts to quite an important specialist collection.'

By far the most imposing items in the room were a George III mahogany pedestal dining table getting on for twenty feet long, and a set of sixteen dining chairs of the same period. These alone were worth tens of thousands of pounds.

The only disappointing area was that of pictures. The room, like the corridor outside, was hung only with portraits of former McFaddon moguls. Each was by a top portrait painter, but they were unexciting. However, what was awaiting me in the Directors' dining room, next door, more than made up for it.

The furniture was chiefly of the same quality and period as that of the boardroom but the pictures were something different altogether. The room was dominated by two massive Venetian scenes by the eighteenth-century English artist, William James, and these were supplemented by nearly twenty good marine pictures of the eighteenth and nineteenth centuries. As far as I was concerned, my cup overflowed.

'What do you think, Mr Harton?' Malcolm Beaumont enquired. 'Am I right? Should these two rooms be separately valued and insured?'

'Absolutely right,' I confirmed. 'You've got some very good pieces here.'

'Okay – what happens now? Do you have to go away and come back with a team of experts?'

'No, I can just get on with it straightaway if that suits you.'

'Excellent!' he said, 'I'll see you're not disturbed.'

I spent several happy hours at McFaddons, and was even treated to a light lunch in solitary splendour in the Directors' dining room. As days went, it was a very enjoyable one; and I had the satisfaction of knowing I was earning a not inconsiderable fee for Hampson's at the same time. I drove back to the office with a song in my heart and a spring in my accelerator foot.

'Unlock the door, Richard. Quick, let me in!'

I was backing into a parking space a few yards from the office when I suddenly became aware of Bob Derby tugging at the passenger door handle and pleading to be admitted. I stopped the car and did as he asked.

'Hello,' he said, smiling broadly.

'Hello, Bob,' I replied rather cautiously. I had never

seen him drunk but it crossed my mind that inebriation might be the explanation for what was definitely very strange behaviour.

'I was just popping out when I saw you – thought I'd have a word,' he went on. 'Had a good day?'

'Yes, very good, in fact. I've been at McFaddon's the . . .'

'Good, good – did they have any early seventeenth-century Italian pictures?'

'Seventeenth-century Italian?' I said, even more bewildered by his behaviour. 'No, there were a couple of William James Venetian scenes, but everything else was . . .'

'Oh, pity,' he interrupted, still beaming away at me. 'I like seventeenth-century Italian pictures – don't you?'

I looked at him hard for a moment. I couldn't smell any alcohol, but something was wrong.

'Bob,' I said.

'Yes, Richard.'

'What's going on? What's this all about?'

'We-e-e-ll . . .' he said, drawing out the word and adding to the suspense, '. . . you know we had a picture sale today.'

'Yes,' I replied, still not sure what he was getting at. After all, it had only been an ordinary sale; as much a clear-out of odds and ends as anything else. There had only been one lot which I had introduced, and that was the picture I'd brought in the previous month from Hillsley House . . . the seventeenth-century Italian oil . . .

Suddenly my collar felt uncomfortably tight and I felt uncomfortably warm. My colour was rising – I could sense that. As my palms became unpleasantly moist, the Chairman of Hampson's maintained his implacable smile.

'Diana Pickering's picture?' I suggested.

Bob Derby nodded vigorously.

'What happened to it?' I asked.

27

'Oh, it sold . . . it sold . . .'

'How much?'

'Guess.'

'Oh, come on, Bob . . .'

'No, go on – guess.'

It was obvious I'd dropped a brick. It must have been more important than I had thought. But, if it was, I wasn't the only one to have missed it: the pictures department had catalogued it quite simply as 'Italian School – Early Seventeenth Century'. That meant Charles Morrison-Whyte, the director in charge of pictures, had not rated it either.

'Oh, I don't know,' I said. 'Two thousand?'

'No!' Bob Derby replied disparagingly. 'More!'

'Five thousand?'

'No! More, more!'

'Ten thousand?'

'More!'

'Fifteen . . .?'

He shook his head and, still smiling, pointed upwards.

'Twenty . . .?'

Still the finger pointed towards the heavens. I could feel a general clamminess seeping over me again. Even my scalp prickled.

'Twenty-five . . .?'

'More!'

'Thirty?'

'Now, let's not be ridiculous,' he said, shaking his head. Then, smiling again, 'It made twenty . . . seven . . . thousand . . . pounds – that's what it made.'

'Oh, my God!' I said, reaching out and gripping the steering wheel as tightly as I could. 'What the hell was it?'

'A good point, Richard. As yet I haven't been made privy to that particular piece of information.'

'You mean we still don't know?'

'Oh, Charles Morrison-Whyte knows all right. But he's under his office desk. Unavailable for comment just at

28

the moment – he's been fending off the press all afternoon.'

It seemed that the panel had been recognised as one of a series of pictures painted by a leading Italian Master around 1600. Unimpressive in itself, set in the context of its companion pictures it became extremely important and fairly valuable.

'No doubt we'll get the full story when Charles comes out of hiding. The main thing is, according to the trade, twenty-seven thousand was a lot of money for it, far more than was made by the last one to be discovered.'

I slackened my grip on the steering wheel and consoled myself with the fact that, at least, major disaster had been avoided. Two people *had* recognised what it was and *had* entered into a little healthy, competitive bidding. A moment later I felt hot and clammy again as the thought of what would have happened if only one of them had spotted it flashed through my mind.

'When did Charles discover what it was really worth?' I asked, clearing my throat nervously.

Bob Derby smiled. 'That depends upon which of the two versions of events you decide to accept.'

'What do you mean?'

'Well, I have no doubt that Charles's official account will involve his recognising the picture for what it really was some time prior to the sale, and then his coaxing the bidding up to the dizzying figure of twenty-seven thousand.'

'And the unofficial version?'

'I suspect that will lean more towards a later recognition of the work's value,' he said thoughtfully.

'How much later?' I asked.

'I'm not sure – sometime between the opening of the bidding and the fall of the hammer I would think.' He grinned broadly again.

'Well,' I said, 'all I can do is apologise for missing it.'

'I shouldn't lose any sleep over it, Richard. It was a pretty obscure item. All joking aside, Charles doesn't miss much, and this one left him cold. Anyway, there is something you can do for me by way of penitence.'

'What's that?'

'You can telephone Diana Pickering as soon as you set foot in your office and let her know what's happened.'

'Okay,' I agreed.

'And, at the same time, you can explain convincingly how it's quite reasonable that, although I've been visiting Hillsley House for twenty years, *I* never spotted a picture worth nearly thirty thousand pounds.'

'Er . . .'

'I tell you, Richard,' he went on, opening the car door and swinging himself round ready to get out, 'I don't even remember having seen the damned thing, let alone having valued it – weird!'

'Er . . . yes . . .' I agreed. 'Weird!'

The telephone at Hillsley House rang for a long time before it was eventually answered: 'Hello – four-one-seven-two – Diana Pickering speaking.'

'Hello, Miss Pickering,' I replied. 'It's Richard Harton.'

'Oh, hello, Mr Harton. Is it about the chairs? . . . I haven't returned that bit of paper about the reserve yet, have I? . . . I've got it right here somewhere . . .' There was the sound of papers being riffled through, '. . . I'll look it out this evening and post i off . . . will that be soon enough?'

'I'm sure it will,' I said, 'but it wasn't the chairs I was calling about: it was the picture.'

'The picture?'

'Yes, as you know, it came up for sale this morning.'

'Oh, yes, I did have some sort of note about it. I've got it here somewhere.' There was a noisy resumption of paper shuffling.

'Well, the turth of it is,' I pressed on, 'it was of considerably greater importance than I . . . we initially believed.'

'Greater importance?'

'Yes – it sold for rather a lot of money, Miss Pickering.'

'Oh?'

'Yes, it realised twenty-seven thousand pounds.'

There was a long silence at the other end, then I heard Diana Pickering clear her throat.

'Twenty-seven thousand pounds, you say?'

'Yes, that's right – twenty-seven thousand pounds.'

'Good . . . Lord!' she articulated slowly. 'That is a bit more than you reckoned, isn't it?'

'Yes, I must apologise for being so wildly out . . .'

'Apologise? You don't have to apologise, Mr Harton. You can make mistakes like that any day of the week as far as I'm concerned. I suppose there's no chance of the chairs making forty or fifty thousand, is there?'

A few minutes after my conversation with Diana Pickering I picked up the telephone once again. This time I could dial the number from memory: it was Sarah's direct line to her office. I felt I should lose no time in informing her that her improvised drinks tray had made just slightly less than her flat would on the open market.

'Oh, my God!' she said, paraphrasing Miss Pickering's own reaction. Then, after a moment's silence, she added, 'How do you think future art historians will explain the ring-marks from our glasses?'

Chapter 4

'Wow!' Charlotte called out shortly after she started opening the post.

'What?'

'Your friend, Mr Beaumont at McFaddon's.'

'What about him?'

'Well, I know you said he was a good client, but he's just turned into a perfect one – he's paid his bill by return.' She stood up and passed the cheque and accompanying letter across to me.

Payment this prompt was unprecedented in my time at Hampson's. Few clients settled their valuation accounts in less than the approved thirty days, while a not insubstantial minority seemed to feel that thirty months was a more reasonable period. Malcolm Beaumont was beginning to look like a real candidate for canonisation. And there was more: in his highly complimentary letter he invited me to contact him about another valuation. I reached for the telephone immediately.

'Ah, thanks for calling so quickly, Mr Harton,' he said. 'Only it struck me that it would be as well if we had the contents of the Managing Director's flat valued as well. I've no idea if the insurance cover is anywhere near the right figure – it's probably miles out.'

'Probably,' I laughed, 'but let's just take some details to start with, Mr Beaumont. Now, the address is . . . ?'

Marlborough Place was just a few minutes' walk from Hampson's. It was as exclusive as anywhere in Belgravia, and the McFaddon's flat was as desirable a residence as one would expect in that area.

Malcom Beaumont had explained it was a relatively recent acquisition, the lease having been purchased a little under two years earlier.

'Does that mean all the contents have been acquired in the last two years as well?' I asked.

'Yes, that's right – no problem there, is there?' he replied.

In theory the answer to his question was 'no', but in practice it was likely to be 'yes'.

'Was the furnishing handled by an interior decorator?'

'No . . .'

So things were not as bad as they might be. By the time interior decorators put their mark-up on a piece the price was usually out of sight. That had been my chief concern – explaining to Malcolm Beaumont the difference between my price and theirs.

'. . . it was all handled by the Managing Director's sister,' he went on.

Every alarm bell and siren in my head went off simultaneously. Suddenly this valuation had all the hallmarks of disaster. Wrongly handled it heralded the end of a beautiful professional relationship between myself and McFaddon's.

'Do you have receipts for most of the items?' I asked, hoping the enquiry sounded reasonably matter-of-fact.

'Yes – why?'

At least that was something – I could work from the receipts.

'Oh, it's just that it's probably best to use the purchase prices as the basis of the valuation,' I said. 'After all, in the event of a claim you would probably replace things through the same source.'

It all sounded terribly reasonable to me.

'No, don't worry yourself about that, Mr Harton, I'm a realist,' Beaumont replied. 'It's pretty small beer to us anyway. I just want to insure it for what it's worth rather than what we paid for it'.

'Are you quite sure?'

'Yes, don't worry. This is strictly between you, me and the insurer,' he said, concluding cheerfully, 'nobody else will know about it.'

One thing was obvious as I looked around the Marlborough Place flat – no expense had been spared. Each and every room looked like something out of one of the glossy monthly magazines which specialise in sumptuous interiors.

I took out my pen, notebook and rule and started to write:

A George III Irish mahogany three-pedestal dining table, raised on turned pillars and outswept reeded supports, with two additional leaves.
    Height 2ft 4in, Width 4ft, Length 12ft 4in (fully extended).

Then came the big question – how much to put on it for an insurance valuation?

It was the sort of piece I would have expected to make in the region of £7,000 to £9,000 at auction. There was obviously no point in erring on the side of caution in this case, so I decided on £9,000 as the hammer price. The next step was to allow for the retailer's mark-up. That was easy – say 100 per cent. That took it to a mere £18,000, which was where it would normally have stopped. But not on this occasion. Malcom Beaumont's assertion that the valuation was strictly between us and

34

McFaddon's insurers was all very well, but when you were dealing with the results of the labours of the sister of the Managing Director, belt *and* braces were advisable. I decided to add an additional 25 per cent to the value of everything. That slapped on a further £4,500 to the £18,000 table.

I jotted down the figure in my notebook – '£22,500' – looked at it, scribbled it out and wrote in '£23,000' instead. After all, what's five hundred pounds among friends?

I looked at the next item and began to write:

'A set of twelve George III mahogany dining chairs . . .'

It may not have been the most exciting valuation I had ever done, but it definitely allowed for some of the biggest retailer's margins I'd ever dreamed of. Still, better safe than sorry, whatever Malcolm Beaumont said.

I knew there was something wrong as soon as the telephone rang. It was a sort of sixth sense one develops for impending doom.

'It's Mr Beaumont from McFaddon's,' Charlotte announced.

'Okay, put him through,' I said. Then, picking up the telephone, 'Hello, Mr Beaumont – what can I do for you?'

'Hello, Mr Harton – well, it's a bit embarrassing actually. It's about some of the things you valued at Marlborough Place.'

'Really – what's the problem?'

'Well . . .' he paused, 'we can't seem to reconcile your valuation with our records . . .'

Damn! I'd gone over the top with my figures. That was obviously what I'd done. I'd been so intent on making the MD's sister look thrifty, I had stupidly overcooked the whole thing. I'd even had a nagging suspicion about it when I'd signed the wretched thing.

If only I'd altered it then. Now it was going to be very awkward.

'There seem to be certain discrepancies,' he went on, 'which I don't really understand.'

'Can you give me an example?' I asked.

'Not really . . . I know so little about it . . .'

'Well, is it to do with values?' I pressed him.

'Er . . . yes . . . certainly values . . . and some descriptions too . . .'

Descriptions? What was wrong with my descriptions? Something strange was going on here.

'. . . so I wondered if you could meet Mrs De Courcy at Marlborough Place . . .'

'Mrs De Courcy?'

'Yes, Mrs De Courcy is . . .'

'Your Managing Director's sister?'

'Yes, that's right.'

I was beginning to feel just a little bit like a patsy. Somewhere inside me a few tingling nerve ends were telling me that Malcolm Beaumont had set me up.

'But I thought the valuation was just between us and the insurers,' I said.

'And so it was,' he confirmed, innocently. 'Unfortunately, it somehow found its way onto Sir William's desk and he started taking a personal interest in it.'

Somehow? Somehow it just happened to land on the desk of Sir William Trench, Managing Director of McFaddon's, and one of the most feared industrialists on either side of the Atlantic. Just wonderful!

'So what do you actually want me to do to resolve this?' I asked.

'Well, Sir William has asked Mrs De Courcy to discuss the whole matter with you and to report back to him . . . could you possibly be at Marlborough Place at nine tomorrow morning. Mrs De Courcy will be travelling up especially . . .'

*

When I had gone along to Marlborough Place to make the valuation, the smartly liveried hall porter had simply escorted me up the four floors in the lift and let me into the apartment. This time he rang through to announce my arrival.

'He's here, Mrs De Courcy,' he said, eyeing me up and down as he spoke. 'Shall I tell him to come up, Madam, or should he wait?'

It may have been a touch of paranoia on my part but it seemed to me that he was treating me with about the same degree of deference he would have afforded a carrier of bubonic plague.

'Certainly, Madam,' he went on, 'I'll tell him right away.'

He put down the telephone, eyed me up and down once more, for some reason paying particular attention to my shoes, and said, 'You're to go up immediately.'

Without replying I turned towards the stairs and slowly made my way to the fourth floor. I saw no point in making a hurried ascent in the lift. Mrs De Courcy could wait.

On reaching the fourth floor landing I found the door to McFaddon's flat a little ajar. I pressed the doorbell and heard a woman's voice call out a sharp and almost palpably unfriendly, 'Come in!'

Mrs De Courcy was in the dining room, standing with her back to the door looking out of the window at the gardens below. She turned as I entered and gave me a look which should have frozen the marrow in my bone.

'Good morning,' she said curtly. 'I am Madeleine De Courcy.'

'Richard Harton,' I replied.

She cast an appraising eye over me in much the same way as had the hall porter a few minutes earlier, then

37

turned towards the window again as if she couldn't bear to continue looking at me.

'You, Mr Harton,' she said, still looking out on the gardens, 'have caused me considerable embarrassment.'

'I'm very sorry if that is the case,' I replied, 'but . . .'

'Of course it's the case!' she snapped, spinning round to face me again. 'What else could your extraordinary, so-called valuation have caused me other than embarrassment?'

I had been prepared for a *reasonably* difficult interview with Mrs De Courcy, but I was still surprised by the vehemence of her opening attack – she actually gave the impression she would happily kill me given a half-suitable opportunity. I found this a little hard to take, particularly since Mrs De Courcy was a strikingly attractive woman. Of medium height, with long auburn hair, she was elegant and timelessly beautiful. She was also obviously used to getting her own way.

I laid my briefcase on the dining table, opened it and took out a copy of the valuation. Closing the briefcase again I looked up at her.

'Perhaps we could begin by going through the individual items where we have a problem.'

She closed her eyes momentarily and shook her head.

'Then we had better start at page one and work our way through to the end,' she said.

'As you wish,' I replied – two could play at that game.

Without warning, Madeleine De Courcy smiled. It wasn't a smile of friendliness or pleasure, it was a smile of complete contempt. It was not a nice smile.

'Yes, why don't we begin by having a look at what we have in this room,' she said, slowly rotating the large emerald and diamond ring which she wore on her left hand.

I glanced at the valuation, then at the dining table.

'The first item is this table,' I said. 'What specific problem do we have here.'

'The price.'

She was not being at all helpful. If she was, as she said, embarrassed by my valuation figures, then that meant she had charged McFaddon's *more* than I had valued the pieces at. It hardly seemed possible. My initial fear had been that I had gone way over the top with my figures, not that I'd undervalued anything.

'And what exactly is wrong with the price?' I asked.

'It is exactly twelve thousand pounds out,' she replied with admirable precision and not a little nerve.

It took a moment for what she had said to sink in, and even when it did I could still hardly believe it.

'Twelve thousand! You mean McFaddon's paid thirty-five thousand for this table?' I gasped.

'Yes, are you suggesting there is something wrong with that?' she replied.

'Well. . .' I was genuinely shocked by the figure she had quoted, '. . . I do think it's a great deal of money.'

'Do you?' she replied, haughtily. 'Well, let's have a look at the chairs next, shall we.'

I referred to the valuation again – a set of twelve George III mahogany dining chairs. I would have expected them to make £5,000 to £6,000 under the hammer. I had valued them at £15,000 for insurance.

'How much?' I asked.

'Eighteen thousand,' she said.

'Oh, we're getting quite close,' I remarked with inadvisable levity.

Madeleine De Courcy's brow darkened like a summer sky suddenly heavy with thunder.

'And what about the sideboard?' I pressed on.

'Fifteen thousand,' she snarled.

I looked at my copy of the valuation again – a figure of £10,000 was set against the piece in question.

And so it went on throughout the flat. Almost every item I had valued had cost McFaddon's anything between 20 and 50 per cent more than the figure I had put on it. Malcolm Beaumont had obviously sat back powerless as these considerable sums of money were being distributed to grateful members of the antiques trade, but then he had seized his opportunity to strike back. Unfortunately I had been his unwitting instrument of retribution, and it was an exceedingly uncomfortable role to play.

'So what do you intend doing about it?' Mrs De Courcy asked, finally.

It was quite an interesting question really. On most of the items we were so far apart on price that to try to agree compromise figures would have been futile. There were also, just as Malcolm Beaumont had said, two or three items on which Mrs De Courcy and I disagreed as to authenticity. There was definitely no room for manoeuvre on those. All in all, I felt there was precious little I *could* do, even if I had felt so inclined – and by that stage I didn't.

'Frankly, I don't think there's anything I can do about it,' I replied. 'Anyway, even if I did increase the figures on the valuation to those actually paid by McFaddon's, in the event of a claim a loss adjuster would tear them to shreds. The annual premium would just be a waste of money.'

While I was speaking, Madeleine De Courcy paced up and down extremely elegantly in front of the fireplace. Abruptly, she stopped and turned on me.

'I bought the majority of these pieces through Jonathan Reid. Do you know him.'

'I know of him, certainly,' I said.

He was an occasional visitor to Hampson's good sales. Smooth, wealthy and clever, he had a sizable private clientele which he pampered, entertained lavishly and charged through the nose. He was a very successful dealer.

'I see,' she continued, rather like a barrister

cross-examining a witness. 'And from your knowledge of Jonathan Reid you believe he's a crook, do you?'

'Certainly not.'

'But surely that's what you're implying isn't it?' she persisted. 'You are saying he charged me thirty-five thousand pounds for a table worth, in your opinion, no more than twenty-three thousand. You are saying he is a crook.' She articulated the last sentence very precisely and quietly, putting great emphasis on the final word, smiling as she did so.

'No,' I replied, equally emphatically, 'I am saying he placed the table in his showroom and put a price tag of thirty-five thousand pounds on it. You then agreed to buy it at the price he was asking. He didn't force you to do it – it was entirely up to you.'

'You make it sound like buying and selling vegetables at the local greengrocer's,' she observed distastefully.

'Well, the principle is the same, whether it's Canalettos or cauliflowers, Mrs De Courcy.'

She winced at my words, looked me up and down once more and said, 'What an extraordinary approach to this business you have, Mr Harton.'

I sensed the meeting was over.

'How did it go?' Charlotte asked, when I arrived back at the office.

'Not good,' I said. Madeleine De Courcy is under the impression that I am, to fine art auctioneering, what Genghis Khan was to the promotion of petit point as a pastime.

'Well . . . ?'

'Don't say another word, Charlotte,' I warned. 'I am not in the mood. Just get me Malcolm Beaumont's number. I have a fee to salvage.'

I quickly discovered there was no real cause for concern. Although he didn't say as much, the Financial Director of McFaddon's seemed delighted that I had

41

refused to make any changes to the valuation.

'I'll see Sir William gets a full report,' he said, with barely disguised glee, 'and I'll also ensure that the cheque for your fee goes into the post this evening.'

'Thank you, Mr Beaumont.'

'Not at all, Mr Harton – I've found this whole exercise most illuminating; most illuminating indeed.'

Chapter 5

'What time do I have to be in Surrey?' I asked.

Charlotte picked up the diary and consulted it. 'Not until eleven,' she said.

I checked my watch.

'Good, I've just got time to stop off at Bailey's on the way.'

Bailey's was the small, independent auction rooms in Twickenham where we sent what we referred to as residual items. Those of a less sensitive disposition might have described the pieces concerned as junk but that would not have been altogether fair. Basically, when Hampson's handled the disposal of a complete house contents, Bailey's took the bits unsuitable for sale in our Belgravia rooms. This could sometimes amount to a spectacular cross-section of domestic furnishings and appliances.

That particular morning, a pantechnicon was due at Bailey's with a load which I had seen the previous week. The carriers were to drop off the items for Twickenham first, then bring on the better pieces to Hampson's. Usually this would have been done the other way round – Hampson's first and then Bailey's. That was why I thought a visit to down-town Twickenham would do no harm – just to ensure nothing went astray.

Not that the ever-conscientious Bailey's staff would have helped themselves to anything. Not any more, anyway. They might have done once upon a time, but now they knew the opportunities for 'mislaying' pieces were few and far between. Everything bound for Hampson's was just too meticulously recorded. Nevertheless, Bailey's still held the general reputation for being a bit of a Bermuda Triangle where ceramics and silver were concerned, so the occasional surprise visit did no harm. It kept the lads on their toes.

'Hello, Mr H,' Harry Sutton greeted me as chirpily as ever. 'How are you, Sir? Good to see you. Cup of tea? It's just brewed.'

Harry was indefatigable. He was everywhere at the same time: a ubiquitous blur, constantly on the move and always in control. Officially Head Porter, he held more sway than the average managing director. I had long ago learnt that nothing happened within the walls of Bailey's saleroom without this energetic, dapper little man either engineering or approving it.

'A cup of tea sounds an excellent idea, Harry,' I said, pausing by the open back of the truck I'd come to check on.

A nice George III bureau, destined for Hampson's good furniture sale, was perched a little precariously near the edge of the tailboard. I ran my hand over the rich, dark mahogany as a strong gust of wind lashed down the narrow street, whipping up the grit into eddies and spinning the old newspapers and cardboard cartons that littered the place high into the air.

'Careful the wind doesn't knock this off here,' I said. 'It's going to make a bob or two.'

'You worry too much, Mr H,' Harry replied, pushing a lock of grey hair back from his forehead and rubbing the dust from his bright blue eyes. 'They've only put it there so they can get at the stuff at the back – all packed whatsit about face as usual.'

As he spoke another blast of wind ripped down the street, rocking the lorry on its axle springs and once again looping his hair over his eyes.

'Cor, let's get inside, Sir,' he said, hunching up his shoulders. 'This wind's going through me like a knife.'

It couldn't have been more than ten or twelve minutes later that I emerged from Bailey's to continue my journey to Surrey. Arthur Porter, better known to all as Polly, was standing by the lorry waiting for the next tea chest to be handed down.

'Morning, Polly,' I said, peering past him into the jumble of furniture and packing cases.

'Mornin' Mr H,' he beamed.

'Where's the bureau?' I asked.

'What's that, Sir?' He fiddled with the control on the hearing aid which he kept at low volume most of the time.

'The bureau – it was standing on the tailboard when I went in.'

'Must have already gone inside,' he suggested.

'It's not for here,' I pointed out. 'It's for Belgravia. It was perfectly clearly marked.'

'Oh, I don't know then,' he said, scratching his bald pate. 'I'll go and check.'

Moments later he returned with Harry Sutton and the foreman of the truck crew.

'What's the problem, Mr H?'

'That bureau, Harry – the one that was on the tailboard. Where is it?'

'Well, if it's not in the saleroom they must have stacked it away again inside the lorry.'

The foreman clambered up and advanced into the depths of the pantechnicon.

'Where's Don?' he asked, when he finally returned to the tailboard.

'Gone for a pee,' Polly replied.

"Ow long's 'e bin gone?'

'I don't know – I haven't been timing him, have I . . . ?'

'Has the truck been left unattended at any stage?' I interrupted.

45

'Yeah,' Polly replied, turning to me, 'but that happens all the time, Mr H. You know that.'

'Yes, yes, Polly. I'm not blaming anybody. I'm just trying to find out what's happened. And since the bureau's not in the saleroom or the truck, and since it was left unattended for a time – albeit a short one – I think we can conclude it's been . . .'

'Nicked!' said the foreman.

'Strewth!' Polly added, once again scratching his shiny head in disbelief. 'But I was only gone a couple of minutes, Mr H. I'd swear on me mother's grave to that. And I was only just inside the door, out of the wind. If there'd been a car or a van come along here I would have heard it.'

'Are you positive, Polly?' I asked.

'Yeah – there's no way anyone drove along here, loaded up that bureau and drove off again. I would've heard 'em.'

'In that case . . .' I began.

'They're on bloody foot!' said the foreman.

'They can't have got far,' Harry said. 'Not round here – there's nowhere for them to go.'

'Let's get after them, then,' I said. 'We'll split up. And one thing . . .'

'What's that?'

'Tell somebody to stay with the lorry.'

I cruised round in my car for about five minutes before I rounded a corner and found Harry, Polly and the foreman already gathered around the bureau. It was lying on its back on the pavement and had obviously been abandoned without ceremony.

'What happened?' I asked, drawing up alongside the thoughtful little group.

'It was a couple of yobs,' the foreman replied. 'I saw 'em, 'ollered out, they dropped it like a brick and was off like bleedin' grey 'ounds.'

Considering what it had been through, the piece

46

didn't look too much the worse for wear. One of the bracket feet was off and there were several bits of veneer lying around it, but that was all. That there was no greater structural damage was a tribute to the eighteenth-century craftsman who built it.

'Could have been worse, Mr H,' Harry Sutton said. 'Do you want us to get it tidied up before it's sent on to Hampson's?'

'No thanks, Harry. We'll sort it out at our end.'

'Whatever you say, Sir. But it's no trouble you know – we've dealt with this sort of thing before.'

I smiled.

'I don't doubt it, Harry. In fact, I'd never imagined for one moment that this was the first bureau to have fallen off the back of a lorry at Bailey's.'

Pamela Orchard's house was not far from Godstone. Set back from the road and surrounded by elderly Scots pines and Cyprus, it offered a fairly gloomy aspect in the best late Victorian tradition. At some point in its history the front of the place had been pebble-dashed, presumably to keep damp at bay. The pebble-dash itself had now all but disappeared under a dense, shaggy overcoat of dark green ivy. Above it, a complex arrangement of white barge-boarded gable ends jutted irregularly into the sky. The wind was still blowing hard as I stood in the open front porch, waiting for somebody to answer my knock. I was actually looking out at the wildly swaying old trees when I heard the door behind me open.

'Miss Orchard?' I said, turning to meet my client. 'I'm Richard Harton of Hampson's.'

Pamela Orchard offered a self-conscious flickering smile of greeting.

'Good morning, Mr Harton,' she said in a soft, tremulous voice. 'Do come in, won't you?'

47

The nervous, enigmatic smile and the near-inaudible, quavering voice seemed at odds with the lady's physical appearance. A little above medium height, squarely built, and with her greying hair wrought into severely permed tight curls, she looked as though she might be a real Tartar. In reality she was quiet, withdrawn and timid.

'I understand you would like the whole contents valued for insurance purposes,' I said, going through the usual routine of confirming instructions.

'I suppose so – if that's what Mr Williams said.'

David Williams was a solicitor with whom I had struck up a good working relationship. The youngest partner in his firm, he tended to get saddled with more than his fair share of the not-so-lucrative private work his colleagues wished to avoid. Undeterred, and fortified with a good sense of humour, David guided his clients through the minefields of law and taxation, almost without exception leaving their affairs in far better shape than they had been formerly. Whether these successes were always appreciated was another matter.

'That's certainly what he asked me to do,' I replied. 'I understand you've never had a valuation of the contents here before.'

'I shouldn't think so . . . certainly not in my memory anyway . . . perhaps Daddy might have had one done . . . but that would have been years ago . . . he died in 1962 . . . Mother handled everything after that . . . I really can't be sure . . . she was always very careful about money . . .'

The words came in short, stacatto bursts, but still in the same shaky whisper: like a little girl, frightened of being punished for speaking out of turn. But Pamela Orchard wasn't a little girl. She was fifty-five if she was a day.

'That's fine,' I said. 'Perhaps you could just briefly show me around the house, then I'll make a start.'

48

She nodded, smiled another weak smile, then turned on her heel, her sensible shoes squeaking on the polished parquet flooring.

'Well, this is the hall,' she said, gesturing about her.

It was rather a dark place, partially oak-panelled and dominated by a heavy oak staircase which rose a dozen steps from the parquet, turned right and promptly disappeared from sight. What furniture there was was good quality Edwardian mahogany which might have been a little at odds with the oak panelling had it not been for the fact that the panelling was almost completely obscured by pictures. There were dozens of them. Mostly quite small and all dating from the last forty years of the nineteenth century. They were chiefly French and Italian with a few German and Spanish works as well. All were of extremely high quality when it came to draughtsmanship, and most were chocolate box interiors packed with dancing girls, beautiful children, seventeenth-century swordsmen or scarlet-faced, scarlet-robed cardinals. The overall theme of the collection appeared to be pure undiluted overindulgence. Most of the subjects were either already very jolly or well on their way to becoming so.

'Well!' I said. 'What an impressive collection! Did your parents put it together?'

'Daddy did. I don't think Mother was ever very interested in them. I think she considered them rather frivolous.'

It was the second time she had referred to her parents in that way: Daddy and Mother, not Daddy and Mummy or even Father and Mother, but the less balanced Daddy and Mother, as though there had been a definite softness for one which had been missing for the other.

She fiddled with one of her cardigan buttons as she glanced over the pictures hanging on either side of the stairs.

'I suppose she found them ... a bit ... well, a

49

bit . . . vulgar,' she added uncertainly.

There would be plenty to agree with Miss Orchard's mother's assessment of the artistic merit of the collection. However, there were plenty more who would be prepared to pay good money for any of the pictures concerned.

'Are they worth anything?' Miss Orchard asked with a genuine naïveté which took me back ten years to when many of my clients had neither known nor cared what their possessions were worth – they just liked them regardless of value.

'Yes, they are,' I confirmed. 'Most of these small oils are worth anywhere between five hundred and a thousand pounds each.'

She looked round in surprise, opened her mouth as if to speak but just shook her head in disbelief instead. She turned back again to the crowded display of ornate gilt frames, bright splashes of colour and sparkling protective glass. 'Are you sure?' she whispered eventually.

'Absolutely certain.'

'Oh dear!' she said, sadly. 'This is awful – whatever is the insurance bill going to be?'

'I shouldn't worry too much,' I consoled her. 'I'm sure Mr Williams will put you in touch with a good broker. Unless you have a lot more tucked away in the house I don't think the damage will be too serious.'

'But that's the whole point,' she said. 'There are a lot more . . . all over the house . . . don't you see? . . . a lot more!'

And Pamela Orchard was not exaggerating. As I followed her around the house, each room produced more and more oil paintings. Not all of quite the same high quality as those in the hall, but every one highly saleable. If Miss Orchard was short of ready cash, as her behaviour suggested, then it was true, she might indeed have a problem when it came to the insurance premium.

In the long corridor on the first floor I paused briefly

to inspect yet another depiction of alcoholic excess. This time it involved several members of a nameless but obviously popular monastic order. It was difficult to see it properly since with all the bedroom doors shut the only light was provided by a dim, single bulb at the far end of the passage.

'I expect you need to see *all* the rooms, don't you?' Miss Orchard asked, as I blinked at the picture.

'Yes, please.'

'Right . . . well . . . this is Mother's . . .' she said, her hand fluttering about the door handle like a butterfly before finally settling and grasping the heavy brass ball. 'I don't think there's much in here.'

One could never tell. There might be nothing but there could be a treasure trove, especially if Miss Orchard had preserved the room exactly as it had been in her mother's lifetime. She certainly struck me as the type of person who would do that sort of thing. I followed her into the room, fairly sure I was going to discover something that little bit unusual or unexpected.

And so I did, for lying in an oversized Victorian bedstead, propped up slightly on a pile of pillows was the ashen, gaunt figure of Pamela Orchard's mother.

For a moment I thought she was dead. Actually, I had assumed all along that she was dead. Miss Orchard had only ever referred to her in the past tense and David Williams had mentioned only the daughter in his instructions.

Frozen in my tracks I gazed on the grey face with its sunken cheeks and dramatic, hooked nose cleaving the air like a shark's fin. It was an Elizabethan face – powerful and masculine rather than soft and feminine. I suddenly knew why Pamela Orchard was such a timid, nervous mouse. The reason was stretched out on the bed in front of me.

'This is Miss Duncan,' my client whispered.

Turning I saw a trim, grey haired lady rising from a chair by the window behind us. She smiled, put down her book on the small table next to her chair and smoothed down her starched, nurse's uniform.

'How do you do,' I whispered.

'It's all right,' Miss Duncan replied brightly. 'You won't waken Mrs Orchard. She's deeply unconscious most of the time.'

'I see,' I replied.

'Mother had a massive stroke almost three months ago. She's barely opened her eyes since,' explained Pamela Orchard. 'It's only willpower that's keeping her alive.'

'I see,' I repeated.

Miss Orchard was markedly more talkative as we completed the tour of the house, as though just going into her mother's room and coming out again had given her a renewed sense of independence.

'I'd never even had a chequebook of my own until Mother had her stroke,' she explained, 'then suddenly I had to start looking after all our financial affairs – stocks and shares, trust funds, deposit accounts – I don't know what I would have done without Mr Williams.'

'I'm sure he's very helpful,' I said.

'Oh, he is. And patient too. I still don't understand it all though. Generally I just do as he advises. Mother would be furious if she knew. He's rearranged all the investments she'd had going for years. If she ever recovers it will be awful . . . oh! . . . I didn't mean it like that . . . I just . . .'

'I understand,' I smiled. 'But, you said earlier that you were concerned about meeting the cost of the insurance premiums. Is that really likely to be a problem?'

Miss Orchard frowned and sighed deeply. 'I just don't know, Mr Harton,' she said, shrugging her shoulders. 'I'm very confused. When Daddy was alive we used to have dinner parties and go away in August on holiday. Then, when he died, Mother said we were poor because he'd been profligate. Now, Mr Williams tells me that we're really quite comfortably off again. I just can't get used to the idea after all these years of scrimping and saving.'

'It must be very difficult,' I agreed. 'But one thing is certain, and that is that your father's collection of pictures is worth somewhere in the region of fifty to eighty thousand pounds. So, if you do ever find yourself in need of funds you only need to sell a picture or two.'

Miss Orchard, who had been listening intently, looked shocked. 'Oh, no, Mr Harton!' she said, 'I could never do that – Mother would never permit it . . .'

An hour and a half later I had completed the valuation of all the rooms on the upper floors with the exception of Mrs Orchard's. I knocked tentatively on the polished oak door. A moment later it was opened by Nurse Duncan.

'Is it convenient for me to do this room now?' I asked.

'Yes, of course, come in,' she said. 'In fact, I'll just pop down to the kitchen while you're here, if you don't mind.'

'Not at all.'

'And don't worry about waking the old lady,' she remarked as she left the room. 'You could march a brass band through here and she wouldn't hear it.'

As the nurse's footsteps faded away down the corridor I set about my business. Working my way around the large L-shaped room as quickly as I could, I wrote down the description, value and dimensions of each item in turn. It was one of those jobs when three hands would have been useful: one for the notebook, one for the pen, and an extra one to grapple with my elderly, extending steel rule.

Old Mrs Orchard's bed stood in a dark corner of the

room far away from any windows. A small lamp glimmered dimly on the table next to where she lay, picking out her waxy features with its yellow light. I stood and watched her for a moment. She was absolutley motionless. There was nothing to suggest she was even still breathing. How on earth the nurse could tell she was alive I had no idea.

I noted down the details of the bedside table and walked around to the huge Edwardian wardrobe which stood against the wall on the opposite side of the bed. It was typical of its type: a combination of full length cupboards, fitted drawers, sliding trays and weighty mirrors. During my years in Sussex I had knocked down plenty of them for twenty pounds or less and been pleased to get rid of them. Now I wrote down an insurance figure of £1,200. Times had changed.

I stretched across the front of the piece to hold the rule in place as I measured the width. Marking the point on the tape with my thumb, I squinted at the badly rubbed numbers. They were so indistinct in the semi-darkness I couldn't read them at all. Clutching the six or seven feet of noisily flexing metal in both hands, I turned and leant forward over the bed a little to catch the light from the bedside lamp.

'Six feet eight inches,' I muttered to myself. Then I suddenly sensed I was being watched.

A pair of grey, watery eyes were staring up at me out of that sallow face on the pillow. For the second time that day in that room I was rooted to the spot. I stood there, hunched over the old lady like a vulture, temporarily just as paralysed as she was. Slowly, she seemed to examine me, then, without warning she let out a strange, gurgling cry. It wasn't particularly loud but it was so unexpected that I leapt back, crashing into the wardrobe behind me. It rocked against the wall, then settled forward again as I spread my arms wide to steady it. When I looked back on Mrs

Orchard her eyes were once again closed.

There was no doubt in my mind that this time she really was dead. To have woken up to find a strange man leaning over her bed was one thing, but for her to have struggled back to consciousness to discover the funeral director measuring her up had to be the last straw. True, I wasn't actually wearing a black top hat with a crêpe band but otherwise, with my dark suit, white shirt and subdued tie, I was every inch the undertaker; with or without the extending rule.

I was just sidling away from the bed when Nurse Duncan returned.

'Everything all right?' she asked cheerily.

'Er . . . yes . . .' I said, wondering whether I should mention that I had killed her patient and therefore terminated what was probably a very lucrative contract for her, '. . . but she did cry out.'

'Oh, yes?' she said, plumping up the cushions in her chair by the window.

'Yes – quite loudly,' I went on, 'and her eyes opened for a moment too.'

'Mmmm . . . ?' she said, apparently sublimely uninterested in the passing of Mrs Orchard.

'I thought she might have taken a turn for the worse,' I continued, contemplating just how blunt I had to be to get Nurse Duncan to spring into action.

'Oh, I shouldn't think so,' she smiled, crossing the room to the bed, 'but let's just make sure anyway.'

I watched in silence as the nurse carefully checked the old lady's pulse. After a while she replaced the fragile looking arm beneath the covers and gently smoothed down the sheets again.

'No – no change,' she confirmed, once again smiling brightly. 'She does have very brief moments of consciousness but they're few and far between. I expect it gave you a start, didn't it?'

'You can say that again,' I agreed, as we walked

towards the door. 'Quite frankly I thought she'd gone and died on me.'

'I'm not surprised,' Nurse Duncan laughed. 'She did the same thing to Miss Pamela once and I needed smelling salts that time.'

'For the daughter rather than the mother, I take it?'

She nodded and looked across at the inert form in the big old bed. 'Mind you, it would be best for both of them if the old lady could just slip away. She's had a long life and doesn't really want to live any more . . .'

'And the daughter's had no life at all,' I added.

'Ah, you're an observant man, Mr Harton,' she said as I opened the door. 'Yes, I think, on this occasion, when one life ends the other will begin.'

Charlotte looked up as I entered the office. She was plainly tired.

'Thank goodness you're back,' she said. 'Where *have* you been?'

'You know where I've been: doing that valuation for David Williams in Surrey.'

'Yes, but why are you so late? I telephoned the house an hour and a half ago and the woman said you'd just left.'

'And so I had,' I replied, looking at my watch. 'I've been slogging my way through the traffic: there's no door-to-door motorway you know. Anyway, what's all the fuss about?'

'Oh, nothing. Nothing at all. Just that while you've been messing about in the country I've been trying to catch up with typing the backlog of valuations; the telephone hasn't stopped ringing; everybody wants you to ring them back urgently; almost every senior member of Hampson's staff has wandered in here expecting tea or coffee as if we're some sort of Lyon's Corner House; Bob Derby has been up and down those stairs half a dozen times whingeing about something fresh each time; and I think I'm going to scream . . . !'

'No, please don't!' I insisted, raising a hand in protest. 'There are valuable ceramics next door and we've already had one breakage today . . .'

'I know – the bureau. That's one of the things our beloved Chairman was complaining about.'

Hampson's jungle telegraph never ceased to amaze me. It was so inexplicably efficient, Bob Derby had probably heard about the broken bureau before the thing had hit the pavement.

'It wasn't my fault,' I protested.

'Tough!' Charlotte said, carefully putting the cover on her typewriter. 'It's not mine either, but he moaned to me about it for ten minutes this morning.'

'All right, I'll go and see him and find out what he's getting so excited about.'

'Right, but don't forget to sign those valuations and letters in your tray if you want them to go in tonight's post. I'm not hanging about this evening. I'm out of this place at five thirty on the dot come hell or high water. I have had enough!'

'Okay, okay,' I said, going round behind my desk and taking the pile of correspondence from the metal basket, 'I'll do them now if it will make you happy. And may I say, Charlotte, what a joy it is to return to my cosy, friendly little office and loyal staff after a hard day's valuing.'

'Knickers!' she replied, and continued tidying her desk.

The Chairman turned out to be in one of his hyper-efficient moods. This was obviously why he had been so troublesome during the day. I found him with his jacket off outside the furniture saleroom instructing a junior porter on the finer points of carrying a table which was far too large and awkward for him.

'There you are,' he shouted as the young man zig-zagged away from us, knees buckling under the burden, his face getting redder with every step he took. 'That's it! That's it! You've got it!'

The porter wheeled left into the foyer and disappeared from sight. A moment later there was a distant crash: it was the unmistakable sound of a drawer dropping out of a table.

'There goes the drawer,' I said.

'I know,' Bob agreed, shaking his head, 'and I told him to be careful of that. Half the trouble with these youngsters is they don't bloody listen.'

'Very likely.'

'Mmmm,' he said, nodding his head in agreement with his own theory. 'But what about this fiasco with the bureau at Bailey's this morning, Richard? I understand you were in on that.'

I explained exactly what had happened.

He shook his head once more, as he picked up his jacket from a nearby chair and slipped it one. 'There's just not enough attention paid to security in this company – things have got to be tightened up.'

'But . . .'

'No buts, Richard. It's all got far too slack. It was pure luck that we got that bureau back at all . . .'

"Scuse me, guv.' Bob was interrupted by a burly man wearing a blue apron. 'I'm s'posed to pick up some urns. They was in today's sale.'

'Yes, just have a word with one of the porters . . .'

'I 'ave, but they're all busy, an' if I don't get goin' soon my guvnor'll lock the ware'ouse before I get back.'

'I'm sure they'll deal with you as quickly as they can. It's just that everybody wants to clear at once at the moment,' Robert Derby explained patiently.

'An' I'm triple parked out there an' all,' the man added for good measure. 'I 'spect the next thing'll be a bleedin' ticket wun' it.'

'Well, I don't . . .'

'I'll 'ave to pay for it you know,' the man moaned on.

'My guvnor don't pay parkin' tickets. 'E makes the drivers pay 'em – tight sod 'e is.'

Hampson's Chairman sighed. I could tell the salvo of complaints was wearing him down.

'Have you got your paperwork?' he asked wearily.

'Yeah – I got it all 'ere,' the man said, pulling a catalogue and two folded bits of paper from his apron pocket.

'Let's have a look,' Bob said, taking the receipted copies of the bills from him and opening them out. 'Oh, it's these,' he went on, pointing to four nineteenth-century Italian marble urns that had been displayed with some other garden statuary in the corridor outside the saleroom. 'You can take these – that's no problem.'

The man looked at the four heavy lumps of carving and frowned.

'I'm on me own,' he complained, 'I got a pair of wheels, but if I start liftin' them bleedin' fings about I'll end up wiv a bleedin' 'ernia.'

'We'll give you a hand,' my employer said soothingly, volunteering my services as well as his own. 'You go and get your set of wheels.'

While the man returned to his lorry I had a look at the urns. 'They're quite nice quality,' I said. 'What did they make?'

'Two and a half, I think,' Bob replied, glancing at the bill to check. 'Oh, no they didn't,' he said. 'According to this they only made two thousand four hundred and fifty. Odd – I could have sworn they made exactly two and a half.'

A metallic rattling from the foyer heralded the return of our friend with his sack barrow.

"Ow we goin' to do this, then?' he asked when he rejoined us. What he actually meant, of course, was how were Bob Derby and I going to do it.

'You hold that thing steady and we'll lift them on,' the Chairman directed.

With much heaving and straining and quite a bit of grunting we loaded the first one onto the creaking sack barrow.

'Do you need a hand getting it onto the truck?' I called after the man as he trundled his first load back down the corridor.

'Nah – I got hydraulics,' he explained, making it sound like some sort of infectious disease.

It was just over a quarter of an hour later when we loaded the final urn onto the sack barrow.

'That's it then,' the man said. 'D'you keep both of them?' He pointed to the bills which Bob had laid on a nearby chair.

'No, just one of them – the Porter's Copy,' Bob Derby replied, handing the other back to the man.

'Okay. See yer,' he grunted, and set off down the corridor and out to his lorry.

'Well, he was all charm, ' Bob commented once the aproned figure had disappeared from sight.

'Yes,' I said, 'and he didn't even offer us a tip.'

He smiled momentarily, then looked serious again. 'Now, what was I saying before we got involved in that? Ah, yes – security.'

I allowed myself an inward groan. I had hoped he'd forgotten.

'That fiasco with the bureau this morning was just the tip of the iceberg, Richard, and it's costing us a lot of money.'

'But . . .'

'No buts – things have got to be tightened up . . . have you got a problem, John?' His rather irritated enquiry was directed at John Adams, the Head Porter of the Furniture Department who was standing behind us scratching his head.

'I don't know – we seem to have lost a lot, Mr Derby.'

'Here we go again,' Bob snorted. 'What is it you can't find?'

'Well, it's ridiculous – it's those Italian urns – Lot 244. I mean, nobody's likely to have spirited them away, surely?'

'No, it's all right, we've just released them to a carrier. Here's the Porter's Copy of the bill.' He handed the piece of paper he had been holding to John Adams. 'I was just going to bring it to you.'

The porter looked baffled as he scrutinised the document. 'But this isn't right, Mr Derby,' he said, eventually. 'I don't know who the 'Jones' is on this bill but he definitely didn't buy those urns.'

'What on earth do you mean? There's the bill, John. You can see for yourself – can't you?'

'Yes, Mr Derby. But here's Architectural Antiques' bill.' He removed a copy of a bill from the catalogue he was carrying, and handed it to the Chairman. 'The urns are listed there as well. Look – Lot 244 – two thousand five hundred pounds. I know they bought them because I was bidding on their behalf.'

Bob Derby stared at the bill, then took back the one he had just handed to John Adams and compared the two.

'What is it?' I asked. 'Some sort of billing error?'

'No,' he said, still staring at the bills, 'not a billing error, just one of the oldest tricks in the book, and I fell for it – we've been conned, Richard.'

I took the two bills from him and looked at them.

'I don't understand,' John Adams complained. 'How can it be a con-trick? The Jones bill's stamped paid. There's nothing fake about that. All right they've got the urns, but it's still cost them two thousand four hundred and fifty pounds. Don't tell me they went to all this trouble for the sake of fifty pounds?'

Bob Derby suddenly looked very tired. 'Do you know what they've done, Richard?' he asked quietly.

'I've got a pretty good idea,' I said. 'I had it done to me once in Sussex.'

61

'Would you like to explain the principle to John, please. I don't think I can do it without crying.'

'Well, John, I think you'll find that somebody giving the name of Jones did buy in today's sale,' I began, 'but it wasn't Lot 244. I suspect we'll discover it was Lot 44 that he bought. And he didn't pay two thousand four hundred and fifty pounds for it, just fifty . . .'

It was a neat little con and all you needed were nerves of steel when you came to pick up your targeted piece. It all revolved around altering the entry on the bill of course.

'All they had to do,' I continued, 'was forge a "2" in front of the lot number and "24" in front of the price. It didn't matter that the price wasn't the right one, it was close enough for any porter not to have given it a second glance.'

'I would have noticed,' John Adams protested.

'Yes, and he made damned sure you didn't get the chance, didn't he?' cut in Bob Derby. 'He saw you in the saleroom, obviously knew you were the one who had actually bid for the urns, and looked around for somebody else.'

'Whom he promptly found,' I added.

Robert Derby glared at me but said nothing.

'How long ago did he clear the urns?' asked John Adams.

'Not long,' I replied. 'Ten minutes, or a quarter of an hour perhaps.'

'Perhaps he's still outside,' he suggested, his voice rising a little with excitement. 'Perhaps he hasn't got away yet; perhaps he's . . .'

'Well on his way to wherever it is he's going,' Bob said, morosely.

'But he can't have got far,' Adams insisted, obviously filled with righteous zeal. 'If we get onto the police right away we can give them a description of the lorry and its registration number. They're bound to pick it up.'

'The trouble with that idea, John', explained Bob Derby, 'is that we have no idea what the lorry looks like, let alone what its registration number is.'

'But surely one of you saw it!'

'No,' I said. 'You see – he had hydraulics.'

Chapter 6

For a routine furniture sale it had really been quite
eventful. In fact, if I'd had any tendency towards
paranoia I would have gone straight back to my office
and locked myself in. However, being relatively
complex-free, I simply eased myself carefully into my
chair and once again very gently felt what seemed to me
to be an egg-sized lump on the back of my head.

'Ouch!' I said, just in case Charlotte had failed to
notice something was wrong.

'What's the matter?' she asked, dutifully.

'I've got a large lump on my head.'

'What did you do – fall out of the rostrum?'

Her question, although doubtless intended to be
humorous, was not that far from the truth. Anyway, I
had once fallen off the rostrum some years earlier in
Sussex. It had been at my old firm, Wilson's, where we
always constructed an improvised rostrum from
furniture included in whatever sale happened to be
taking place. Ideally the base would be a big, strong
dining table covered with a rug and old table cloths to
protect it. On top of that we would stand a small table,
also covered with a large velour cloth, and finally a nice,
comfortable dining chair with arms would be added.
This arrangement generally worked very well although
we usually tried to make sure the large table came from
a probate lot. This was because if the owner did happen
to be in the land of the living he or she inevitably had a

fit when they saw the use their pride and joy was being put to. This could be very disruptive if it occurred in the middle of a sale.

At the auction in question we'd had quite a struggle to find a suitable table to fill the bill. Eventually we had chosen a modern oak refectory table which had the advantage of being part of a house contents where we knew no members of the late owner's family would be attending the sale. Its disadvantage was that it was probably about eighteen inches shorter than it might ideally have been. Nevertheless, I didn't see any great problem arising from that – there still seemed to be more than enough room once the whole thing was set up.

What I had failed to appreciate until that day was just how much I fidgeted during a sale. The better it was going, the faster it was selling, the quicker the bids were coming, the more animated I became. I certainly had no idea I tended to ease my chair gradually further and further away from the side table at which I sat. It was a discovery I made at Lot 464. I had barely finished reading out the lot number when the view in front of me changed dramatically. Instead of the faces of the two hundred or so people in the auction room, I suddenly found myself staring up at a frighteningly fast moving vista of fluorescent tubes and skylights. I had pushed my chair back just an inch too far and the back legs had slipped over the edge of the table. Fortunately for me, the largest and strongest porter in our team had, in the nick of time, foreseen what was going to happen and had just managed to get behind me when I fell off. So, no sooner had I become reconciled to the idea of meeting my maker, than the whole process was suddenly reversed. Fluorescent tubes, skylights, walls and people all passed before my eyes again, but this time as if they were part of some sort of slow-motion action replay of my life. My burly saviour was quietly and without fuss heaving both me and my chair back into the vertical plane.

'Not on this occasion,' I replied to Charlotte's question.

'What happened, then?'

'I was hit by a clock.'

'A clock?'

'Yes – a longcase clock.'

'Go on then,' she said. 'You're obviously dying to tell me about it.'

'Well, it was like this,' I began. 'I was sitting in the rostrum, minding my own business, taking the furniture sale . . .'

All I had done was to ask for the windows to be opened. It wasn't an unreasonable request. It was one of those days when London was at its stickiest and grimiest. There was no breath of air and the heat rippled back from the pavements turning the city into one big sauna.

Although the furniture saleroom at Hampson's was shaded from any direct sun it was still hot and stuffy. The further into the sale I got the more difficult it became to get the bidding going. The assembled company was becoming very drowsy. Given another quarter of an hour they would all be asleep.

'I think you and I are the only one's still awake,' I whispered to Patrick Faulkner, the Furniture Director.

He was standing next to the rostrum with his nose in his catalogue. As he looked up I saw tiny rivulets of perspiration trickling down his florid face. He mopped his shining brow and replied, 'Speak for yourself, dear boy. *I've* been dozing gently through most of the sale – I've already missed two bids for clients.'

'We'd better do something to wake them up,' I said, completing another unsold entry in my book, 'or we may as well pack up and go home.'

'Sounds fine to me – it's a pretty awful sale, after all.'

He had a point. It was definitely not one of Patrick's

better sales, and that, just as much as the weather, was helping to contribute to the sluggish pace. However, there was another factor at work as well: a tall, sharp-featured dealer called Sefton-Clare, who was exactly what an auctioneer didn't need on a day like this.

Mr Sefton-Clare was a skilled and doughty campaigner when it came to wrecking auctions. He was well aware that a fast, tightly run auction produces higher prices than a slow one where the bidding is dictated by the buyers on the floor rather than the auctioneer in the rostrum. Consequently he had, over the years, formulated a certain technique designed to throw any auctioneer off his stride.

To begin with, he rarely stayed still for more than a couple of minutes at a time. Instead, he would wander about the saleroom having brief snatches of conversation with any other dealers he knew. These chats would usually take the form of observations on the lot currently being offered, or comments on the sanity of the buyer of the previous piece:

'That one still doing the rounds is it? It was at Sotheby's last month!. . . I've got a *pair* in stock he could have for the price he's just paid for that *one*!. . . five hundred pounds! She must have money to burn . . .!'

Of course, his none too subtle remarks caused the dealing fraternity little concern; they knew what he was up to. It was the inexperienced buyer whose confidence was sapped by his critical commentary, and it could be more than a little distracting for the auctioneer too. Not as distracting, however, as it was when he actually bid for something.

One of his favourite tricks was to stand almost directly in front of the rostrum with his back to the auctioneer. From that vantage point he could usually identify who was bidding against him, and having done so he would scowl at them or laugh or just shake his head in apparent disbelief every time they made a fresh bid.

This was intimidating for the bidder, often amusing for everybody else in the crowd, and annoying for the auctioneer because he couldn't see what Sefton-Clare was actually up to. But when it came to annoying auctioneers, nothing worked like the way he delivered his own bids.

He would either throw up a languid hand or call out his next bid very loudly. In either case he would do it just a second or so later than was desirable, usually just as the hammer was on the way down but before it had actually fallen. This had the potential to turn any sale into a stop-go marathon with the bidding on various lots having to be reopened because Mr Sefton-Clare's shouts and waves were just in time, even though the piece had been temporarily knocked down to somebody else. This particular technique could be countered as long as the auctioneer was firm and as long as there were lots of bids coming from other people. All you had to do was ignore him and take the bids from elsewhere in the room. On a day like this, however, when three quarters of the assembled company appeared to be fast asleep, Sefton-Clare was in ascendancy: he was difficult to ignore.

'. . . at one hundred and twenty pounds, then . . . at one hundred and twenty . . . at one hundred and twenty . . . are you all finished with it at one hundred and twenty pounds . . . ?' I enquired, surveying the sleepy scene with little hope in my heart that we would ever make it to the £150 reserve figure in my book. As I raised my gavel, Mr Sefton-Clare broke off the conversation he'd been having with another dealer who was seated away to my right and made for the showing table where the piece concerned, a chair, was being displayed.

'Wait, please, Sir!' he implored as he loped across the room, his half-moon spectacles pushed back on his balding head, his expression one of deep seriousness.

'Just a moment!' It was as though his life suddenly depended on it.

I held the gavel high in the sultry air as he wrenched the lot from the porter and went over it in minute detail.

'. . . at one hundred and twenty pounds,' I reminded him. 'Will you bid me one hundred and thirty?'

He stood back, looked at the chair, stepped forward, examined it again, then suddenly threw his hand aloft.

'. . . one hundred and thirty . . .' I confirmed, '. . . one hundred and forty . . .' I continued, plucking a non-existent bid from a sleepy looking woman in the middle of the room, '. . . may I say one hundred and fifty . . . ?' The question was addressed to Mr Sefton-Clare who still hovered by the showing table.

He flipped his spectacles down from his forehead onto the end of his nose, peered at the underside of the chair once more, shook his head theatrically and strode away towards the back of the saleroom.

'. . . at one hundred and forty pounds, then . . .' I said, and in the sure and certain knowledge that I wouldn't get another bid from any other member of that moribund gathering, I brought the hammer arcing down.

'One forty-five!' Sefton-Clare's bellow reached me just a split second before the head of the gavel cracked against the woodwork of the rostrum. He was in time, and even if he hadn't been I would have reopened the bidding anyway. After all, you never missed the opportunity of selling a lot to somebody bidding against a reserve – especially if it was Mr Sefton-Clare.

There was a problem, however: the bidder was indulging in another of his disruptive tactics – he was trying to reduce the size of the bids. As an auctioneer I always tried to increase the bidding by approximately 10 per cent. That meant I would take £5 bids from £50 to £100, £10 bids from £100 to £200, and so on. Now my adversary was trying to reduce the increment from £10 to £5. This was the last thing I wanted, especially since the next bid would be £150 – the magic figure at which I could actually sell the chair. No, it was essential that Sefton-Clare bid £150 otherwise *I* would end up bidding it. I would then have the job of explaining to the owner, who just happened to be attending the sale, how it was that although her chair had reached its reserve figure, it was still unsold. I knew only too well that all the elucidation in the world would fail to satisfy her: disappointed vendors were like that.

'You were in time,' I cooed to Mr Sefton-Clare's back, 'but bid me one hundred and fifty . . .'

'One forty-five!' he repeated doggedly without turning.

'One hundred and fifty,' I replied firmly.

At that moment he spun on his heel to face me, his features contorted with rage.

'How dare you!' he demanded. 'How dare you! It's my money – I'll do what I like with it! You've got no right to tell me what to pay – I'll bid what I want!'

It was an extraordinary outburst, and completely unexpected since I had never seen the man in any way emotional before. He had always been so calculating in everything he did. Mind you, his little tirade had performed a service of sorts: there was no trace of somnolence in the room anymore. Though absolutely silent, everybody was wide awake, as if an electric current had been run through their seats. This was entertainment and they had no intention of missing it.

'I'll bid what I want!' Mr Sefton-Clare repeated indignantly, glowering at me.

'Of course,' I replied quietly. 'You bid what you want, but I will accept what I choose. And just at this particular moment, I will accept one hundred and fifty pounds. Will you bid it?'

For a moment or two, Sefton-Clare continued to glare

at me from the back of the hushed saleroom. Then his expression melted into a smile, and with a wink he said, 'Very fair, Sir – one hundred and fifty pounds it is!'

Seconds later I brought down the hammer for the final time on the lot in question.

But all that excitement had occured some thirty or forty minutes earlier. Now even Mr Sefton-Clare appeared to be wilting.

'Can't you open the windows, Patrick?' I asked. 'It'll wake them up a bit if we can get some air in here.'

Patrick Faulkner looked slowly around the room without any obvious enthusiasm.

'Most of them have got furniture in front of them,' he observed, as if that ruled out the possibility of any action on his part.

'Yes, but some of them haven't,' I pointed out. 'At least open the ones behind us.'

He glanced round at the windows in question.

'If you insist,' he said grudgingly, 'but it won't make a scrap of difference. There's no breeze at all out there – in fact, it's hotter outside than it is in here. It'll probably make it worse.'

'I'll risk it, Patrick,' I insisted. 'Just open the windows, please.'

'Oh, all right.' He beckoned to one of his porters. 'But it won't do any good.'

He was wrong. Almost immediately a gentle zephyr insinuated itself into the hot, sluggish saleroom air. As further windows were opened the breeze grew in strength, little by little, until it was just robust enough to disturb the loose papers which lay next to my auctioneer's book. It was glorious, and it was having an immediate invigorating effect on the assembled company. Heavy eyelids were blinking open, catalogue pages were once more being turned and heads were being craned to see which lot was being sold. I began to feel I had a live audience once more.

'Right – Lot 243,' I announced. 'The George III mahogany . . .'

My reading of the catalogue description of a rather nice little chest was brutally terminated by a tremendous blow on the back of my head. The weight of my assailant bore down on me following the initial attack so that I found myself very nearly flattened in the rostrum, with my nose buried deep in my auctioneer's book and my arms thrust straight out to either side.

It's said that people often see stars and hear bells ringing when they receive a blow on the head. I can't say I saw any stellar activity but I certainly heard bells. No sooner had I been pinned down than the thing on top of me launched into a loud and fairly melodious Westminster chime. It was at that point that I realised the aggressor was a large, ornately carved and somewhat top-heavy Edwardian longcase clock which had been standing immediately behind the rostrum.

'Get this thing off me!' I spluttered into my book.

'Hold on . . . hold on . . .' said a voice behind me, then I felt the weight being lifted.

Gingerly I started to sit up straight. I immediately took another solid smack on the back of the head. This time the glass door on the front of the hood had swung open and delivered the Parthian shot.

'Sorry, Sir . . . sorry, Sir . . .' chorused the porters behind me. 'Watch out! The hood's coming off . . . grab it . . . grab it!'

I ducked forward, put my hands over my head and waited for the next hammer blow. It crossed my mind as I cowered there that this was the sort of thing that didn't happen at Sotheby's or Christie's.

'All right, Sir – we've got it now. You're okay.'

I lifted my head once more and peeped out over the front of the rostrum. Had I expected a sea of concerned faces I would have been bitterly disappointed. The faces were there all right but the expressions of concern were absent. The view I got must be the sort stand-up comics dream of: everybody in the room appeared to be convulsed.

I looked to my right where Patrick Faulkner was clinging to the side of the rostrum wheezing gently as large tears joined the little lines of perspiration which were still running down his face – a face which was now almost scarlet. He looked up.

'Oh, dear . . . I thought you'd had it for a moment there, dear boy . . .' he gasped. 'I did warn you . . . opening that window . . . would only make things worse . . .' He dissolved into a fresh bout of asthmatic wheezing.

I turned in the rostrum and looked at the big longcase as the porters finished tethering it to the wall.

'What the hell happened?' I asked.

'It just blew over, Sir,' John Adams replied, manfully succeeding in keeping a straight face. 'It's a bit top heavy, and once the breeze got behind it . . . well . . .'

'Yes,' I said, 'I get the general picture.'

I turned to face the room again. The laughter was beginning to subside but it seemed no time to try and stand on my dignity. I brought the gavel down loudly to restore order, and a respectful hush once again settled on the room.

'I don't suppose anybody's got the time?' I asked.

Still gently stroking the lump on my head, I sat back in my chair and looked across at Charlotte.

'Anyway,' I said, 'enough of my tedious, run-of-the-mill morning. Has anything interesting happened here?'

'Nothing mind-blowing,' she replied, in between picking at a lunchtime sandwich, 'but some solicitor called with instructions for a probate valuation.'

'Did it sound any good?'

'Difficult to tell. The deceased was in some sort of

business, but the solicitor said the house is really quite small.'

'Okay – where is it?'

'Well, that's the point – it's in the Lake District.'

'The Lake District! That's one hell of a trek for a small house.'

'I know but you always say we must never say no to probate work.'

'I know, but . . .'

'So why don't you make a weekend of it?'

'What do you mean?'

'God, Richard, you are dim sometimes,' Charlotte said, shaking her head in exasperation. 'You can charge expenses for an overnight stop, can't you?'

'Yes.'

'Well, why don't you book it in for a Thursday or Friday, take Sarah with you and have a long, romantic weekend?'

'Oh,' I said. 'I hadn't thought of that.'

'No, Richard,' Charlotte said, 'I didn't for one moment think you had.'

Chapter 7

Despite leaving London at lunchtime on the Thursday so as not to get entangled in rush-hour traffic, it had still taken us a good five hours to get to Merethwaite House Hotel.

Although the weather was now quite grey it didn't detract from the landscape which surrounded us as we drove up the long tarmac drive to the hotel.

'Good Lord,' Sarah said, stretching in the passenger seat beside me. 'What a pile!'

It was true. I doubt anybody would have described Merethwaite House as an architectural gem, but it was imposing. Perched precariously on the side of a fell, its solid grey structure brooded over the patchwork of green fields which dropped away below it. Behind, the steep hillside climbed, to disappear eventually in a pall of low cloud which hung over the castellated roof of this very Victorian mansion.

Although a few cars stood outside the massive front doors there was a feeling that the place was not teeming with guests.

'It's quite chilly,' Sarah said, as she stood by the car admiring the view.

'Never mind, it's a pleasant change after the last couple of weeks in London,' I replied, retrieving my briefcase from the back seat and locking up. 'Let's go in and see what the room's like.'

Merethwaite House had been the personal recommendation of the solicitor handling the probate valuation. I had naturally regarded it with some suspicion since his client was due to pay the cost of at least one night's stay, but when Charlotte checked up on it she found it had quite a reasonable reputation and that its room rates were not particularly cheap. As a result, Sarah and I had decided to book into Merethwaite for two nights and then decamp to a bed and breakfast for the Saturday evening, driving back on the Sunday.

We located the reception desk tucked below the stairs in a suitably baronial entrance hall. It was unattended so I rang the bell and waited.

'Look at this,' Sarah said, pointing to an easel with a rather ugly plastic notice board on it.

I wandered over to see. It was one of those displays which welcomes the arrival of corporate guests. It seemed that a double glazing company's sales force was due to descend on the hotel on the Saturday afternoon: just about the time we would be leaving.

'That was a close one,' I observed.

'Yes,' Sarah agreed. 'Short of filling the place with merchant bankers I can't think of anything worse.'

We were still studying the notice board when a member of the hotel staff appeared on the scene. He was in his late forties or early fifties, had a toupee which looked like an old ginger Tom, and seemed to be wearing just the faintest hint of rouge.

'Good evening, Sir, Mad-am,' he said, with a Welsh lilt as he minced elegantly across the hall to the reception desk. 'Sorry to have kept you waiting, but we're just a little short-handed at the moment. what can I do to help you?'

'You have a double room for us,' I said, 'in the name of Harton.'

'Oh, yes?' he replied. 'Let's have a look now.' He scanned the large ledger which lay open on the desk in front of him. 'No Har-ton,' he said eventually, 'but we've got a double room down for Bar-ton – I expect that's you. These silly girls just don't listen.'

I shrugged my shoulders. 'My secretary confirmed it in writing,' I said. 'You should have a letter there . . .'

'Yes, don't worry about it,' he said cheerily. 'It happens all the time. If you'd both like to register I'll get your cases – is your car locked?'

I gave him the keys and we both watched him spellbound as he made his way outside. He walked just as though his legs were tied together at the knees.

'What an amazing little man,' Sarah said. 'Do you think he runs the place single-handed?'

'No – he's obviously got a team of silly girls who just don't listen,' I said. 'Watch out – here he comes again.'

'All done?' he asked as, regardless of the considerable weight of suitcases he was carrying, he glided effortlessly across the hall. Putting down the bags he slid behind the desk again, spun the register around and checked it.

'Mr Har-ton and Miss Bish-op,' he read, smiling. 'I see.' He studied the entry for a few seconds more, then turned and took a key from the board behind him. 'Room thirty-two – I'll take you up now.'

Sweeping up our cases just as painlessly as he had carried them before, he set off in the opposite direction to that indicated by the signs for the lift.

'We'll have to use the service lift, I'm afraid,' he explained. 'The engineer's working on the passenger one – should be done any time now.'

We followed him down a narrow passageway to a large and aged lift. Dragging back the heavy concertina door he permitted us to enter first, then clambered aboard himself, closed the door and pounded the third-floor button two or three times. There was a distant whirring noise, the lift shuddered, then with a jerk it left the launchpad and clanked its way onward and upward.

Our guide, who was standing just inside the door, next

to the control panel, regarded us with a tolerant, almost indulgent smile. I felt the need to break the silence.

'The hotel doesn't seem too busy at the moment,' I observed, for want of anything more incisive to say.

'No, Sir – it's the lull in between the storms, if you see what I mean. We've just got rid of one big sales conference and we've got another one starting on Saturday.'

'The double glazing lot?' Sarah said.

'Yes, Miss,' he replied, as what was obviously a shudder ran through him. 'I know I shouldn't say this, but they're a real bunch of animals. They were here last year – all short-sleeved shirts and polyester ties. They'll arrive here at four to four thirty, and be paralytic by eight. I don't know why they bother to have a meal. They're too drunk to appreciate it when they eat it and they throw it up later anyway.'

The lift crashed to a halt so violently that it left Sarah and me staggering about like a couple of the double glaziers our friend had been describing.

'Whoopsee!' he said. 'Be careful. I'll lead the way, it's a bit of a long walk.'

It wasn't really too bad, although the corridor which led to the main landing was rather dark. There was also a strong, acrid smell which hung on the air; as though someone had been burning plastic nearby.

'What's that smell?' I asked.

'What smell's that then?' our porter enquired out of the gloom ahead.

'Smoke of some sort, I think,' Sarah replied.

'Oh, that!' he said, skilfully opening the door onto the landing almost without breaking his stride, let alone putting down the cases. 'I've got so used to it already I don't notice it any more . . . your room's just down here by the way – not far now.'

'But what is it?' I asked again, as we trotted along behind him across the landing, which seemed brilliantly lit after the darkness of the service corridor.

'Smoke – it was everywhere,' he explained, heading down another passageway.

'Where did it come from?'

'Why – the fire, of course,' he answered. 'Ah, here we are: room thirty-two.' He put the cases down and put the key in the lock.

'What fire?' Sarah asked with a note of concern in her voice.

'The one in the kitchens,' he said rather absent-mindedly but with no trace of annoyance. As though a fire in the kitchens was a perfectly normal event and our cross-examination just one of the natural burdens a porter has to bear.

'When was that?' Sarah went on, now clearly alarmed, as we followed him into the room.

'This morning,' he replied, mincing around the large Edwardian bed to the window. 'Lovely view, look.'

'I hope it wasn't a serious fire,' I said.

'Oh, yes – it was awful. Pretty well gutted one of the kitchens – not the main one though, so it could have been worse. Mind you, the last fire engine's only just gone.' He turned back to the window again. 'It's a shame it's got so hazy – you could see for miles this morning.'

'You're sure it's all quite safe now?' Sarah persisted.

'Oh, yes, Miss,' he said, smiling at her, 'safe as houses.'

He was about to go when I realised our room seemed to be lacking something. 'Where's the bathroom?' I asked.

'Oh, yes – almost forgot in the excitement,' he said, opening the door. 'Just across there.'

Through the doorway I could see another door on the other side of the hall. It had a 'Private' sign on it.

'It's for your own private use, so I've put the sign up. You won't be disturbed.' He gave what looked suspiciously like a wink and slipped out of the room closing the door behind him.

79

Later that evening as we made our way downstairs for pre-dinner drinks, Sarah and I agreed that Merethwaite House did at least have a certain creaky, eccentric charm.

As soon as the porter had left us with that suggestive flutter of his eyelid, we had got down to business: not what he seemed to have had in mind, simply a search for the nearest fire escape – just in case. We had eventually located it not far from our room. It was a very small doorway, more of a hatch really, which was halfway up the wall and led out onto the battlements. Climbing on a chair I squeezed through it and followed a line of duckboards and ladders for some distance over the undulating lead-covered peaks of the hotel roofscape, returning eventually to my starting point.

'Where does it lead to?' Sarah asked.

'Back here,' I said. 'As far as I can see we're supposed to mill round out there until any fire goes out.'

The bathroom had also been well worth a visit. It was about the same size as our bedroom but contained only essential bathroom furniture which gave it a vaguely cavernous air. The bath itself was a massive bit of Victorian ironwork which stood raised up proudly on a sort of dais in the middle of the room. It was the type of bath that meant business – there was nothing frivolous about it. The room was without windows but it did possess a large skylight which was placed so as to permit a little amateur astronomy as one lay back in the tub. It was all very civilised in its own way, but I could not help but feel that the occasional creaking board in the corridor outside was the passing ghost of a long dead house guest from a far more glorious past.

'Good evening, Sir . . . *Miss* . . .' our friend from the afternoon greeted us pointedly when we entered the bar. With a change of jacket and the addition of a bow tie he had been transformed from porter into cocktail waiter. I was beginning to believe Sarah was right: he was running the place single-handed.

We took our drinks by the huge fireplace where a display of fresh flowers filled the grate. Then we made our way through to the oak-panelled dining room.

We had both prepared ourselves mentally for the possibility that the waiter (or waitress) might well turn out to be that same familiar figure with the Welsh lilt and the Ginger Tom toupee. On this occasion, however, it was not to be. Instead we were greeted by a young girl with a local accent, what was almost certainly all her own hair, and a slightly nervous smile.

Once seated at our table we looked around the large, rather brightly lit room. Only four of the tables were occupied, underlining what we had been told – that we were in the lull between the storms.

'I think we're the youngest here by about forty years,' Sarah whispered.

'Yes,' I agreed. 'I suddenly feel incredibly young.'

'With the exception of two elderly ladies who were chatting quietly at one table, the other six guests looked to be married couples.

'Have you noticed that none of them are speaking?' Sarah asked quietly.

'Yes,' I said, looking at the silently masticating white and grey heads.

'I suppose they just don't have anything to say any more – sad, isn't it?'

'Oh, I don't know,' I replied. 'It might not be that. It might just be that their dentures don't permit eating and talking at the same time.'

Sarah scowled at me.

'Well, *I* think it's sad,' she continued. 'They were probably all deeply in love one day and now it's come down to this: silent meals in empty hotel dining rooms. It's depressing.'

'At the risk of seeming mercenary,' I said, 'we could be perfectly adequately depressed at home for nothing.

Being depressed here, however, is costing my client and me a small fortune.'

'You're right,' she said with a bright smile. 'Anyway, they're probably perfectly happy like that.'

As she spoke there was a sudden explosion at the far end of the room.

'Well, I'm going up! You can do what *you* goddam like!'

The speaker was a tall, heavily built man with a red face and a shock of white hair. From his accent he was clearly American, and from his impassioned outburst he was clearly upset with his companion.

What little conversation there had been in the dining room had ceased, and all eyes were temporarily focused on the departing broad-shouldered figure and the silent partner still seated at the table. I judged her to be some years younger than him, and at that moment she was very obviously bitterly unhappy. She stared straight ahead, avoiding the gaze of her fellow diners, and I noticed that as she raised her glass to her lips her hand trembled slightly. But, otherwise, she maintained an admirable outer calm.

The big man's ill-tempered display did at least do some service for the moribund conversation of the other guests. Heads were soon shaking at each table and a low, indistinct murmur became audible above the clinking of cutlery on china.

Sarah and I continued to watch the lonely figure. She sipped from her glass once more, then rose from her seat, picked up her handbag and, smiling faintly to the suddenly embarrassed couple on the next table, walked slowly from the room.

'The poor woman,' Sarah observed. 'What a dreadful old boor that man must be.'

The episode did little to brighten up the evening and even Sarah and I found ourselves finishing our main course in silence. By the time the plates had been cleared away we were the only ones left in the dining room.

'Would you like to see the sweet trolley?' the young waitress enquired.

A few moments later she was slowly and self-consciously going through the list of delicacies available: '... fresh fruit salad ... strawberry shortcake ... chocolate gâteau ...'

'What would you like?' I asked Sarah.

'Oh, I'm full really,' she replied, 'but perhaps I'll just have some fruit – an orange, I think.'

Most of the top tier of the trolley was given over to an impressive pyramid of fresh fruit topped by a large pineapple. It did all look very good.

'An orange?' asked the waitress, with the implication that this was an unexpected and unusual request.

'Yes, please,' Sarah confirmed.

For a moment the girl's hand hovered beside the great pile of fruit, then she plunged in. I held my breath: for some inexplicable reason she had chosen a fruit from the very base of the pyramid. There were others dotted about the structure which were obviously of much less importance to its continued stability, but she had chosen one from the base.

For a few seconds the edifice remained intact, then in one big rush it collapsed completely. The hapless waitress made an unavailing lunge but it was useless; the pyramid simply disappeared before her eyes as its component parts cascaded from the trolley and sped off to the four corners of the room. As the last apple bounced onto the carpet and trundled away under a nearby table Sarah and I sat, once again silent, desperately avoiding any eye contact. With admirable poise, the brightly blushing waitress placed the orange on Sarah's plate and turned to me.

'And for you, Sir?' she asked.

I concentrated as hard as I possibly could on not collapsing into uncontrollable laughter. Fortunately what I wanted wasn't on the trolley, it was on the sideboard next to a decanter of vintage port.

'I think I'll have a little of the Stilton and a glass of port,' I said.

The waitress looked blank.

'The Stilton,' I repeated gently, pointing towards the fine half-cheese.

She looked over at the sideboard then back at me. 'The Stilton?' she said, just as doubtfully as she had confirmed Sarah's fruit order.

I nodded.

Still avoiding looking at each other, we watched her as she made her way through the litter of fresh fruit to the sideboard. She paused looking down at the cheese, then picked up the knife which lay next to it. Another pause, then she replaced the knife and returned to our table.

'I'm afraid we don't have any Stilton,' she said.

It was my turn to pause. I cleared my throat. 'But,' I began, 'that's a Stilton on the sideboard – and a very nice one by the look of it.'

The waitress looked thoughtful for a moment, then her face broke into a disarmingly bright smile. 'I don't know how to cut it,' she confessed. 'I'm new here – it's only my second day.'

'Would you like me to do it?' I asked.

'No, Sir, don't you worry – I'll go and get somebody. I won't be a minute.'

A short while later she returned with our old friend, the porter-cum-barman. He looked around the room in disbelief.

'Oh dear, oh dear,' he said eventually. 'You told me you'd had a *little* accident with the fruit. This place looks like Covent Garden market on a bad day.'

The waitress said nothing.

'Oh, well, you pick it all up, Trudy, and I'll see to the gentleman's cheese.'

Trudy nodded and set about her task.

'I'm sorry, Sir,' the factotum apologised when he delivered the cheese and the port, 'we're a bit short-handed today what with the fire and everything. Now – where would you like your coffee? In the lounge? Or shall I just get Trudy to throw it over you in here?'

We elected for the solitary splendour of the lounge – as opposed to the solitary splendour of the dining room – and passed the next three-quarters of an hour there without further mishap.

'Well,' Sarah said, replacing her cup on the table, 'after all this excitement there's just one thing I have to say to you, Richard.'

'Oh, yes,' I replied. 'And what is that, pray?'

'I'm going up! And you can do what you goddam like!'

Chapter 8

The same four couples as on the previous evening occupied the dining room when we came down for breakfast. We exchanged greetings with two of them as we took our table.

'There they are in the window,' Sarah whispered.

'I know,' I said. 'I saw them when we came in.'

The large, red-faced man was engrossed in his newspaper while his wife nibbled at a bowl of cereal.

'He looks such a brute,' Sarah went on. 'I wonder what the attraction is.'

'Perhaps he's stupendously wealthy,' I suggested.

'Perhaps,' she said. 'Anyway, he seems quiet enough now.'

'Yes,' I agreed. 'But to change the subject: what are you going to do with yourself this morning?'

'I haven't really decided. I might go for a walk. How long do you think the valuation will take?'

'I don't know. It's supposed to be quite small, so I should be finished before lunch.'

'Well, why don't we . . .'

Sarah's suggestion was interrupted by a bellow from the window table: 'What did you say?' boomed the old man.

His wife said something in reply, but very quietly.

'What?' the man bellowed once more.

Again the woman said something which didn't carry to our table.

'Dammit! Why don't you speak up?' he thundered, his face almost purple. 'I can't hear a goddam word you say! Why don't you speak so I can hear you?'

This time I could pick out odd words in her reply: 'Please . . . looking . . . hate it . . . please . . .'

'What d'you mean, people are looking?' he roared. 'Of course they're not goddam looking! Why should anybody be interested in you, Julia? Why d'you think anybody would be interested in what you've got to say? Eh? Tell me that, Julia? Just look around you – nobody's looking at you – are they?'

I suppose, at that particular moment, he was right: nobody was looking at her. Suddenly, everyone was deeply involved with their menus, cornflakes or scrambled eggs. Just a second earlier, however, every eye in the place had been fixed on Julia and her tormentor. It was such compelling stuff it just couldn't be ignored. But, in the end, good old British reserve won through and we all pretended we had seen and heard nothing.

The man rose to his feet, picked up his newspaper and once again strode dramatically from the room. A boor he might have been but he sure knew how to make an exit.

As the muted murmur of conversation returned once again to the sunlit dining room, the much verbally abused wife gathered her things together, and with near superhuman dignity got up and left.

'She certainly handles humiliation with style,' I observed after she had gone.

'So would you if you'd had as much practice as she has,' Sarah replied. 'I just don't understand why any woman would put up with what she seems to endure on a daily basis.'

She was right. It was impossible to fathom. Perhaps it was that the old man had not always been like that; perhaps the woman had memories of better days to

87

sustain her; or perhaps it was just habit – more difficult to break than it was to suffer the daily onslaughts quietly. Whatever the explanation, she had definitely developed the ability to cope.

When I walked to my car half an hour later she was seated nearby on the edge of the lawn at an easel, a pristine sheet of white paper pinned to the board in front of her and a box of watercolour paints by her side. She was absolutely still, staring out over the fields to the distant lake and the harsh fells which rose beyond. Dressed almost entirely in white and wearing a broad-brimmed straw hat, she looked serenely Edwardian.

'It's a wonderful view,' I observed, as I threw my briefcase into the car. 'Do you paint a lot?'

'Yes,' she said, smiling, apparently not at all shy or reticent. 'My husband and I spend about four months a year travelling. He plays golf and I paint. It works very well.'

'Well, good luck,' I said, climbing into the car, not at all sure why I had actually made that particular remark.

'Thank you. Goodbye.' She smiled once more and turned back to the panorama below her.

I never saw either of them again. By the time I returned to the hotel later that morning, both she and her husband had checked out.

The valuation address turned out to be a very ordinary brick-built house which must have dated from between the wars. It was small and dowdy and was set in a ragged little garden next door to a large, old prefabricated concrete garage. My expectations had not been high but it still fell short of them. I began to suspect I would be back at Merethwaite House before Sarah even laced up her walking shoes.

Charlotte had arranged for the local estate agent to meet me, and the highly polished Rover parked on the uneven, cracked concrete slab outside the garage suggested he was nothing if not punctual. As I clambered from my own vehicle the front door of the house was thrown open and a man in a pale blue suit bounded out to meet me. He was in his mid-thirties, a little puffy around the face, and with a lock of blond hair which hung down limply over his forehead.

'Mr Harton? You're in good time! Good to meet you – I'm Denis Evans. Come in, come in! I'm just measuring up for the particulars. It's not much of a place but you can sell anything and everything in this area nowadays! I wouldn't have thought there was anything for you though. I don't know why they bothered to drag you all the way up here. They might as well have used the local man. He's very good. I put a lot of work his way. It's all junk here as far as I can tell. Mind you I don't know much about furniture and that sort of thing so I could be wrong, but it all looks like rubbish to me. I collect limited edition china. Do you know anything about that? It's a pretty specialist market of course, most of the buying and selling is direct – one collector to another. But I expect you know that. After all, you are the expert. How are you?' He shook my hand vigorously as he concluded his opening remarks which seemed to have been delivered without any pause for breath.

'Very well, thanks,' I replied, careful not to get involved in offering any sort of opinion on the limited edition porcelain market.

'Good, good. Let's go in then you'll see what I mean. Mind the step – it needs some attention.' He rattled the loose brick with his foot, then carried on into the house. 'See what I mean about it being junk,' he went on as we surveyed the rather squalid little hallway. 'How some people live – I don't know!'

'I understood the late owner was a businessman,' I said.

'Oh, he was,' he laughed, 'and never without work I'm sure.'

89

I must have looked puzzled.

'He was an undertaker, Mr Harton. The neighbours say he was a nice old chap but a bit eccentric in later years.'

We moved through into the dining room, then the sitting room. It was the same everywhere: dingy paintwork, ancient wallpaper, nasty 1930s and 40s cheap furniture. It was really quite depressing.

'Well, this isn't going to take me very long,' I said, as we trudged upstairs. 'It looks like a figure of two or three hundred maximum will cover the lot.'

'That's what I thought,' Mr Evans replied. 'Complete waste of time dragging you up here . . . what's that you've found in there?'

He was referring to the contents of a large, painted plywood cupboard at the top of the stairs. I had opened the double doors expecting to find nothing more exciting than bed linen only to be confronted with a little boy's wonderland instead.

'Toys,' I said, 'and a lot of them.'

The old cupboard was packed as full as it could be. Every shelf sagged under the weight of its load. I removed a large flat box and blew away the woodworm dust which had fallen onto it from the shelf above.

'What's that?' asked the estate agent, craning his neck to get a better look over my shoulder.

'An electric train set – Hornby Dublo. It doesn't go back any further than the 1950s but it looks to be in excellent condition.'

'What's it worth?' he asked, this time almost elbowing me aside in his excitement.

'No idea,' I admitted, replacing the train set and looking through some of the neatly stacked Dinky toys on the next shelf down. 'I'll just list the whole lot and check the prices when I get back to London . . . oh look!'

'What? What?'

'A car transporter – I always wanted a car

transporter . . . never got one though.'

Denis Evans gave me a very strange look then cast his eye over the contents of the cupboard once again.

'Some of those boxes look as though they've never been opened,' he said.

'Yes, the toys inside are going to be in mint condition,' I replied. 'That's what collectors get excited about – top condition, original boxes and wrapping. They'll pay a lot of money for this lot if it comes up under the hammer.'

'Yes, it's the same with limited edition china,' Mr Evans replied. 'What sort of money do you think it's all worth?'

'Well, I'm no expert, but some of these are pre-war and they'll range anywhere between a hundred and five hundred pounds a piece.'

There was a sharp intake of breath from the estate agent.

'Good God!' he said.

A wardrobe in one of the bedrooms held a small treasure trove of 1930s American model railway equipment, so it was with quite a sense of expectation that I opened the door of a large built-in cupboard in the late owner's bedroom.

My companion and guide could scarcely contain his own enthusiasm and very nearly barged me aside as the contents of the cupboard were revealed.

'Clothes!' he said, his voice redolent of the deepest disappointment. 'Nothing but ancient suits and stuff.'

'Well, he had to keep them somewhere I suppose, and this is more appropriate than the larder.'

Evans gave a contemptuous sniff and tugged at one of the old suits on its hanger.

'It's almost threadbare,' he said. 'I wonder why he bothered to keep them at all. I shouldn't think he'd worn any of them for years . . . hello!. . . what's this?'

The old suit had swung aside to reveal a previously

91

hidden shelf tucked away behind the elderly garments. It was fixed to the wall at a height of about four feet, and though it was a substantial slab of pine it still bowed in the middle under the weight of the load it carried.

'Magazines by the looks of it,' I said, reaching out to take one.

'*Meccano Monthly*, I suppose,' Evans said.

'Ah!. . . not exactly . . .' I replied, examining the cover of the periodical I'd picked up, 'although this one does seem concerned to some extent with how things are made.'

'I say! I see what you mean. Will you look at that!'

Our late client's tastes had obviously been far more catholic than we might initially have imagined. When he wasn't admiring his collection of children's toys it seemed he gained equal pleasure from studying the female form in its most natural state.

Encouraged by the magazine I was holding, Evans took one from the shelf himself and opened it at the centrefold. His eyes first became rather slitty then opened very wide indeed, making his pink face look even puffier.

'I say!' he repeated.

'Mmmm . . .' I murmured studying his double-page spread, 'extraordinary . . . I wonder how they got the horse to stand still.'

'Who knows,' Evans muttered dreamily, his eyes standing out like bright blue marbles. 'Who cares?'

I stuck my head inside the cupboard and rummaged around. It quickly became evident the collection of magazines on the shelf was no more than the tip of the iceberg. Many more of them were piled high in the darkness on either side of the cupboard. It was really quite an extensive library.

'Some of these are ancient,' Denis Evans said, burrowing his way deep into one of the stacks. 'Look, this one's dated June 1954.'

He flicked through the pages rapidly, gave a snort of disappointment and discarded it in favour of a more lurid and recent publication.

'1950s treatise on naturism not to your taste?' I asked.

'Pretty tame by these standards,' he replied, blowing out his cheeks and shaking his head as he stared goggle-eyed once again at the latest centrefold.

'Well, I'd better get on,' I said, moving to close the cupboard door.

'Hold on. What are you going to do with this lot then?' he asked.

'Do with them? Why, nothing,' I replied. 'They're not of any sale value as far as I'm concerned so I won't be including them in the valuation . . .'

'Not of any value, you say?'

'No. There probably is a market for them somewhere, but I don't know where it is and I don't intend finding out.'

'So you're just going to leave them here?'

'Yes, of course – they're part of the estate, valuable or not. I've only had instructions to value the contents of the house, not to dispose of anything.'

Denis Evans, still clutching one of the magazines, looked first thoughtful then cunning.

'But we can't leave them here – can we?' he said eventually, flicking through the pages once again.

'Why not?'

'Well – I mean – they're pornographic, aren't they?'

'So what?'

'Well – people will see them.'

'Which people?'

'Prospective purchasers of the house – it could be most embarrassing.'

'Put a sheet over them with a "Do not touch" sign on it,' I suggested.

'No, no, that's no good,' the estate agent clucked dismissively. 'They'll have to be removed.'

93

'You'd better contact the solicitor then.'

'Oh, surely that's not necessary,' he went on. 'After all, you said they're valueless.'

'I said they're not of any *sale* value. That doesn't mean the late lamented didn't prize them so highly as to have bequeathed them to somebody in his will.'

'That's not very likely is it?'

'No, but it's possible. For all we know he might have left them to anybody, from the British Library to the local Women's Institute.'

Evans looked frustrated as he stared through the open doorway into the dark cupboard.

'It's no good – they really can't stay here,' he reiterated.

'Then telephone the solicitor and get his permission to dump them,' I said. 'I shouldn't think there'll be any problem.'

'Can't you do it?' he asked.

'No!' I replied abruptly. 'It really doesn't concern me.'

'But then I could load the wretched things in my car and just take them away now if you'd give me a hand. It wouldn't take long and then it would be all over and done with . . .'

'Mr Evans,' I interrupted, 'if you want to take those magazines away it's between you, the solicitor and the executors of the estate. It's nothing whatsoever to do with me.'

'Mr Harton, I want to make it quite clear that my only concern in this matter is to protect the sensibilities of my clients. I have no other interest at all in what happens to these disgusting . . .'

'Of course not,' I agreed. 'So just explain that to the solicitor when you contact him and I'm sure he'll assist you in any way he can.'

'Oh, very well,' he said with obvious reluctance. 'But I still think it would be much more sensible if we just . . .'

'I really must get on,' I said, relieving him of the

magazine he was holding. I tossed it back into the cupboard and closed the door. 'Now, are there any outside effects?'

'I don't know,' he replied sulkily. 'I haven't looked. Here are the garage keys – help yourself.'

I caught the bundle of keys he tossed to me and turned to go downstairs.

'I'll go and take a look now,' I said. 'Are you coming?'

'Er, no, I'll join you in a minute or two. I just want to finish measuring up here first.'

I strolled down the concrete path which led from the house to the double garage. The lawn on each side was unkempt and rather brown with the occasional tuft of lush, green growth. There were several lumps, bumps and depressions where flowerbeds had been incorporated into the sward without even being properly levelled. Whatever else the late incumbent had been, he was not a gardener.

The window of the garage was hung with a dirty old net curtain which made it impossible to see in, so I started trying the keys in the lock of the side door.

The third one proved successful. I stepped into the murky half-light of the garage and looked around. The bay immediately inside the door was empty but the other one contained something covered completely in old white sheets and grey blankets. From the long, straight-backed outline it was evident the object hidden under the covers was an elderly car. I walked over to it and pulled the sheets away from the front where they were gathered over what was obviously a bonnet mascot. Revealed was the unmistakable figure of the Spirit of Ecstasy and below that the angular outline of a Rolls Royce radiator. Quickly, I stripped away the rest of the covers to find an impressive, early 1930s saloon. Although the leather upholstery was worn and the black paintwork was faintly crazed she had obviously been lovingly cared for. To preserve her she

95

was raised up on blocks, so it was clear she hadn't been out of the garage for some time.

I have never been a great car enthusiast but I must admit I fell in love with that one at first sight. There was nothing skittish or racy about her, unlike the sports limousines and coupés of the same period. She was austere and unbending: a car for bearing grieving relatives at a sedate pace. It was a car for following a hearse on that last unhurried journey.

I needed more light to inspect her properly so I unbolted one of the sets of double doors and threw them open. As the morning sunshine flooded in a strange sight caught my eye. It was Denis Evans reeling about in the driveway clutching the top of his head. It seemed that he had been fiddling with something in the back of his car when, startled by the sudden crash of the opening garage doors, he had jumped and cracked his skull on the boot.

'Are you all right?' I asked, when the worst of his howls and expletives had subsided.

'No,' he replied, still holding his head. 'I've split my head open . . . I know I have . . . It's bleeding . . .'

'Let me have a look,' I said, wandering over to where he was staggering around.

'Be careful! Be careful! It's bleeding I tell you.'

I prised his hand away and conducted a brief examination of what was a very minor cut on top of a fast growing lump.

'You'll live,' I said.

'Does it need stitches? It does doesn't it? It needs stitches!'

'No,' I assured him. 'It's only a scratch – really.'

'Ha! It's all right for you to say that. It's not your bloody head.' He stroked the injured spot once more as he spoke. 'Anyway, if you hadn't opened the door like that I wouldn't have done it. Why did you do that?'

'I'm sorry, but I didn't know you were there,' I said.

'You must have tiptoed past the garage. What were you up to – smuggling out some of those copies of *Penthouse* and *Mayfair*?'

Rather than respond to my lighthearted remark with a laugh or even just a smile, Denis Evans was immediately seized by what appeared to be an attack of apoplexy. His normally pink face flushed scarlet, his head shook violently and his jowls wobbled.

'I . . . I . . . I . . . was . . . I was simply . . . simply . . .' he spluttered incoherently.

It was a moment or two before it dawned on me that my flippant remark about the magazines had accidentally struck a bulls-eye – Mr Evans had indeed been making off with the late owner's collection of soft porn.

'I just wanted to . . .' he blustered on, '. . . to be able to explain to the solicitor exactly what sort of . . . of things . . . stuff . . . er . . . material is involved . . .'

'Quite!' I agreed brightly as I walked around to the boot of his car.

'. . . so I thought it best to take . . . er . . . borrow . . . a few to quote from . . .'

'A few?' I questioned, picking out an example from the untidy stacks of magazines in the back of the Rover. 'You've got enough material here to research a PhD!'

'Well . . . I . . . I thought that if . . . if . . .'

'Have you seen what's in there?' I asked, changing the subject and pointing towards the open doors of the garage.

'No. What is it?' he replied, slamming the boot shut, only too grateful to talk about something else.

'An early 1930s Rolls Royce,' I said as I followed him into the concrete museum. 'It must have belonged to the undertaking business.'

'Amazing!' he said, running his hand along the bonnet, all his former embarrassment suddenly forgotten. 'The neighbours told me the old man used to have one – that was why he had this garage built – but they thought he'd sold it some years ago. Amazing!'

'Yes, I think it's a beauty – although I don't think it's likely to be of huge value, unlike some of its counterparts of the same period.'

'No? How much?'

'I don't really know, but less than ten thousand I suspect. I'll have to check up on it when I get back to London.'

'I see,' Denis Evans said, rather haughtily I thought. 'More research, eh? What with knowing nothing about that or the Dinky toys you're going to be busy aren't you?'

'I suppose so,' I replied. 'But then so are you.'

'How's that?'

'Well, look at all the homework you've got in the boot of your car.'

'Your Mr Evans sounds the archetypal estate agent,' Sarah laughed.

'That's a bit harsh on the other members of the profession,' I said, lacing up my boots in preparation for our afternoon's walking. 'I don't think there are that many Denis Evans clones about.'

'Perhaps you're right but I'm not so sure.'

'No, no – I'm convinced there are very few estate agents who would make a habit of stealing large quantities of soft porn from dead undertakers. Come to that, the opportunities must be few and far between.'

'You have a point,' she said. 'Anyway, it was pretty tame stuff by the sounds of it.'

'I don't know – some of it was quite exciting.'

'Oh, really!'

'Yes – there was this horse . . .'

Chapter 9

Adrian Taylor's home was a picturesque old Kentish farmhouse standing in open country a few miles to the east of Tenterden near the county border with Sussex. It was part clad in pristine white weather-boarding, with an undulating, faded, clay tile roof, through which the main timbers showed like the ribs of some great writhing animal.

Set just to the north of the house was a group of outbuildings including two converted oast houses, one of which Mr Taylor used as the nerve centre for his import-export business. Most of the other buildings were given over to garaging, storage, or loose boxes for the ten or more horses which occupied the fields surrounding the farm.

Perhaps, in the end however, it was the spectacular views from the farm rather than the farm itself which made it such a desirable place to be, if only for a day doing a valuation. From almost every vantage point, and particulary looking north, the fields and orchards of the 'Garden of England' stretched away into the distance.

It was a bright, clear July morning when I first visited Amhurst Farm. The drive down from London had been a pleasant one, against the traffic and with an enjoyably cool breeze from the car's open window. It was clearly an ideal day to spend away from the oppressive humidity of London, and Amhurst looked a' very suitable place to choose.

The front door of the farmhouse was propped open and I was met on the step by Adrian Taylor.

'Mr Harton – nice to meet you. You obviously had a good journey – you're very prompt.'

He was tall, grey-haired and sparely built, with a friendly smile and a firm handshake. His tanned face and open-necked shirt suggested he was an outdoor person, although I noticed he walked with a slight limp, his right foot turning inwards.

'Come on in,' he went on. 'I think it's going to be a real scorcher again today. You can see the heat haze already out there – look.' He pointed through the window at the end of the hall to the distant Weald beyond. 'I must say, I'd rather be on my boat than in my office today, but that's the way it goes.'

I agreed. Not that I'd ever been faced with that particular choice.

'You tell me what you need from me,' he said, ushering me into a large oak-beamed drawing room, 'then I'll disappear into the office and leave you to it.'

I explained all I needed was a brief tour of the house and a rundown on anything that wasn't to be included in his insurance valuation.

'Everything's to go in as far as I'm concerned,' he replied, 'but I'll leave it entirely to you. My wife and I inherited pretty well all the things in the house and we've never had a valuation done before so we haven't a clue what anything's worth.'

I smiled to myself as I followed him around his home. He was the ideal client: affable, no half-baked ideas about what he owned or what things were worth, and he was happy to let me get on and do the job as I thought fit.

'There's quite a bit of silver in here,' he said, opening a door to a pantry just inside the kitchen. 'I expect you'll want to see that, won't you?'

'Yes,' I confirmed, stepping into the closet to cast an eye over the collection, and thinking once again what an ideal client Adrian Taylor was. Only too frequently one would finish a valuation, at the end of an afternoon, only to have the owner produce a sea of silver from nowhere. That extra couple of hours' work never seemed to be fully compensated for by the additional fee.

'You've got some very good pieces here,' I went on.

'Have we? Oh, good. Most of it came from my wife's family. Lord knows where they got it from. Oh, are they any good?'

His question concerned four small, circular, silver salts. They were decorated with swags and lion masks and each stood on three paw feet.

'Yes, they are,' I confirmed, checking the hallmarks. 'They're by Paul Storr, made in 1815.'

'Oh – the year of Waterloo, wasn't it? Was Paul Storr particularly important?'

'Important enough for these to be worth four to six thousand at auction.'

'You're kidding!'

'No, I'm not. And then there's this . . .'

It was a small silver-gilt cream jug fashioned in the shape of an ornate shell, encrusted with leaves and masks and with a fabulously ornate handle.

'What about it?' Adrian Taylor asked. 'Has that been around since Waterloo as well?'

'Well, I can't find any marks on it, but I think this has been around since a little before Culloden.'

'Now, you've got me there – when was that?'

'1745, but I think this dates from, probably, five years earlier.'

'So it's not by Paul Storr?'

'No, I think it's probably by Paul de Lamerie.'

'And he was important too, was he?'

'Well, I would be very surprised if it didn't make in

the region of three to four thousand were it to come up under the hammer.'

He gripped hold of the doorpost and closed his eyes momentarily. When he opened them again he reached out, took the jug from my hand and placed it back on its shelf.

'No more, no more!' he said, wincing. 'You're scaring me to death. I'm not sure I really want to know all this. You just write it down and I'll pluck up my courage for when the valuation drops through the letter box.'

'Okay. I'll get started,' I said.

'Right. Now, my wife's out all day, but there's some cold lunch for us. So when you're ready, come out to the office, we'll have a drink then a bite to eat in the garden. The office is in the second oast – all right?'

'Fine,' I said. 'I'll come and find you at about a quarter to one.'

The morning went well. The only interruption to my labours being my own occasional lapses of concentration when I found myself staring through wide open windows at the broad expanse of hedgerows and fields shimmering in the sunshine. Despite these distractions the valuation was more than three-quarters finished by the time I wandered across the yard to my client's office. I was observed with a casual lack of concern by two chestnut mares, standing nose to tail on mutual fly-whisking duty, under a giant horsechestnut tree in the nearest paddock.

'Up here,' Adrian Taylor called, as I entered the cool of the old brick-built oast. 'I'm on the next floor.'

I clambered up the open, wooden stairs and arrived in a spacious, circular office. It was comfortably equipped, with a mahogany partners desk positioned to benefit from a huge picture window which commanded an uninterrupted view of all points east. Mr Taylor was standing by an open drinks cupboard.

'Gin and tonic?' he asked. 'Or would you prefer something else?'

'No, no – gin and tonic will be fine,' I replied, crossing to the window.

'Magnificent, isn't it?' he said. 'I'll never tire of that view, it's . . .' As he turned to bring me my drink he stopped in mid-sentence. 'I'm talking about the wrong view, I see,' he concluded, handing me the glass.

He was right. My attention was focused not on the rolling panorama of Kent, but on a small oil painting hanging just to the right of the massive window. It was a free and lively sketch of a valley with trees in the middle distance and a silvery band of water snaking away out of sight. It was an unmistakably English scene, and had I not known just how unlikely such a find would be I would have said it was by the hand of none other than John Constable.

I stood back, took a sip from my glass and put it down on the corner of the desk.

'Do you mind if I look at the back?' I asked, stepping up to the picture once more.

'Not at all – be my guest. There is an inscription I believe.'

I took the picture down from the wall. It was painted on a wooden panel about seven inches by nine inches. Inscribed on the back was: 'Oct 1812'.

'What do you make of it?' Adrian Taylor asked.

'Well, if I didn't know better,' I replied, 'I would say it was an extremely important picture.'

'What makes you say that?'

'Quite simply: it has all the hallmarks of a John Constable sketch.'

'Oh, it is a Constable,' he said, as if everybody had one, 'but I don't think it's very special, is it?'

I turned the framed panel over in my hands and looked at the strong, confident brushwork: the work of an artist as intent on recording the scene in his own mind as on that simple piece of wood. It seemed to me that it was a remarkable picture.

'I'm quite sure if this picture had a provenance it would command a very high price,' I said.

'What – you mean some sort of history?'

'Yes.'

'Oh, I've got something to that effect,' he said, taking another slurp from his gin and tonic. 'I think it's in my desk somewhere. Hold on, I'll have a look.'

He walked round to his chair, sat down and proceeded to ransack the drawers of the desk with considerable enthusiasm.

'Ah, this looks like it,' he said after a period of concentrated silence. 'I think it's all in here.'

He was holding a battered old manilla envelope. The stamp bore the sharp, bearded profile of George V.

'Yes, this is all the bumf on it. See what you think.' He slid the envelope across the desk to me.

'It was bought by my grandfather from an old friend of his during the 1920s,' he went on. 'I don't know what he paid for it, but not much.'

'Fifty guineas, according to this,' I said, taking an old, yellow, hand-written receipt from the bundle of other papers the envelope had held.

'Sounds about right. He was quite a shrewd operator was my grandfather. My father always said it didn't matter to the old boy what it was he happened to be buying or selling. It was the fun of putting a deal together that he loved.'

'He certainly put a good one together here,' I said. 'If these papers are what they appear to be, there's a direct link with the Constable family.'

'Really? I haven't looked at them for such a long time I can't remember what they say.'

'Quite a lot: apart from anything else there's mention of John Charles Constable owning this picture.'

'And who was he?'

'The artist's eldest son,' I replied, 'and the person

responsible for the disposal of the picture collection following his father's death.'

'Oh, I see,' Adrian Taylor said. 'That's quite good I suppose, isn't it?'

Delightful man though my client was, it was evident that he and I were still on different wavelengths when it came to our individual perceptions of the importance of his picture.

'Mr Taylor,' I said, 'what do you think this picture's worth?'

'Well, as it happens, I do have some idea because, some years ago, an old friend of mine, who's a bit of a collector, said he thought it was probably worth in the region of six or seven thousand. That's why it's out here: the office has got a burglar alarm whereas the house hasn't, you see.'

'That was some time ago you say?'

'Yes, so no doubt it's worth a bit more than that now.'

'How much would you say?' I asked.

'I would have thought . . . probably . . . oh, I don't know – say, ten to fifteen thousand.'

'I see,' I said, picking up the picture once more and examining it again. 'Well, I think I should warn you that I believe this painting could be worth considerably more than that.'

'Really? What had you in mind, Mr Harton?'

'Well, if the provenance can be confirmed as correct, I can't imagine that it could possibly be worth less than fifty thousand, and I think it would probably make nearer seventy.'

Adrian Taylor was in the process of raising his gin and tonic to his lips when I gave him my opinion of the value. As I mentioned the figure he froze. Then he silently mouthed the words 'fifty' and 'seventy' and drained his glass in one large gulp.

'Good God!' he said at last. 'Are you sure?'

'Yes, I'm pretty confident that's the sort of range we'd be talking about,' I confirmed. 'Of course it's all subject to our pictures department having a look at it and satisfying themselves as to its authenticity.'

'Quite,' he said, nodding his head in agreement but still looking dazed.

'So perhaps I could get Charles Morrison-Whyte, our Pictures Director, to come down and have a look . . .'

'No!' He almost shouted the word. 'No! Take it away. Just take it away. I don't want it in the office, or the house, or anywhere any more.'

'Are you sure?'

'Yes, Mr Harton, I'm absolutely certain.'

'All right, I can certainly take it back to London today . . .' I hesitated, concerned he hadn't given it enough thought, '. . . as long as you're absolutely sure.'

'Mr Harton – I've never been more sure about anything in my life. How can we possibly keep it here? In the twinkling of an eye it's just turned from a pretty little picture into a massive liability. We couldn't even go away for a weekend without lodging it at the bank. We'd have to move it to the house and wire that up like Fort Knox. I'd never even be able to look at it again without having pound signs flash up in front of my eyes. No, there's nothing else for it, it must be sold, and the sooner you take it away the happier I will be.'

Chapter 10

Charles Morrison-Whyte sat, expressionless, behind the desk in his opulent but rather intimidating office. With its mahogany bookcases and leather-covered chairs it always made me feel like a guest in a select gentlemen's club – one where I would never qualify for membership.

Charles had listened impassively to my brief account of the discovery of Adrian Taylor's picture. Despite his customary lack of enthusiasm, for once he hadn't continued to go through the papers on his desk while I was speaking. That in itself was a good sign. Instead, he had just stared at the small oil painting I had given him.

'This is all the paperwork he had,' I said, placing the old envelope on the blotter in front of him.

He made no reply but turned the picture over again and re-examined the inscription on the back. He then laid it down the correct way up on his desk and removed the sheaf of papers from the manilla envelope. One by one, and still without speaking he read the documents, placing each, in turn, face down on the desk next to the picture. Finally, he picked it up again and stared at it, his forehead wrinkling into a frown as his eyebrows arched above his small, almost black eyes. He pursed his lips, then spoke for the first time.

'How much do you know about John Constable, Richard?'

'I'm certainly no expert,' I confessed readily.

He placed the picture on the desk again, lightly rubbed together the tips of his fingers to remove any lingering dust, then leaned back in his chair and with both hands smoothed back the silver-grey hair from his temples.

'His dates were 1776 to 1837,' he began. 'He is regarded as second only to Turner in terms of his importance as a British landscape artist.'

That much I knew.

'This picture,' he tapped the gilt frame as he spoke, 'would appear to be a view of Dedham Vale and it looks to have been painted from a viewpoint close to the one he chose for "Dedham Vale – Morning" – a picture he exhibited at the RA in . . .' he paused for a moment as he cast back through his memory for the date, '. . . 1811, I think.'

He picked up the picture again, turned it over and looked at the inscription once more, but this time with the aid of a powerful magnifying glass which was always lying on his desk.

'This inscription appears to be rubbed and incomplete. Only the month – October – and the year – 1812 – are legible; the day has been completely obliterated.'

He laid down both the picture and the magnifying glass, got up and went over to the larger of his bookcases. Opening one of the glass doors he removed a volume, thumbed through it quickly then replaced it, closing the door once again.

'I shall have to do some research,' he said, returning to his seat. 'I know Constable visited Dedham twice in 1812, and I believe the second visit was from September to November, so the inscription on this picture would correspond with that.'

I felt just the faintest tingle of excitement as one of the pieces of the jigsaw dropped into place.

'What I can't remember,' he went on, 'is how many pictures are recorded from that visit – it's either two or three. Whatever it is, I'm certain the whereabouts of each of them is known.'

'So this would be a hitherto unknown work?' I said.

'Mmmm,' he murmured, nodding and once again looking at the painting. 'And as you will appreciate, establishing the authenticity of a work of the potential importance of this one is a delicate matter.'

'What about the provenance?' I asked, pointing to the bundle of papers. 'Isn't the paperwork of some help?'

'Some,' he conceded, frowning again, 'but most of it's hearsay, you know. There's not much contemporary material there. As an account of the picture's descent to the present owner it's credible enough, but it doesn't amount to proof.'

'What about the connection with Constable's son?'

'Same there: it's wonderfully credible but there's absolutely no proof that it's true. No, I shall have to do a lot of research before I come down one way or the other.'

'Okay,' I said, 'take all the time you want. I'm sure the owner won't mind.'

'All right – I'll keep you informed of any progress.' His head bowed over the picture once more.

'Just one last thing, Charles . . .'

'Yes,' he said, looking up again.

'. . . if it is right – what do *you* think it will fetch?'

'Oh,' he replied immediately, 'I think you were probably just about right, Richard – somewhere in the region of sixty or seventy thousand.'

'Well, what did old misery guts have to say?' Charlotte asked when I got back to the office.

'Who? My friend, Charles?'

'Oh, obviously it must have been good if you and Charles Morrison-Whyte are suddenly on cordial terms.'

I smiled.

109

'Charles and I are always on cordial terms, Charlotte . . .'

'Ha!'

'. . . it's just that sometimes it doesn't show.'

'Anyway, what's old lemon features' verdict? Is it right or wrong?'

'He can't say yet – he's got to do a lot of research, but I got the impression that under that ice-cold exterior there was something closely akin to excitement building up.'

'More likely to be acid indigestion, Sweetie.'

'You could be right,' I agreed. 'It is difficult to tell with Charles. Anyway, any messages?'

'Just one: Bernard Thornton phoned to say if you want to see half a dozen examples of really good Oriental ceramics then get over to the porcelain department right away.'

'I'm on my way.'

I rarely passed up an opportunity to visit Bernard's domain. For one thing, he was such a wonderful character, no visit was likely to be boring if he was around. A large, bear-like man, he took no interest at all in the politics of the company and was on record as having forgotten to attend more board meetings than any other director. He was frequently outrageous, always interesting, and never anything other than generous with his expertise – which was considerable.

As I stepped from the lift into the ceramics reception area I almost bumped into him, gingerly making his way towards his office clutching a plastic cup of coffee in each hand.

'Hello . . . can't stop . . . these things are hot . . . ah! – thank goodness!' He dumped the cups onto the reception counter and blew on his fingers to cool them. 'Good to see you, Richard. Have you come to see my prize exhibits?'

'Yes,' I said. 'Charlotte says you've got some good Chinese pieces for sale.'

'I have indeed. Come on, I'll show you.' Spurning an offer of help he picked up the coffee cups once more.

'No, no, I can manage,' he insisted, wincing as he adjusted his grip on each of the flimsy vessels. 'You just follow me and prepare yourself for something special.'

'Just what is it that I should be preparing myself for?' I asked.

'Well, there's a very good Ming blue and white bowl, a Song Jar, a Yuan jar...' Moving very carefully to prevent the coffee from spilling, Bernard turned, pushed the door open with his behind and backed slowly into his office, '...a Quinlong stem-cup, a...'

His inventory was brought to a halt by a dull thud, followed a moment later by a loud crash. Both noises emanated from just inside the office and coincided with the moment the door had swung open.

Bernard stood petrified in the doorway, staring at me, eyes wide and panic-stricken. I could almost see his brain working as all the dreadful possibilities presented themselves for consideration.

'Oh, my God!' he said eventually, his voice no more than a whisper. 'Not the Ming! Please Lord – not the Ming!'

Still he stood there, unwilling to confront what had actually happened. Eventually the suspense proved too much and, followed closely by me, he turned and entered the office. Carefully, he placed the still unspilt cups of coffee on his desk then he peered nervously behind the door.

On top of the built-in work unit was the usual haphazard array of pottery and porcelain. In the middle of it all was a strikingly beautiful Chinese blue and white fruit bowl about a foot in diameter.

'It wasn't the Ming!' Bernard gasped, momentarily closing his eyes in an ecstasy of relief. Then he opened them again and leant over the unit to examine the floor below. 'Bugger! It was the Song.'

I too peered over the unit. Sure enough, lying on the floor below were the shattered remains of what was once a black glazed pot of some description.

'What exactly was it?' I asked as we both surveyed the wreckage.

'It was a glazed jar,' Bernard replied with a faintly wistful air. 'About eight inches high, produced at some stage during the Song dynasty.'

'Had you actually put a date on it?'

'Not really, although I suppose we're probably talking 1100 to 1200 Anno Domini.'

'As early as that, eh?'

'Oh, yes,' he said, wandering round to the other side of the unit and bending over the shards. 'After all, that's quite late for Song – the dynasty began in 560 and didn't grind to a halt until 1279.'

'Oh,' I said.

'Hmmm,' Bernard mumbled as he collected together the bits and piled them on top of the work unit.

'Yes,' he said, standing up and regarding the heap of pieces, 'over seven hundred years without as much as a hair-line crack and then it gets sent to the Hampson's ceramics department . . .'

'Well, these things will happen sometimes,' I tried to console him.

'Hmmm,' he murmured again, still staring at the jar fragments. 'I'll make a note of that on the accident report when I submit it to Bob Derby – I'm sure he'll be wonderfully understanding.'

'What's the financial damage likely to be?'

'Oh, it's not too bad really – about fifteen hundred I suppose.'

'I thought you were going to say thousands,' I admitted.

'No, fortunately not, despite its age. Now, if it had been this . . .' he carefully lifted the fruit bowl clear of the items which surrounded it, '. . . then it would have

112

been an altogether different matter.'

'This is the Ming piece I take it,' I said, as he handed the bowl over to me.

'It certainly is: Xuande period – 1426 to 1435. Isn't it exquisite?'

It was. The finest porcelain, beautifully decorated with restrained images of flowering peonies and trailing foliage. The reign mark, just below the rim of the piece, was a minor work of art in itself.

As I held up the bowl in my left hand I tapped it gently with my other hand. Instantly, a pure, bell-like sound rang out. The clear, resonant chime lingered on and on until it eventually, almost imperceptibly, faded away.

'And dare I ask what it would have cost Hampson's had it been this which you'd just swept up?' I said.

'Somewhere in the region of twenty-five thousand,' Bernard replied brightly.

I stopped holding the bowl in just one hand and passed it back very carefully to Bernard. As I did so, William Baron, Bernard's assistant, arrived on the scene from the storeroom.

'Ah, William,' Bernard greeted him jovially, 'I was just showing Richard our collection of fine Chinese porcelain.'

'Some lovely pieces, aren't there, Richard?' William said.

'Yes,' Bernard Thornton replied quickly. 'Richard was particularly interested in the do-it-yourself Song dynasty jar.'

'Do-it-yourself?' William Baron looked puzzled, then he spotted the shattered pot. 'Bloody hell! How did that happen?'

'Somebody put it on the work top – along with the Ming bowl I might add – so that I could knock it off with the damned door when I arrived with your coffee a few moments ago. I wonder who that could have been?'

113

The director of the ceramics department glared accusingly at his assistant.

'Well, don't look at me,' William defended himself. 'You told the porters to bring them for cataloguing.'

'No I didn't.'

'Yes you did – first thing this morning.'

'Did I?'

'Yes – you said you wanted to get them done and put away safely before some idiot smashed something.'

'Oh, yes, I do seem to remember something about it now you come to mention it. But I didn't suggest the bloody fools put everything just behind the door where it would all get knocked over by the first person to come into the room.'

'Bernard,' William Baron said patiently, 'the only reason the door opens that far is because you insisted on removing the doorstop because you kept tripping over it.'

Bernard Thornton opened his mouth to speak, obviously decided against it and turned to me instead.

'You haven't seen the Yuan jar yet, have you?' he asked. 'Now, where is it? Ah, here we are . . .'

Chapter 11

'Has he gone?' Charlotte asked.

I nodded.

'I've never seen him like that before,' she said. 'It was quite unnerving.'

I knew what she meant. A visit to our office by Charles Morrison-Whyte was a rare enough occurrence in itself, but that he should have been so happy, almost skittish, was definitely an all time first.

'I think that's the first time I've ever heard him really laugh,' I said.

'I know,' she said, 'and all over one little picture.'

To refer to Adrian Taylor's oil painting as a little picture was technically correct of course. Only seven inches by nine inches, it was certainly not an epic work, but what it lacked in size it had suddenly gained in historical importance since Charles had just dropped in to confirm that he believed it was indeed the work of John Constable.

He had done a lot of research over the ten days since I had brought it in to him, and sought some fairly high level academic opinions on the work. In the end, the general consensus was that it was a previously unrecorded work which had passed on the artist's death in 1838 to his eldest son, John Charles. John Charles had been very close to his father and had taken charge of the disposal of his pictures. However, there was no record of it having been included in the two-day sale which had taken place in May of that year, so it was felt that John Charles had simply retained it as part of his personal collection of his father's art which he housed in his rooms at Cambridge. The theory then fell in with the chain of events set down in the dog-eared manilla envelope: that the picture had passed out of the family either on, or shortly after, John Charles's own untimely death from scarlet fever in 1841.

It knitted together very nicely and all I had to do now was give Adrian Taylor the good news and get his formal instructions to go ahead with the sale. And a formality was all it would be, because he had made it quite clear at the outset that the picture would have to be sold if it turned out to be right, and there was no doubt about that now.

It was Mrs Taylor who answered the telephone. She explained that her husband was out and that he was expected back shortly. Then she asked whether we had come to a decision about the authenticity of their Dedham Vale picture.

'Yes,' I said, 'we believe it is by John Constable and we would be pleased to sell it with that attribution.'

'Does that mean it's definitely worth the sort of money you thought, Mr Harton?' she asked.

'We believe so,' I replied.

'Goodness!' she gave a deep sigh. 'It's all a bit of a shock to us, you know.'

'But a nice one I hope,' I said.

'Oh, yes,' she said, 'a nice one.'

But somehow she didn't sound as enthusiastic as I would have expected. It crossed my mind that perhaps she was less convinced than her husband about the wisdom of selling the picture.

'Anyway, it's all very exciting,' she continued, making an effort to sound keen, 'and I'm sure my husband will call you just as soon as he gets in. I know he wants to speak to you anyway. Goodbye, Mr Harton.'

'Goodbye, Mrs Taylor,' I said, replacing the receiver.

'What's wrong?' Charlotte asked.

'What?'

'What's wrong? You suddenly look worried.'

'Do I?'

'Yes. What's the matter?'

'I don't know,' I said, still pondering on my brief conversation with Mrs Taylor. 'But I get the impression something is.'

'Why? What did she say?'

'Oh, it wasn't anything she said. More the way she said it. I just got the impression she wasn't altogether happy about the idea of selling the picture.'

'But she didn't actually say so?'

'No – it was just her tone: as though she knew something I didn't. And she said her husband wanted to speak to me anyway.'

'So?'

'So I can't think of anything he'd need to speak to me about, unless . . .'

'Oh, come on, Richard!' Charlotte said, sitting back in her chair and laughing. 'There are a dozen things he could want to talk to you about. Apart from anything else, he's got his insurance valuation now. It's probably a question about something in that.'

'Yes,' I said, 'you're probably right.'

But I didn't really think she was. I felt in my bones that something was wrong. I'd had too many years dealing with too many clients not to sense when a job was going sour.

If I'd had any doubts at all about my instinct, they were immediately dispelled by Adrian Taylor when he telephoned fifteen minutes later.

'Hello, Mr Harton. My wife's given me the good news on the picture . . . but I'm afraid I've some bad news for you.'

'Oh dear – what news is that?'

117

'Well, there's no point in beating about the bush: I'm afraid I can't let Hampson's handle the sale of the Constable.'

Although it was what I was expecting, that didn't make what he'd just said any the more palatable. In one brief sentence Adrian Taylor had snatched away not just the best discovery I had made since joining Hampson's but the best piece I had stumbled over in my entire career.

No matter how prepared for the news I might have thought I was, it still left me stunned. So much so that no immediate reply came to mind. Then I realised exactly what it was Mr Taylor had said. He had not said *he* wasn't going to sell the picture, he had said he wasn't going to let *Hampson's* sell the picture.

'What exactly is the problem?' I asked.

'Quite simply, the picture isn't mine,' he replied.

'I don't understand,' I said.

'There's no reason why you should, Mr Harton. I didn't mention anything about it while you were here because it's not something I ever give any thought to. Suddenly, however, what I've always regarded as a technicality has become rather more than that.'

'I'm afraid I'm still not sure what you mean.'

'No, I'm not surprised; I'm not explaining this very well,' he said. 'The fact is I put a lot of my possessions into trust some years ago just in case anything happened to me . . .'

'Well, if you're concerned about the tax angle . . .' I began.

'No, no, it's not that,' he went on. 'Although it was my accountant who was the first to raise any objection to the proposed sale.'

'But, why?'

'He's one of the trustees. My solicitor is another and my younger brother is the third. When they heard of the possible value of the picture they all decided, as one,

118

that . . . well, to be quite frank . . . that Hampson's is just not big enough to handle the sale.'

'But, that's just not true,' I protested.

'I know, I know,' he agreed. 'As far as I'm concerned, you've behaved with great professionalism, and if the decision were mine Hampson's would handle the whole thing.' He paused. 'Unfortunately, it isn't up to me and the trustees have made their decision: they intend to instruct Faulkner's to sell the Constable.'

'Is it too late for me to speak to them?' I pleaded. 'Perhaps I can convince them . . .'

'There's no point, Mr Harton. Really – you'd just be wasting your time. In fact I've already fought your corner hard enough to have caused a bit of ill-feeling with my solicitor, and I don't want that to get any worse.'

'May I ask who your solicitor is?' I enquired.

'Yes, he said he'd used you a couple of years ago; you may remember him. His name's Jim Parkinson. He's with –'

'Hallworth, Jolly and Phillimore,' I said.

'That's right. Obviously you do remember him. He's a nice chap although he can be a little bit stuffy sometimes. Anyway, initially he insisted it should go to Christie's, then my brother said it just had to be Sotheby's but in the end . . .'

I didn't bother to listen any more. Any thoughts I might have had of salvaging the sale were dashed at the very mention of James Parkinson's name. It was true, he had instructed me to make a probate valuation a couple of years earlier. It had been an emergency; I had fitted it in on the same day as his telephone call; it had been the filthiest, most disgusting flat I had ever set foot in, but I had discovered a piece of Russian silver worth £1,000 to £2,000 which he hadn't even known existed. On that occasion Mr Parkinson had rewarded my diligence by sending the piece of silver to Christie's. No doubt the same company had been the recipient of all his subsequent valuation work as well.

'What do you want to do about collecting the Constable?' I asked.

'Oh ... er ... I think the intention was to ask Faulkner's to collect it direct from your salerooms. Would that be all right?'

'Yes, I'll see the picture is ready for release to their carriers.'

'Thank you, Mr Harton ... and may I say, very sincerely, just how sorry I am about this – it really is not my doing at all.'

'No, Mr Taylor,' I said. 'I do appreciate that.'

Charlotte and I sat glumly silent for some minutes after the call, then she spoke:

'I've just thought of something.'

'What's that?'

'It's something even worse than losing the sale of the Constable.'

'Go on, cheer me up. What is it?'

'You've got to break the news to Charles Morrison-Whyte.'

'I know,' I said. 'I'm just plucking up the courage to go and see him.'

'He's going to take it very badly.'

'Yes.'

'I should have a drink before you do it,' she suggested.

'No,' I replied, 'but I fully intend to have several *after* I've done it. In fact, Charlotte, I shall probably get plastered tonight.'

'I think we should definitely go on somewhere,' Philip Lawrence said, draining the remains of his pint.

'Where do you suggest?' I asked.

'Well, I do happen to have temporary membership of a particularly salubrious casino that's recently opened not a million miles from here.'

120

Although, in my earliest days at Hampson's, I had quickly realised my companion was a man of many parts, I had never supposed gambling to be one of his vices. When he wasn't managing the silver and jewellery departments he always seemed to be thrashing golf balls about the countryside. The smoke-filled atmosphere of the gaming room didn't seem to be his sort of environment at all.

'Since when have you been a gambler?' I asked.

'Since I first bet a whole week's pocket money on my champion conker, about twenty-five years ago,' he replied, his blond head bowed as he contemplated his empty glass.

'Did you win?'

'Did I hell – the second shot the other chap had at it, the damned thing shattered into a thousand tiny pieces. All I was left with was a piece of string.'

'Tragic,' I said. 'How much did you lose?'

'Sixpence,' he replied. 'And those were the days when sixpence could buy you enough cheap sweets to make you throw up and still leave change for a taxi home.'

'I remember it well. But I'm surprised such a traumatic experience didn't put you off gambling for life.'

'No, we Lawrences are made of sterner stuff than that. The next day I took him on for a shilling with a new prototype model and cleaned up. From then on I was bitten.'

'And now you've graduated from conkers to casinos,' I observed.

'Yes, but I always let my membership lapse before I lose too much money. However, tonight I feel lucky!'

Unlike Philip, my formative years had not been spent gambling the contents of my piggy bank on the outcome of dubious sporting contests. Probably as a result of which I had never set foot in a casino. This meant our arrival half an hour later at Latchford's – a newly opened gambling club a short walk from Hampson's – was a whole new experience for me.

No sooner had we got through the door than we were greeted effusively by a man who both looked and behaved like a head waiter. A moment later I had been signed in and Philip and I were on our way to the mahogany-panelled bar. Two large gins and tonics later we were on our way out again, this time to the mahogany-panelled gaming room. It was large with a low ceiling and soft lighting. The air was heavy with the aroma of Havana cigar smoke.

'We'll get some chips,' Philip said, 'then you can have a go at whatever you fancy: black jack, baccarat, roulette . . .'

'Which requires the least experience and intelligence?' I asked.

'Roulette – it's pure luck.'

'Then that's the one for me.'

There were four roulette tables; two of them quite busy, the other two not so. What surprised me most was the clientele gathered around these green baize outcrops. It was made up almost exclusively of elderly ladies wearing huge lumps of expensive jewellery and with strange coloured hair rinses – every shade from champagne to electric blue. Each of them seemed to be weighed down with knuckle duster diamong rings and yards of heavy gold chain. I stood quietly behind one group and listened. It was evident from the conversation that they all knew one another and that Latchfords had already become a regular meeting place.

'Oi! Twenty-eight again! How can that be? How many times is that tonight?'

The questioner shrugged her shoulders and moved the pile of chips on the table in front of her backwards and forwards impatiently.

'Two, three times, maybe,' replied a round and rather jolly-looking woman on the other side of the table as she reached out two jewel-encrusted hands and pulled her winnings towards her.

'Three, at least three, maybe four,' added a third while she rearranged her own much more modest pile of chips. 'It's just like last night only then it was . . . what was it?'

'Fourteen,' suggested another. 'Last night it was fourteen, all the time fourteen . . . unless *I* put money on it of course. Then . . .'

'No more bets, please,' intoned the stone-faced croupier as he spun the wheel one way and with a flick sent the small white ball rotating in the other direction.

Round and round it went, every eye at the table following it. Then it circled slowly down the high sides of the wheel to meet the revolving, numbered segments. It rattled noisily in and out of several numbers then eventually came to rest.

Necks were craned at the still-turning wheel.

'Eighteen, black,' announced the croupier, instantly gathering in the losing bets.

'Ah, eighteen!' confirmed the gem-encrusted jolly lady on the other side of the table. 'I thought so. I thought so. I knew it would be eighteen that time.'

'Ha!' snorted the woman who had so recently complained about number twenty-eight. 'Eighteen again – always it's eighteen after the twenty-eight. It's crazy – there's something wrong with this wheel I think . . . no, I *know* there's something wrong with it!'

'Beginning to get the idea?' Philip asked from behind me.

'Not really,' I replied, 'but I love the punters.'

'Yes, the North London blue rinse set,' he said. 'All wealthy, all widowed, all lonely. They're just the same as you'd find in any bingo hall up and down the country except this lot have got a lot more money – at least they had when they arrived. Come on, let's go to a quieter table and I'll explain the odds.'

We took our seats at a table which, save for the presence of a rather bored looking croupier, was deserted.

'Now, as you can see,' Philip began my tuition, 'the table is split into three blocks of numbers: the first dozen – one to twelve; the second dozen – thirteen to twenty-four; and the third dozen – twenty-five to thirty-six. If you bet on any single number the odds are thirty-five to one – all right?'

'Yes,' I nodded.

'You can also bet on whether the winning number will fall in the first, second or third dozen.'

'I see,' I said, 'so that means a bet on a block of numbers, not on an individual number.'

'That's right. The odds on that bet are two to one.'

'Okay,' I said.

'You can also bet on whether the number will be odd or even,' he continued in a patient, almost scholarly tone, 'and whether the colour will be black or red. The odds in both cases are even.'

'Er . . . right.'

'You can bet high or low – on whether the first eighteen or the second eighteen will contain the winning number. The odds there are even as well.'

All this business about odds and evens was beginning to sound confusing.

'You can also bet on smaller groups of numbers.'

'I can?'

'Yes, you can bet on three consecutive numbers, like ten, eleven, twelve – they'll pay you out at eleven to one if any one of those comes up; or you can bet on a group of four numbers – in that case it's eight to one; or you can . . .'

'Yes, yes,' I said hastily, 'I think I'll try to absorb that lot before you tell me any more.'

'Probably wise,' he agreed. 'Anyway, let me try to demonstrate how it should be done . . .'

124

'Place your bets, please,' the croupier requested in a particularly flat way.

'The knack is to try to cover your bets, like this,' Philip said, dropping his voice to a whisper as he began to spread small columns of twenty-five-pence chips on the table.

'No more bets, please,' said the croupier, spinning the wheel.

'You see what I've done?' Philip whispered. 'I've used two pounds' worth of chips to cover numbers thirteen to twenty-one, so if any one of those comes up I win a minimum of four quid. I also put a pound on the first dozen at two to one, and another pound on even numbers at even money.'

The ball swooped down on the revolving wheel and ricocheted around loudly.

'That's what you could call a well-spread risk,' Philip said, concluding the summary of his bets.

'Number twenty-five, red,' the croupier announced, expertly sweeping away Philip's chips in one deft move and adding them to the bank's stock.

'So, how much did you lose there?' I asked quietly. 'Four pounds?'

My mentor jutted out his chin and tapped two of his remaining chips together impatiently.

'Yes,' he said, sharply. 'That's how it goes sometimes.'

'Place your bets, please.'

'Let's try again,' he muttered, once again rapidly deploying small columns of chips about the table. 'This time we'll cover one to nine; we have a pound on evens again and another pound on second dozen.'

'No more bets please.'

'This time we've cracked it,' Philip said, his tone fully mirroring the confidence of his words.

'Number thirty-four, black,' the croupier chanted, once again sweeping up most of Philip's chips, but this time diverting some to the stake he had on even numbers.

'How much did you win?' I asked in hushed tones.

'I didn't win anything,' he replied, this time with a real touch of acidity. 'I just didn't lose as much as I might have – that's what I meant by covering my bets.'

'So how much did you lose?'

'Well, I bet four pounds and got two back.'

'So you've lost six pounds so far?'

Philip raised an eyebrow and gave me a sidelong look.

'Since you've become such a skilled observer,' he said, 'perhaps you'd like to show me how it should be done.'

'Place your bets, please.' The croupier now sounded terminally bored.

I picked up a pile of four twenty-five-pence chips, hesitated for a moment as I tried to decide what I should do with them, then for want of a better idea I put the lot on number five.

My companion shook his head.

'That's it, is it?' he sighed.

'Er . . . yes . . . I think so.'

'What about covering your bets?' he hissed. 'What about odds and evens, low and high, first dozen, second dozen . . .?'

'Oh,' I said. 'I forgot.'

I picked up some more chips and put a pound on the first dozen and another on odd numbers.

'No more bets please.'

My companion shook his head slowly as the small ball shot round and round above the rotating wheel.

'Number five, black,' the croupier confirmed, bulldozing a large pile of chips towards my stake on number five.

'I don't believe it!' Philip sighed, resting his head in his hands.

'How much have I won?' I whispered.

'Thirty-five pounds on the number, two pounds on the first dozen and a pound on the odd numbers: a total of thirty-eight pounds,' he confirmed without raising his head from his hands.

'Oh,' I replied. 'That's quite good isn't it?'

He gave me another sidelong glance and rose from his seat.

'I think I'll play a little black-jack,' he said, 'before I throttle you, or burst into tears or both.'

'Okay,' I said, grinning. 'Good luck.'

Philip shook his head again and strode off towards the black-jack tables.

He returned about twenty minutes later with a refreshed pile of chips and a happier look on his face.

'How's it been going?' he enquired.

'Not bad,' I replied in a low whisper. 'Nothing spectacular, but you should see these two play!'

The two I referred to had joined my table shortly after Philip had taken himself off to play black-jack. They were unconnected as far as I could tell but they both played roulette very seriously indeed.

One of them was young, Middle Eastern, very expensively dressed and encased in gold jewellery, while the other was a grizzled old Australian with a deeply furrowed brow and a very abrupt manner.

The bearded younger man had arrived with a massive pile of high denomination chips and had thrown himself into the play with considerable flair although no apparent enjoyment. Every spin of the wheel saw great mountain ranges of chips towering above the baize from one end of the table to the other. In fact, there were always so many of his chips piled up out there that on several occasions I hadn't placed any bets myself in case I knocked over one of his teetering columns.

No such concerns seemed to trouble the Australian gentleman who, I had sensed, was becoming increasingly annoyed with our conspicuously wealthy companion. Not least of all because the two of them always seemed to be going for the same number at the last minute. A collision of hands was inevitable and when it eventually happened the Australian's chips ended up spread liberally all over the table. He had appeared pretty irascible when he arrived, and that experience had done nothing to improve his outlook on life.

While this tense little drama had been playing itself out I had continued, available space permitting, to play my own modest game. On one occasion, knowing instinctively it was right, I'd placed five pounds on number nineteen. There was no doubt in my mind. It was just one of those moments when I *knew* I couldn't lose. At the very last moment the smooth young Arab placed £3,000 worth of chips on the same number. It was going to be a big payout.

'Zero.'

I watched stupefied as the croupier swept away my hard-earned five pounds along with every other chip on the table. I just couldn't believe it. I glanced up at the bearded man. He was sipping a glass of orange juice and showed no sign of emotion at all. He had just lost £3,000 on that one number, let alone what he'd dropped on his other bets, and he was behaving as if he were no more than a casual observer. Whereas I had just lost a fiver and was mildly suicidal. We seemed, somehow, to approach the game differently.

'Good God!' Philip whispered, tugging at my sleeve. 'Look at that little lot.'

The man opposite us had just stacked another tower of chips on the table. This time on numbers sixteen and seventeen.

'There must be ten thousand there,' I said.

I had been about to place a fifty-pence stake on number twelve but I withdrew my hand and surreptitiously replaced the chip on the pile in front of me. I just felt I was in a different league somehow.

'No more bets, please,' the croupier called as he set both ball and wheel spinning yet again.

Several spectators had gathered at the table now, and there was absolute silence as the small white ball slowly circled down onto the revolving wheel. This time it rattled around furiously, seeming first to settle on a red number then popping out again to come down on a black.

'Number sixteen black,' called the croupier.

'Phewww!' Philip whistled softly. 'Our affluent friend has just brought home the bacon at odds of seventeen to one.'

'A hundred and seventy thousand!' I gasped. 'He's won a hundred and seventy thousand pounds?'

Philip nodded and rolled his eyes.

But after a moment's hesitation, instead of paying the man out, the croupier suddenly but smoothly pushed the £10,000 pile of chips back towards its owner.

'I'm sorry, Sir,' he said, 'but your bet was above the table limit and therefore it was void.'

'No,' the bearded man said, his reply curt but without any note of anger or surprise. It was the refusal of a man who was used to getting his own way.

'I'm sorry, Sir,' persisted the croupier, 'but . . .'

'No,' repeated the man. 'Pay me.'

'I can't pay you, Sir, because . . .'

'Pay me.' There was no change in tone, still no hint of anger. The only feeling he seemed to be experiencing was boredom.

'I'm afraid I can't pay . . .'

'Get the manager,' he said quietly, taking another sip from his orange juice, not even bothering to look up at the now uncomfortable croupier.

'But I . . .'

'Get the manager,' he repeated, examining his finely manicured nails.

'Certainly, Sir,' the croupier said, giving way with relief rather than reluctance I thought.

'That was very naughty,' Philip said, as the croupier

made his way across the gaming room to the office, a low buzz of conversation started among the spectators.

'Yes,' I said, 'surely he should have rejected the bet at the outset rather than after he'd spun the wheel?'

'Of course he should,' he agreed. 'Can you imagine our friend over there being handed back his chips if he'd lost?'

'Frankly, no.'

'No, nor can I. Hello . . . here they come. This should be quite interesting.'

Accompanying the croupier was a heavily built man with greying hair. He caught the younger man's arm when they were still several yards away and asked him something. The croupier pointed to the Middle Eastern man and said something in reply.

There seemed to me to be no hesitation at all on the part of the manager. He simply nodded, said something further to the croupier and turned and walked away.

'Would you believe it?' Philip whispered. 'He's only going to pay him! A hundred and seventy thousand quid! What about that then?'

Throughout the delay, the man opposite us, with a mere one hundred and seventy thousand at stake, had sat quietly continuing his inspection of his manicure. Every now and then he would push back a cuticle or remove a speck of dust from beneath his chalk-white nails, but otherwise he didn't move.

At the other end of the table, the grizzled old Australian was also quiet. But he wasn't inspecting his finger nails. Instead he just glared at the bearded man. It obviously meant a lot to him that payment had been refused.

'My apologies, Sir,' the croupier said, on his arrival back at the table. 'It was my error. I do apologise most sincerely.'

First a gasp then a murmur of excited conversation went round the group of spectators. The Middle

Eastern man simply nodded and watched impassively as the columns of chips were shovelled in his direction. His apparent apathy was breathtaking.

I glanced down the table at the Australian: he now appeared to be almost consumed with rage. His face had darkened by a shade or two and, on the table in front of him, his big hands were gripped into square, bony fists, the knuckles standing out livid and white. He was in the same condition as gelignite when it sweats: highly unstable and likely to go off at the slightest provocation.

'Place your bets, please.'

The old man seemed to muster all his self-control as he dotted a handful of chips about the table. Once again, he and the bearded man made physical contact as the younger of the two spread around several thousand pounds' worth of the brightly coloured discs.

Again, the old man summoned up a bloodcurdlingly ferocious glare. Again, the Arab remained quietly unconcerned.

'No more bets, please,' cautioned the croupier as with a flick of his finger he sent the ball spinning away on its orbit.

'God dammit man!' the elderly Australian bellowed, first raising a fist then bringing it crashing down on the green baize so hard as to make the piles of chips jump and dance. 'Why the hell don't you do that properly?'

All eyes were at once on the croupier. He opened his mouth to reply, looked perplexed, then closed it again. It was obvious he had no more idea what the old man was complaining about than I had.

The ball clattered onto the revolving wheel and came to rest.

'Er . . . twenty-three, red,' announced the visibly upset croupier.

For the first time I noticed he was really quite young – twenty or twenty-one, perhaps. His earlier, rather bored attitude had made him seem more mature and self-possessed. Now he seemed very unsure of himself. He even fumbled the chips as he was paying out to one of the blue rinse ladies who had just started playing our table.

'Well, answer me!' roared the old man, half rising, fists still clenched.

'I . . . I'm sorry, Sir, but . . . I . . . I don't know what you're referring to.'

'He doesn't know what I'm referring to,' the angry Antipodean repeated in sarcastic mincing tones, looking round the table for support but conspicuously avoiding eye contact with the Arab.

I looked at Philip to see if he had any idea what he was getting at. He raised his eyebrows and mutely shook his head. It seemed he was in the dark as well.

'I'm referring to the way you spin that bloody wheel, Man,' the Australian continued. 'That's what I'm bloody well referring to. Do it properly!'

The shaken croupier looked even more confused but simply nodded.

'Place your bets, please,' he muttered with little of his former authority.

'No more bets, please,' he went on, picking up the ball and pressing it against the dished rim of the wheel. Then, with his customary flick he sent it on its way.

'Are you trying to be funny?' roared his protagonist from the other end of the table. 'Is that it? Do you think you can make a monkey out of me you little . . .'

'What seems to be the trouble?'

It was a quiet, calm voice. It was that of the manager who, unseen in all the excitement, had moved in to join his beleaguered croupier at the wheel.

'It's that bloody little poofter . . .'

'No more bad language, Sir, if you please,' the manager insisted, holding up his hand, 'or I'm afraid I shall have to ask you to leave.'

132

The old man glowered at him but said nothing.

'Now, if you would like to tell me what the problem is . . .'

'He doesn't spin the wheel both ways,' the Australian snarled through gritted teeth.

'I'm sorry, Sir?'

It was the manager's turn to look puzzled.

'I've played roulette all over the world,' the man went on, his high colour slowly returning to normal, 'and that includes Vegas and Monte Carlo, and they all roll the ball clockwise and anticlockwise – alternately. Your man, here, only sends it clockwise . . . that's wrong . . . that's all . . . that's all . . .'

As he stumbled to a conclusion, he reminded me of a small boy who having thrown a tantrum about something trivial then feels rather embarrassed about the whole business.

'I see,' said the manager, smiling pleasantly. 'Well, there's no such house rule here, but I'm sure my croupier will have no objection to doing as you request.' He turned to his young employee: 'Will you, Martin?'

The question had the tone of an unambiguous order.

'No, Sir,' the croupier replied.

'Excellent – then it only remains for me to wish you good luck, gentlemen . . . and ladies, of course.' He smiled once more at the assembled company then swept away leaving peace where he had earlier found conflict.

The croupier paid out the previous call, then cleared his throat.

'Place your bets please, ladies and gentlemen.'

A few moments later he pressed the ball against the rim of the wheel.

'No more bets, please, ladies and gentlemen.'

A second later the ball flew out of the wheel, soared a good seven or eight feet in the air, arced over the next roulette table narrowly missing a spectator, and bounced away merrily towards the black-jack tables.

Mortified, our croupier stood following first the flight then just the general direction of the missile. Some moments passed before the ball was returned to him by one of the underdressed waitresses who roamed the gaming room dispensing free sandwiches, coffee and soft drinks in return for the odd gambling chip. This one had been particularly attentive to our Arab friend but had been greeted with a marked lack of enthusiasm.

Giggling, she held out the ball to the blushing croupier. He took it, placed it in position on the wheel once more and again cautioned: 'No more bets, please, ladies and gentlemen.'

Whether it was just accumulated nervous tension or whether there was some congenital reason for his being unable to make the little white ball travel anticlockwise around the wheel, I don't know. But, whatever the cause, once again I sat and watched as the thing soared away on exactly the same course and trajectory as before. On this occasion, however, one of the gamblers on the next table got in the way. It struck the man firmly just below the left eye. He let out a yelp, clutched at his cheek and looked all around him for the unseen assailant.

This time, everybody at our table had followed the missile from launch to impact, and since the man it hit was quite large and self-important looking, the entertainment value was enhanced no end. The whole group, including the old man who had started all the trouble with his bad-tempered complaint, was rendered helpless with laughter. Only the young croupier failed to see the joke.

It was the bearded man opposite me who was the first to regain some self-control.

'Yes, yes, very good!' he said as, with a cream silk handkerchief, he wiped away the tears. 'Yes, yes, very good! Very good indeed!'

*

It was two thirty in the morning when Philip and I eventually staggered out of the restaurant bar into the night air. He sniffed suspiciously and coughed.

'Ugh! Whatsat smell?' he asked.

'Fresh air,' I replied, clutching at a parking meter for support.

'Horrible!' he said, looking around, trying to get his bearings. 'Did we bring the carsh – I mean the cars?'

'No, we walked . . . I think,' I said.

'Yeah, I think we did too. Good thing. I don't think it'd be a good idea to drive anywhere jush now.'

'No,' I agreed, still clinging to the meter. 'We might be over the limit.'

He nodded profoundly and stumbled towards me.

'Shall we share a cab?' he suggested.

'But we don't live anywhere near one another . . . do we?'

Philip grabbed hold of the meter and thought for a moment.

'No, you're right,' he said. 'We don't.'

'That's what I thought,' I mumbled. 'I'll see you tomorrow, then.'

'Yeah.'

'Jush one thing,' I said.

'Whatsat?'

'That Arab did win a hundred and seventy thousand and then lose it all again, didn't he? I mean, I didn't dream it, did I?'

'No, it happened all right,' he said, still clinging to my meter. 'That's why the manager didn't mind paying him – he knew he'd get it all straight back.'

'S'pose so,' I said. 'How much have you got left?'

'About a tenner – and you?'

'About the same,' I confessed.

'Oh, well,' he said, as he peeled himself off the meter

135

and staggered unsteadily away, 'at least it's taken your mind off that picture.'

'What picture'sh that?' I asked as he disappeared round the corner.

Chapter 12

'What do you make of it?' Charlotte asked as she leant over my shoulder rereading the article once again.

'I don't know,' I said.

'But what do you think? Is it likely to be true?'

'Well, he's certainly done his homework. So true or not, a lot of people are going to think twice about it now.'

'So, what would you do if you'd been going to buy it?' she persisted.

'I suppose, in all honesty, I'd turn my back on it and walk quietly out of the saleroom.'

She went back to her desk, perched on the edge of it, and looked serious.

'But if it's wrong,' she said, 'there's going to be a lot of egg on a lot of faces, isn't there?'

'I suppose so.'

'Well, aren't you worried that some of it might be on yours?'

'Not as worried as I would be now if I was head of the British Pictures Department at Faulkner's.'

'No, I can understand that,' she said. 'He must have really loved it when he opened his newspaper this morning.'

It would definitely have put me off my cornflakes. Just three months after we had lost Adrian Taylor's Constable to the more socially acceptable and, admittedly, much larger auctioneer's, Faulkner's, the

137

picture was in the news. And not for the sort of reason auctioneers like: it had been publicly denounced as a copy or, worse still, a deliberate forgery of the artist's work. I suspected the appalling hangover I suffered the day after losing the picture would rank as nothing against the one Faulkner's Picture Director would be nursing before too long. He was in deep trouble.

From the outset Faulkner's had concurred fully with Charles Morrison-Whyte's conclusions. They had advertised and hyped the picture as a long-lost work by the hand of John Constable, and had highlighted just how effortlessly it fitted into the jigsaw of established historical fact and documentary evidence. All had been going absolutely swimmingly without a dissenting voice, until, that is, the article had appeared in the paper that morning.

It was a well reasoned piece by a specialist writer who had turned up some old archive material which, at the very least, suggested the picture might have been executed by a hand other than John Constable's.

The material in question was a short series of letters between a Victorian art dealer and one of his regular coterie of collectors. One of the items discussed in the correspondence was a small oil painting believed by the collector to have been the work of Constable. The dealer was adamant that the picture had, in fact, been painted as an exercise by a young student some years after John Constable's death. He was able to be so firm on the matter because, he claimed, he actually knew the student concerned. He went on to stress that it had never been the student's intention to defraud anybody. He also made it clear, however, that he held less charitable views on the motives of the dealer currently trying to persuade his client to purchase the work. On that point the tone of the letter was distinctly icy.

Of course, all this might have been dismissed as nothing other than professional jealousy, had not the

138

dealer enclosed a letter from the erstwhile student in support of his case. In the letter the painter had described the picture in considerable detail, and although the dimensions he gave, being from memory, were only approximate, the rest of the minutiae recorded did seem to point to his painting and Adrian Taylor's being one and the same.

Where the whole business became really steamy was in that the journalist had very responsibly taken his findings to Faulkner's and asked them if they would re-attribute the work. Faulkner's had apparently suggested that the journalist should go away, take his findings with him, and never darken their lofty portals again. As I skimmed through the article once more, I had no doubt they were at that very moment questioning the wisdom of their high-handed action. And since the sale was due to take place just two days later, they didn't have a lot of time to undo the damage done.

'What do you think they'll do?' Charlotte asked.

'My bet is they'll quietly withdraw the picture from sale and do some more research on it,' I said. 'Adrian Taylor won't be interested in selling it if it's only a copy, and it would be foolish to try and bluff their way through without some hard evidence to refute these claims.'

'So you think they'll just resolve it all behind the scenes.'

'Yes, Faulkner's are intelligent enough to know there's nothing to be gained from a public slanging match with the press. They'll just cut their losses and retire gracefully.'

It was with ill-concealed delight that Charlotte greeted me on my arrival at the office the following day.

'Good morning, Boss,' she bubbled. 'Have you by any chance seen the . . .'

139

'Yes,' I said, 'I have.'

'Oh, bother! I was looking forward to watching your face as you read it. So what do you think now?'

'I think they must be mad,' I replied. 'Stark, raving mad!'

My face probably had been a picture as I'd read the letter from the head of Faulkner's British Pictures Department in that morning's paper. It was a curt rebuttal of the previous day's article. The trouble was he had failed to produce any real evidence with which to counter the newspaper's case: he seemed to be falling back on arrogance rather than argument. The letter was no more than three paragraphs of huffing and puffing.

'So why have they done it?' Charlotte asked. 'You said the last thing they'd want would be a slanging match with the press . . .'

'And that's exactly what they've walked into,' I said. ' I know – it just looks like insanity to me. All I can think is they've got somebody who's straining to buy it and this has been done to keep his confidence up, or . . .'

'Or what?'

'Or the Director of Faulkner's British Pictures Department has had a rush of blood to the head and has decided to risk his reputation on this one picture.'

Charlotte looked thoughtful, then she grinned wickedly.

'Presumably,' she said, 'if the picture fails to sell tomorrow, he'll be expected to commit hari-kari on the rostrum after the sale.'

'No,' I replied, 'that's only for Oriental works of art specialists – this man will probably just be garrotted personally by the Chairman of Faulkner's.'

'Considering the accuracy of your predictions so far, I should think it's more likely I'll read in tomorrow's paper that he's just become Company Chairman.'

'That is a possibility,' I admitted.

*

Good sales at Hampson's tended to be crowded affairs, but not on the same scale as important sales at Faulkner's.

The British Pictures sale was taking place in the Oak Room on the first floor, but the scrummage began downstairs in the reception area. There was definitely no shortage of interest in the event, and as I eased my way through the mêlée towards the main staircase it was obvious there was no shortage of money either.

There were the usual knots of dealers scattered around, heads bowed in rapt conversation swapping information and disinformation – probably in roughly equal proportions. But there seemed to me to be a lot of private buyers as well. There were certainly a lot of very expensive and fragrant ladies present. By the time I had battled my way to the top of the stairs my olfactory nerves had been numbed by an assault more diverse and relentless than one would have encountered in Harrod's Perfume Hall. As I eased my way into the Oak Room I mused on the idea that the old assertion was quite true: you could smell money. What was more, a Faulkner's crowd actually smelt as though it had a greater level of disposable income than a Hampson's crowd. I suddenly felt very inferior.

The head of Faulkner's British Pictures Department was probably no more than thirty-five years of age, but one had to admit that seated in the polished oak rostrum he had considerable presence. His scraped-back, wavy, dark hair and heavy, horn-rimmed spectacles lent him a certain gravity, nicely at odds with the calculated flippancy of the polka-dot bow tie he was wearing. If he exuded anything it was confidence, and judging by the prices realised by the first dozen lots it appeared to be well founded. All of them soared effortlessly above their estimates. It showed the promise of being another record-breaking sale.

As I observed the sure-footed performance of the man in the rostrum I couldn't help feeling he knew something about the Constable that I didn't. This was not the swan song of a man destined for professional oblivion; this was the self-assured exhibition of a man who believed himself to be on the way to the very pinnacle of achievement. It crossed my mind that Charlotte could well be right: I might just be looking at a future Chairman of Faulkner's.

'. . . at seven thousand pounds, then . . . any more bids at seven thousand . . .?'

His ivory gavel descended, slowly at first as he watched for a late bid, then sharply.

'. . . Burlington – seven thousand pounds . . .' he cooed into his bank of microphones, smiling and nodding at the extremely attractive woman buyer as he did so.

He noted the details of the sale then looked up and away to his left at the small landscape now being displayed by the senior porter.

'Which brings us to Lot 36,' he went on. 'A most important picture – Dedham Vale by John Constable – what will you bid me? Bid me thirty thousand . . .'

Just like that. I had to admire his nerve. Not even a veiled reference to the controversy over the work's authenticity which had raged so recently in the pages of one of the country's most respected broadsheets. Either he really knew something I didn't or he was one hell of an actor.

'. . . thirty thousand I am bid . . .' he confirmed, pointing aggressively to the middle of the room: my own technique when nobody had moved a muscle.

'. . . thirty-five thousand . . . forty thousand . . . at forty thousand . . . forty-five thousand . . .'

There was no need to look round to see where the bids were coming from. There was no need because I knew there were no bids. He'd had me fooled for a while all right, but now I knew the game was up – nobody was

142

going to touch Adrian Taylor's 'Constable'. In the end, all the bluff and bravado had not been enough to see off that well-written article.

'... at forty-five thousand then ... are you all finished at forty-five thousand pounds ...'

Taking one last look at the man who had just ceased to be in the running for the chairmanship, I turned to go. Behind me the gavel cracked down once more as, forcing a path through the crush in the doorway, I popped out into the open space at the top of the staircase. I paused for a moment, listening to the progress of the next lot, when a familiar voice called out behind me.

'Hello, Mr Harton – what a pantomime, eh?'

For a man who had just failed to sell a picture which had been expected to make anything up to £100,000 and which was now completely discredited, Adrian Taylor looked pretty chirpy.

'Hello, Mr Taylor,' I said. 'What can I say?'

'Oh, "How about a drink?" would do, I think,' he said, grinning. 'Have you got time – there's a nice little pub round the corner.'

'Yes, of course,' I said. 'But I feel rather guilty. After all, I started all this and ...'

'Nonsense, my dear chap. It's not your fault. It's been an interesting experience as far as I'm concerned.'

We wandered slowly down the wide staircase, across the reception area, busy with people clutching brown paper parcels and carrier bags, and out into the sunlit street.

'I must say, you're taking this very well,' I told him.

'And why not?' he laughed. 'As you couldn't have failed to notice, my wife and I have a very pleasant lifestyle; we're certainly not hard up and we didn't need the money. The only reason we were selling the picture was because we couldn't afford to keep it – if you know what I mean ...'

'Yes, I understand perfectly.'

143

'So, now, suddenly we can afford to keep it again and I'm delighted. I liked that little painting when I thought it was worth a few thousand, I didn't like it any more or less when it suddenly became worth tens of thousands. And I still like it just as much now it's apparently worth sod all. I'm just looking forward to having it back where it belongs – on my office wall.'

'Mr Taylor,' I said as we stepped from the glare of the London street into the dark little pub, 'you should be a collector.'

'No thanks,' he replied, shaking his head, 'I wouldn't be able to stand the excitement.'

Chapter 13

'Is it all right?' Charlotte asked.

'Excellent,' I said. 'As far as I'm concerned you can send it to them.'

'Okay, let me have it back when you've signed it and I'll post it at lunchtime.

I flicked through the top copy of Mr and Mrs Templeman's valuation once more. It was an extremely professional piece of work. It had been a large, comfortable house, and both Templemans had inherited nice pieces from their respective families. I had enjoyed doing the job; both clients had been very charming; and the fee, at £1,500, had made it fairly profitable.

I signed the two copies of the valuation and the covering letter then carefully slotted it all in the accompanying envelope and sealed it. I always did that final job myself, just to make sure nothing went astray at the last moment.

As I dropped the large, manilla package into Charlotte's mailing tray the telephone rang.

'Hampson's Valuation Office,' she murmured in her most seductive answering voice. 'Oh, hi! How are you?'

It obviously wasn't a client.

'Oh, I'm fine . . . but you haven't been in for ages . . .'

Probably one of the seemingly endless chain of Charlotte's friends who would periodically crash into the office, usually hot foot from exotic climes and

145

shattered romances. Their arrival never did a lot for Charlotte's productivity but they were a colourful bunch and they did tend to brighten the place up.

'. . . yes, he's here . . .'

Perhaps I was wrong. This caller actually seemed to wish to speak to me.

'. . . oh, not too bad,' she went on, grinning mischievously across at me. 'He actually made the coffee when he got in this morning – that's the second time this year . . .'

Apparently this was one of *my* friends.

'. . . yes, I'll see if Sir will take your call, Madam . . . see you soon . . . pop round – we'll have lunch and I'll give you all the up-to-date dirt on him,' she giggled.

I sat waiting patiently for this one-sided character assassination to end.

'Okay . . . bye . . .' She pressed the button on the telephone to transfer the call to my line. 'It's Sarah for you,' she said.

'And just where were you last night?' enquired the voice on the other end of the line before I could say anything.

'I didn't get back from Devon until gone eleven,' I explained. 'I did say I might be late.'

'You could have phoned.'

'You know what it's like trying to find a telephone that works in a motorway service area. Anyway, I didn't think you were . . .'

'All right you're forgiven this time,' she said, obviously not really having been particularly concerned from the outset. 'And just to prove it I've actually got a bit of business for you – have you got a pencil and paper handy?'

'Yes, fire away.'

The details were those of an elderly lady who lived in Bayswater. She had, Sarah explained, fallen on hard times and needed to liquidate some assets as quickly as possible.

'I'm told she's got some valuable rugs,' Sarah went on, 'although I have to say I haven't been dealing with it personally so I don't know for sure.'

'I thought it sounded a bit outside your commercial sphere,' I observed. 'Who's been dealing with it?'

'Our new boy – the Honourable Patrick Lush.'

'He's the one I met – with the acne and the halitosis.'

'That's right, although I must say the poor chap's halitosis has got much better – shame about the acne though.'

'Is he still dealing with it?' I asked.

'What – the acne?'

'No, Sarah – the job.'

'Oh, well, yes but he's swamped with work at the moment so I said I'd help him with this one since I knew you – professionally of course.'

'Of course,' I said.

'Anyway, the good lady's expecting a call from nice Mr Harton, so see what you can do.'

'Right.'

'And are you coming round for supper this evening?'

'Yes, please.'

'Okay, I'll be back by seven thirty – and don't be late.'

'Yes, Ma'am,' I said, replacing the receiver.

Mrs Barbara Cochrane lived in a modest third-floor flat off Queensway. She was a petite, smart lady, probably in her early seventies. She wore a wig, but not I assumed out of vanity or a desire to look younger, since it was silver grey, almost the same colour as her tired eyes. Although there were no obvious symptoms for me to see, I got the impression that Mrs Cochrane was far from well.

However, if her health was failing, it did not stop her from handling the opening of our meeting with cool efficiency.

'I'm told my by advisors that I have to raise what seems to me to be a considerable sum of money, Mr

Harton,' she said, sitting opposite me in the sitting room with a notebook and pen cradled at the ready in her lap. 'It's something to do with essential repairs to the roof of this building and it seems that the tenants, and there are only three of us now, are liable.'

'I see,' I said, already glancing round the room and doing some mental arithmetic.

'Personally, I think it's got more to do with the owner wanting our leases back. He's been trying to get us out for five years now, and he thinks he's found a way of achieving it at last. Perhaps he has. Anyway, my solicitors tell me I must try to raise the sum involved. Hence your presence.'

She smiled and arranged her hands calmly and deliberately on top of the notebook and pen which lay in her lap.

'May I ask how much you need to raise?' I asked.

'At least twenty thousand pounds,' she replied. 'Perhaps as much as twenty-five.'

'And would it all have to come from the sale of pieces in the flat?'

'Oh, yes,' she said, smiling again. 'I don't have any secret hoards of cash tucked away anywhere, Mr Harton.'

I glanced around the sitting room once more. The furniture was not spectacular, there were no ceramics to speak of, and only a couple of unimportant pictures. On the floor, however, were seven or eight of the rugs Sarah had mentioned when she first called me about the job. They were good but on their own would fall a long way short of Mrs Cochrane's target figure.

'I take it you'd like to raise the amount needed by selling as few items as possible,' I said.

'Mr Harton, I don't *want* to sell *anything*, especially not my beautiful rugs, but what choice do I have?'

'I understand,' I assured her. 'Let me have a look around and I'll see what suggestions I can come up with.'

'Be my guest,' she said, sinking back into the big armchair and slowly closing her eyes.

As I wandered about the flat two things became clear: firstly, I was going to be hard pressed to raise the sort of money Mrs Cochrane was talking about without selling every rug in the place; secondly, if the amount of prescribed drugs there were anything to go by, she was a very sick lady.

When I returned to the sitting room she was still lying back in her armchair with her eyes closed.

'Mrs Cochrane,' I said gently.

'It's all right, Mr Harton,' she replied, slowly opening her eyes and smiling once more, 'I'm not asleep. It's just that I do get very tired now.'

Despite her fatigue, she listened intently to everything I had to say about the various permutations open to her, and made notes as I spoke. When I had finished she sat in silence for a moment looking down at the open book in her lap. Then she closed it and placed it, along with her pen, on the small table beside her chair.

'So the only way I can raise the money I need is by selling all my beautiful rugs,' she said eventually.

'I'm afraid so, Mrs Cochrane,' I confirmed. 'Naturally, Hampson's would be very happy to handle the sale for you, but I do realise it's the last thing in the world you would choose to do.'

'The last thing in the world,' she echoed sadly, staring down at the rug on the floor in front of her.

We sat in silence for several minutes, then she looked up again.

'They were my husband's, you see,' she explained. 'He worked in the Middle East for many years. We lived all over the place. When the oil company he worked for was nationalised he stayed on to help train the new, local staff – he was fond of the people. The government out there expressed its gratitude by sacking him a year before he was due to retire. They kicked us both out of the country and stole the pension he'd been contributing to for thirty years. He wasn't a bitter man, Mr Harton but he felt so betrayed it just broke his health. He had a heart attack eighteen months after we came back to live in England. It was very cruel.'

I just nodded. I could think of nothing adequate to say.

'Do you know what the most horrible thing is, Mr Harton?' she asked, neither expecting nor waiting for a reply. 'It's that some days I can't remember what he looked like – after all those years. I sit here and close my eyes and try to remember the exact shape of his face, the line of his mouth, and it just won't come right you know.'

'I don't even have any photographs any more. We lost all those when they expelled us. There's a little one in a locket somewhere but I've misplaced that now – I really must find it.'

She seemed to sink down even deeper into her chair. Then she suddenly brightened and sat up again.

'Oh dear! Just listen to me. You don't want to hear all this.'

'Not at all,' I said. 'You go ahead and talk about it if it makes you feel better.'

'Oh, I've said it all really, but thank you for listening anyway, Mr Harton. It's just that, somehow, I feel that if I lose these rugs I'll lose him completely, forever. Do you know what I mean?'

Once again I nodded.

'Of course you don't,' she smiled. 'Why should you? You're young with all your life ahead of you.'

She rose a little unsteadily from her chair.

'I won't take up any more of your time but I will think very carefully about what you've told me and let my solicitors know of my decision.'

She showed me to the door and as I stepped into the musty smelling corridor outside I turned to say goodbye.

'And if there's anything you'd like to ask me,' I added, 'please don't hesitate to give me a call.'

'Thank you, Mr Harton,' she said, shaking my hand almost without gripping it at all, 'but I think you've told me all I need to know – probably what I already knew really. I'm sure I'll be able to make up my mind about what to do now. In fact, if I'm honest I already know what I must do. Goodbye, Mr Harton . . . and thank you again.'

As she closed the door and I made my way along that dingy corridor a feeling of the bleakest depression came over me. Old age could be harsh but old age in London could be appalling. I pulled up my coat collar as I descended the cold, unswept, carpetless stairs. It was a relief to step back onto the street. That too was dirty, but at least it was bathed in the bright, clean late September sunshine.

I looked up at the third floor and noticed for the first time that two small panes of glass were broken in one of the windows of Mrs Cochrane's flat. A few jagged shards remained while the holes themselves appeared to be covered with bits of cardboard. I hadn't noticed the damage when I had gone round the flat, so it must have been in one of the rooms I hadn't seen.

'Probably the bathroom,' I thought as I turned my back and headed for Hyde Park.

It was nearly three weeks after my visit to Mrs Cochrane's flat that we received an unexpected visitor at the office.

'Good morning, Sir,' he said. 'I'm Detective Sergeant Hill. I wonder if I might ask you a few questions. It won't take very long.'

He was of medium height and stocky build. His face and tone of voice gave away nothing, but he still made me feel vaguely uneasy.

As Charlotte retreated to the kitchen to get a cup of coffee for our visitor, he took a seat across the desk from me and removed a notebook from his inside pocket. He consulted it in silence for a moment then looked up.

'I believe you've recently valued some property for a Mr and Mrs Templeman, Sir,' he said.

'Yes, that's right,' I confirmed..

'Was it with a view to your purchasing some of the items?'

'No, no – it was an insurance valuation: just to enable them to insure their house contents for the correct amount.'

'So you weren't interested in buying any of the things concerned then?'

'No, certainly not,' I said. 'Hampson's are auctioneers. We don't buy and sell in our own right. We just act as agents and offer pieces for sale on behalf of our clients.'

'I understand,' he said, looking down at his notebook, then back up at me. 'But would you, personally, have been interested in purchasing any of Mr and Mrs Templeman's antiques?'

'No, certainly not,' I repeated, indignantly.

I had no idea what the sergeant wanted but whatever it was he was doing nothing to allay my initial feeling of discomfort.

'I see,' he said, once again glancing at his notebook then back at me.

I noticed that his hazel eyes had a greenish tint, the right more so than the left. It gave them a certain intensity which I had not noticed when he'd first started talking.

'It's just that Mrs Templeman said you mentioned how much you liked one or two of their antiques,' he went on quietly.

'Yes,' I said, 'I did. I often tell clients when I personally like an item. It's just intended as a compliment, nothing else.'

'I see,' he said again, staring at me, still without any identifiable change of expression.

'Sergeant . . .'

'Yes, Sir.'

'Are you going to tell me what this is all about – clearly something has happened.'

'Yes, Sir,' he replied, 'it has – Mr and Mrs Templeman's house was burgled two days ago.'

'Oh no!'

'I'm afraid so. And the thieves were very selective; they seemed to know exactly what they were after.'

'That's awful.'

'Yes, Sir. They took their time and creamed off every high value piece in the house while the Templemans were out.'

'So they knew what they were doing,' I said.

'Well, it was certainly a professional job, Sir. No question of it being kids or opportunists.'

'How did they know the Templemans would be out?' I asked.

'Oh, they made sure of that. They sent them a pair of the best tickets for a West End show for that night.'

'What?'

'Oh, that's an old trick,' Charlotte said, handing Detective Sergeant Hill his coffee, and sitting down at her desk once more. 'They send them, along with a letter on smart company paper saying you've won them for being the millionth customer for somewhere or other, then they . . . they . . .'

Charlotte faltered and stopped as she became aware of the policeman's gaze which had now become fixed on her.

'You're very well informed, Miss,' he observed laconically.

'My boy friend told me . . . he works in the City,' she said, as though his employment in the City of London automatically explained away his in-depth knowledge of the methods of the criminal underworld.

'I see,' the sergeant replied. 'Well, they do say all the crooks aren't in prison.'

153

Charlotte blushed, made a face as the policeman turned away and busied herself shuffling a pile of papers on her desk.

'Well, this is all very interesting,' I said, breaking the awkward silence, 'and, of course, I'm very sorry for the Templemans but what exactly has it all got to do with me?'

Detective Sergeant Hill looked faintly surprised by my question.

'We suspect the thieves were working from your valuation, Mr Harton,' he said.

I sat and gaped across the desk at the policeman for some moments before I managed a reply. Even then it was hardly adequate.

'What?' I gasped.

'We believe the thieves were in possession of a copy of the valuation you did for Mr and Mrs Templeman, Sir.'

I shook my head in disbelief.

'Are you suggesting that ... that ... that I was in some way involved in the burglary of the Templemans' home, Sergeant?' I asked, choosing my words with some, though probably not enough, care.

'No, Sir, but we do believe those responsible for the crime had access to your valuation.'

I sat, still stunned at the implication of what he was saying.

'But the Templemans had two copies of the valuation,' I pointed out. 'One of those could have fallen into the wrong hands.'

'Yes,' he agreed. 'But since they sent one straight to their insurers and the other is lodged with their solicitor, it doesn't seem likely.'

I turned to Charlotte.

'Get me our copy of the Templemans' inventory, please,' I said.

As she scurried off to the filing room I explained the

154

security system we had set up to safeguard against our copies of inventories falling into the wrong hands.

'The inventory – the detailed list of items and values – is filed separately from the rest of the client's file. There is nothing on it to indicate the name or address of the client concerned. It is linked in each case to the relevant client file by an index card and without that you can't match the inventory to the address of the client.'

'Where are your index cards kept?' the Detective Sergeant asked.

'During the day they're in our filing room, and this office is never left unattended. At night they're stored in the strongroom in the main building. You see, Sergeant, it's just not possible for anyone to have stolen the information from here.'

'I accept that it would be very difficult, Sir,' he acknowledged as Charlotte returned with the Templeman inventory and handed it to me.

'And, as you can see,' I went on, 'our copy is safe and sound.'

I passed it across the desk to him.

He took it and leafed through the first few pages.

'A George II mahogany bracket clock,' he read, 'the dial and backplate signed "Delander, London" ... seven thousand, five hundred pounds.'

'It was a very nice clock,' I said.

'Was, Sir?'

'Yes ... I meant it was ... when I saw it ... it was ... ' Once more I began to feel very uncomfortable. Almost guilty, while knowing I had nothing to feel guilty about. ' ... I'm sure it still is,' I concluded clumsily.

'Not at the Templemans', it's not,' Sergeant Hill observed, closing the file and passing it back to me.

'Oh, well, all I can say is, I'm sorry. You can at least see that nobody has got their hands on our copy of the valuation.'

155

The policeman said nothing, then rose to leave.

'Well, thank you for your time, Mr Harton,' he said. 'I suspect we'll be in contact again.'

'Of course,' I said, 'we'll do anything we can to help, but I can't really think . . . '

'Does the name Sheila Phillips ring any bells with you, Sir?' he asked as he buttoned up his raincoat.

'Sheila Phillips? Sheila Phillips?' I racked my brains knowing the name was familiar from somewhere. 'I think I did a valuation for a Sheila Phillips about six months ago, didn't I Charlotte?'

'Yes,' she said, after a moment's thought. 'It was an insurance valuation; just off the Gloucester Road, wasn't it?'

'That's right,' I said, 'it's all coming back now – she's got a lot of very nice jewellery.'

'Not any more she hasn't,' Detective Sergeant Hill said, pulling up his collar.

'You mean . . .'

'Good morning, Sir, Miss. We'll be in touch.'

As I heard the street door slam behind the sergeant I slid slowly back into my seat.

'Do we have any brandy in the cupboard, Charlotte?' I asked.

'Yes, but it's not even ten thirty yet.'

'I don't care, Charlotte. I need a drink. This is medicinal.'

When I arrived at Sarah's flat that evening she was sitting in the kitchen sucking her pen contemplating the crossword puzzle in her morning paper.

'Not finished it yet?' I asked, piling my briefcase and coat on the chair just inside the door.

'No, it's been murder at the office today,' she said, without looking up. 'I'm too exhausted even to focus on the clues, let alone unravel them.'

I leant over, kissed her, and slumped onto one of the

other two chairs. It was hard and uncomfortable.

'How's your knowledge of criminal law?' I asked.

'Why do you ask?' she replied. 'Don't tell me another consignment of valuables has gone missing in the Twickenham Triangle.'

'No, I've told you before, that sort of thing's all in the past. Bailey's is an example to us all these days.'

She laughed. 'I suspect they've just got so clever down there that you don't even know they're doing it any more.'

'Doing what?'

'Whatever it is you don't know about,' she said. 'Anyway, if it's not Bailey's, who is in trouble with the law?'

'Me,' I replied.

'You?'

'Me,' I confirmed.

Sarah sat and listened quietly to my account of our morning's visit from the long arm of the law.

'What a hoot,' she said eventually. 'I wonder who's doing it.'

'I don't know,' I said, 'but it appears the boys in blue are convinced it's me.'

She shook her head.

'No, they're just shaking the tree to see if any rotten apples drop out,' she said, folding up her newspaper and putting it to one side.

'That's all very well,' I went on, 'but you haven't heard the best of it yet.'

'You mean there's more?'

'Yes. As Charlotte and I were leaving this evening the telephone rang. It was another client. I'd done an insurance valuation for her three months ago. And guess what . . .'

'Cleaned out?'

'Exactly the same as the others. No show tickets this time though. They must have just watched the place until she went out – she's quite elderly and lives on her own.'

Sarah looked doubtful.

'It's probably not got anything to do with the others,' she said. 'Burglaries are ten a penny these days. It's just a coincidence.'

'No,' I insisted, 'from what she told me they knew exactly what they were after. For instance, she had a little display table in her drawing room. Most of the pieces in it weren't of any particular value but there was one thing that was: it was a little Fabergé box and cover carved out of nephrite . . .'

'Nephrite – what's that?'

'Jade – they used to think it relieved nephritis – kidney disease.'

'I wonder why?'

'I've no idea,' I said, a little impatiently. 'The point is it's quite a subtle, understated piece. The average house-breaker wouldn't give it a second glance, but this lot took it and didn't as much as move any other item in the table out of place. They didn't even look at any of the other pieces. Don't you see – they knew exactly what they'd come for.'

'How much was it worth then?'

'I'd put an insurance value of seven and a half thousand on it,' I said.

Sarah whistled.

'It doesn't look good,' I said.

'No,' she said. 'I suppose you are likely to get another visit from your friendly, local CID.'

'So what should I do?'

'There's nothing you can do, except tell the truth. You know you and Charlotte haven't been leaking secrets to London's underworld, and there's nobody else in Hampson's who could have done it. So, clearly the information's coming from elsewhere.'

'But, where?'

'I don't know – you'll just have to sit back patiently and wait for the long arm of the law to find out who done it.'

'That's all very well, but just at the moment the finger of suspicion on the end of the long arm of the law seems to be pointing at me.'

'You worry too much,' she said, leaning over and squeezing my hand.

'So would you if you'd met Detective Sergeant Hill.'

'Never mind him. You didn't want to go out tonight, did you?'

'Not particularly.'

'Good, I'll fix some scrambled egg and bacon and we can watch television for a change.'

She got up, went to the fridge and fished out the ingredients.

'Oh, I nearly forgot,' she said as she began to lay out the rashers in the grill pan, 'I'm going to have to get you to go back to Mrs Cochrane's – you know, the old lady with the rugs.'

'She's decided to sell I suppose.'

'No, the whole situation's changed rather a lot I'm afraid.'

'In what way?'

'She was found dead in her flat yesterday by a cleaner.'

'Oh, no!' I said. 'I'm sorry about that. She was a nice old dear, although I think she was terribly lonely. What was it – a heart attack?'

'No,' Sarah said, looking up from her supper preparations. 'According to the police it was suicide. Mrs Cochrane slashed her wrists with a shard of glass from a broken bathroom window.'

159

Chapter 14

As if the gale force wind wasn't enough, no sooner had
we got out of the car than a fresh downpour of cold,
stinging rain began. Sarah wrestled momentarily with
her umbrella then gave up the struggle and, with some
difficulty, folded it down again.

'Come on,' I said. 'It's that door over there – run!'

We plunged across the flooded street and huddled in
the doorway. Sarah dragged the bundle of keys from
her pocket. A moment later we were standing in the
peeling entrance hall of Queen's House. I recognised
the same damp mustiness from my first visit to Barbara
Cochrane's flat. It had got no better, perhaps a little
worse. It was difficult to tell.

'What a dump,' Sarah commented.

'It gets worse the further up you go,' I said.

We trudged up to the third floor, through the litter
and fallen plaster to the door of Mrs Cochrane's own
neat little home.

Once again Sarah went through the keys in the
bundle she carried.

'Security lock,' she said, inserting one of them in the
door and turning it. 'And now just the Yale.'

This time she didn't turn the key immediately.
Instead she looked round at me.

'The police said it was rather unpleasant when they
went in,' she said. 'I don't suppose it will be any better
now. I mean the place won't have been cleaned.'

160

'No,' I said. 'I can arrange for that to be done when we move the contents out.'

'Yes,' she said, 'that's what I thought.'

The next moment the door was open and we entered the tiny hallway where I had last spoken to Barbara Cochrane. Nothing seemed to have changed. It was still neat and tidy although rather dark now since the doors leading off it were all closed.

'I was just thinking,' I said, as I took my notepad from my briefcase, 'the last time we were on a valuation together was the one in Essex. Do you remember it?'

'How could I forget,' she smiled. 'The housekeeper was dying in the kitchen as you were valuing the pots and pans around her. You very nearly ended up spending the night there looking after her, and when that proved unnecessary you asked me out instead.'

'Yes, isn't it strange how one thing leads to another sometimes?' I said. 'Anyway, I suppose this is no time for reminiscing – we'd better get started. At least it doesn't look too bad in here. Are you ready for the rest?'

'Yes, let's get it over with.'

I opened the door to the sitting room and looked inside. At first glance it seemed unchanged from my previous visit. All the furniture was arranged as before and the rugs were positioned as I remembered them. I stepped into the room and turned to speak to Sarah. There, on the wall next to the open door was a long, red-brown smear. It was unmistakable. It was blood.

'Ah,' I said. 'It appears the police were right.'

Sarah followed me into the room, turning to look at the livid stain as she did so.

'Ugh!' she groaned, giving an involuntary shudder and grabbing my arm. 'How horrible.'

'I know I shall get into trouble for suggesting this,' I said, 'but you could always wait outside in the car.'

'No I can't,' she replied, squeezing my arm tightly, 'I

have to go through her things. We don't have any of her personal papers yet.'

'All right,' I said. 'Her bureau's over there. If I find anything else as I'm going round I'll bring it in to you.'

'Thanks.'

She walked over to the bureau, opened it, pulled up a chair and sat down. A moment later she was deeply engrossed in her late client's paper's.

A thin trail of dried blood led across the floor to the door on the far side of the room. There was more around the handle.

The door opened onto a small, dark passageway. At one end of it was Mrs Cochrane's bedroom, and at the other end, the bathroom which I hadn't bothered to look at on my first visit. I went into the bedroom.

It was devastated. There was blood everywhere: on the walls; on the floor; all over the bed and curtains. All the drawers from the chest, the wardrobe and the two bedside tables had been emptied onto the bed then thrown onto the floor. The place had been ransacked.

I made some notes, then returned to the sitting room where Sarah was still studying the contents of the bureau. A small wastepaper bin beside her was already overflowing with discarded letters and documents.

'Anything of interest?' I asked.

'Oh, hello,' she said, looking up and smiling. 'I didn't hear you come in.'

'You did seem very absorbed.'

'Yes, it was this,' she said, holding up a small book bound in red leather. 'It's Mrs Cochrane's diary. She kept it meticulously, right up to the day before her death. Did you know she had cancer?'

'No,' I said. 'But I gathered she was very unwell. The place is full of pills and potions.'

Sarah flicked through some of the pages again.

'She'd had several bouts of chemotherapy which made her feel dreadfully ill and made her hair fall out.

162

She was very upset about that.'

'That explains the wig, then,' I remarked.

'Yes,' she said, still looking through the pages of tightly packed, tiny writing.

'Sarah.'

'Yes.'

'Did the police mention anything about the bedroom having been ransacked?'

She looked up from the diary and thought for a moment.

'Yes, they did,' she said. 'They thought she'd been searching for something but they didn't know what. They were positive the flat hadn't been broken into or anything like that.'

'Where was the body discovered?'

'In the bathroom, I think. I understand it's really not very nice at all in there.'

I valued what was in the sitting room, then, leaving Sarah still seated at the bureau, I made my way along the passage to the bathroom. I hesitated for a few moments before grasping the cold, white china door handle and turning it.

It was an old-fashioned room with a high ceiling. There was a big cast-iron bath and matching wash basin, both with large chromium-plated taps. The walls were painted cream and the cracked tiling around the bath and above the basin was also cream. The small window which I had seen from the street on my previous visit still had its two broken panes. One hole was covered by a piece of card, probably from a shoe box. The other was open to the wind and rain. As a fresh gust howled in through the jagged glass teeth still embedded in the old hard putty, the door behind me squeaked pitifully then slammed shut.

Startled for a moment, the full horror of the scene suddenly registered. The room was simply covered in blood. Just like the bedroom, it must have witnessed

163

some dreadful frenetic activity before poor Mrs Cochrane had finally slipped to the cold linoleum floor to die exhausted and alone. What had been going through her mind? I could not even begin to guess. According to the police there had been no note. Probably she felt there was nobody left to whom she owed an explanation. Whatever her final thoughts had been, she had taken them to the grave with her. Nobody else would ever know them now.

I stooped and peeled a tiny, unevenly shaped disc of blood-stained paper from the soiled floor just behind the wash basin pedestal. Turning it over I could just make it out to be a photograph. I ran the tap for a moment and wiped the image clean. Staring back at me were a young couple, she blonde and petite, he broad-shouldered with slicked-back dark hair. Their hopeful happiness was radiant. Caught all those years ago by some nameless photographer, it still shone out.

I dried the picture on my handkerchief and returned, slowly, to the sitting room.

'How's it going?' I asked.

'Almost finished, I think,' Sarah replied. 'Is there anything I should see through there?'

'No,' I replied. 'Nothing.'

She looked round at me.

'Is it bad?' she asked.

'Pretty gruesome,' I said, handing her the little photograph.

'What's this?'

'I think it's what Mrs Cochrane ransacked her room for. It's a photograph of her wedding day. I think it was once in a locket.'

'They look so happy. It's awful to think it all ended up like this – with two complete strangers picking over their lives and just selling everything or throwing it away. It's just awful.'

'I know,' I said. 'Let's get out of here. I keep

164

remembering things she said when I was last here. I think she actually decided then that this was what she would do. It didn't mean anything at the time, but now it all falls into place. It's a very unpleasant feeling.'

'You mustn't worry about it. There was no way you could have known. Come on – let's go.'

'Okay,' I said. 'I'll arrange to get the place cleared and cleaned up as soon as possible. Most of the furniture's perfectly saleable, and the rugs will make twenty thousand or more – amazingly there doesn't seem to be a mark on them. I suppose the shark landlord will get the main share of the proceeds?'

'The freeholder – yes, I'm afraid so. I don't suppose he'll even have a twinge of conscience about it,' Sarah said as she took one last look at the sitting room before closing the door. 'I've got the diary by the way. I'll see it's incinerated.'

'Good.'

We stepped out once more into the mildew and decay of the third-floor landing. I watched Sarah as she locked the door before we made our way downstairs.

'It's strange she didn't confide in her diary about the planned suicide, don't you think?' Sarah asked as we reached the street door.

'Didn't she allude to it at all?'

'No, although the very last entry was rather cryptic.'

'What did she say?'

'Just "too tired to remember". That's all.'

Detective Sergeant Hill was comfortably seated by my desk, a cup of coffee in one hand and a sale catalogue in the other. His raincoat was draped over the radiator but looked quite dry. I assumed he had been awaiting my return for some time.

'Detective Sergeant Hill,' I said. 'What a surprise. I do hope you haven't been waiting long.'

'Not really, Sir,' he replied. 'Anyway, it's a lot nicer in

than out today, as you seem to have discovered. I take it the nearest parking space was some way off.'

Unimpressed by his piece of Holmesian deduction I removed my sodden coat and pointedly threw it over his on the radiator.

'Actually, it was about a quarter of a mile away,' I replied, easing my way past him to gain access to my own chair. 'It's always the same on sale days, especially when it rains.'

'And it really has chucked it down this morning, hasn't it, Sir?'

'Yes, it has. I'm absolutely soaked.'

He smiled and looked back at the catalogue he was holding.

'Your young lady very kindly gave me this to keep me amused while I was waiting,' he said.

Charlotte, who with head bowed had been conspicuously busy checking a draft valuation, looked up and grimaced at the detective, then bent over her self-imposed task once more.

'I must say, I'd never heard of netsooks before,' he went on.

'Net-*skis*,' I said.

'What's that, Sir?'

'Net-*ski*,' I replied. 'It's pronounced net-*ski* even though it's spelt *n-e-t-s-u-k-e*.'

'Is it really?' the sergeant said, apparently genuinely interested. 'I must remember that. But what were they for, Mr Harton? Just decoration or what?'

'They're toggles,' I said.

'Toggles?'

'Toggles.'

He looked blank and stared for a long time at the group of carved wood and ivory examples illustrated on the front cover of his catalogue.

Under normal circumstances I would have been only too happy to have given him a brief history of the

Japanese art of *netsuke* carving, but these were not normal circumstances.

After all, he was a member of the Metropolitan Police Force. He'd implied only a few days earlier that I was somehow involved in a series of burglaries, and now he was sitting in my office, drinking my coffee, drying his feet and discussing Oriental art. No, these were not normal circumstances.

'When you say "toggles", Mr Harton,' he said at last, 'what exactly do you mean?'

I gave up. It was probably going to be quicker to tell him all I knew about the subject than it was to wait until he got bored with asking. Anyway, he was making it sound like an official enquiry.

'The traditional Japanese form of dress is, as I'm sure you know, the kimono,' I began.

'Yes.'

'A kimono has a wide waistband called an *obi*, and the wearer would hang things from the *obi*.'

'What sort of things?' he asked.

Detective Sergeant Hill was obviously hungry for knowledge.

'I was coming to that,' I pointed out. 'One of the things would be an *inro* . . .'

'What's an –'

'A small flat box,' I pre-empted the rest of his question, 'made up of up to five sections, used for containing medicines. You'll find some in the catalogue there.'

The policeman thumbed through several pages.

'Oh, yes – here they are. I see what you mean.'

'They would be suspended by a pair of silk cords which were threaded behind the *obi*. Obviously, if there was nothing on the other end of the cords they would just pull straight through and the *inro* would be lost.'

'So they put a toggle on the end.'

'Exactly – the *netsuke* came into being, probably

167

initially as no more than a piece of bamboo or a small lump of wood, but then they came to be regarded as fashion accessories.'

'Fascinating,' Sergeant Hill said as he once again looked through the illustrations in the catalogue. 'You're asking a lot of money for some of these, aren't you? I mean, this one for instance – "An ivory study of a rat, Kyoto . . ." What does Kyoto mean?'

'It's the region of Japan where it was carved.'

'Oh, I see,' he said. Then he returned to the catalogue description: ' "An ivory study of a rat, Kyoto, eighteenth century, the tail forming the *himotoshi* . . ." ' He paused and looked blank. 'The *himotoshi*?'

'Where the silk cords are threaded through.'

'Oh, I'm never going to remember this lot . . . "the tail forming the *himotoshi*, signed, 1¾ins – £2,500/3,000." I mean that is a lot of money, Mr Harton. Will somebody really pay you that much for it?'

'Almost certainly. Probably more,' I said. 'And don't forget, that's not an asking price, just an estimate. We don't own the pieces in that sale, or any other. We're just . . .'

'I know, I know,' he interrupted, with the first grin I had seen since I'd met him, 'you're just offering them for sale on behalf of clients – I remember.'

He took a final look at the catalogue then closed it and set it down on my desk.

'I think you've heard there's been another burglary, Mr Harton,' he remarked, slowly changing like some sort of chameleon back to the stone-faced policeman.

'Yes, if it's Mrs Masters you're referring to. She called me yesterday.'

'So I understand. She told you what was taken, did she, Sir?'

'She told me about the Fabergé box if that's what you mean.' I made a conscious effort to stop fiddling with the letter opener on my blotter.

168

'Yes,' he said, peering down rather absent-mindedly to inspect his now dry shoes. 'What did you make of it, Mr Harton?'

'In what way?'

'Well, would you have expected a common or garden burglar to have taken that box?'

'Not on its own, no Sergeant, I wouldn't.'

'No, that's what we thought. We would have expected him to have taken everything from that display table or nothing at all.'

'Yes,' I agreed, nodding resignedly.

'So, how do you reckon he knew what to take, Sir?'

'Could have been a Fabergé expert I suppose,' I suggested sarcastically.

'No, Mr Harton,' Sergeant Hill grinned for the second unnerving time in five minutes. 'No, he was working direct from your valuation. The cheeky so-and-so actually took a copy of it with him to the house.'

'How can you be so sure? Did he leave it behind or something?'

'No, he destroyed it but he told us all about it when he confessed.'

'Confessed! You mean you've caught him?'

'Yes, Sir – we picked him up this morning. He couldn't wait to tell us all about it.'

'But how . . . ?'

'Oh, even we get it right sometimes, Mr Harton. We've also got the bloke who was supplying your valuations to the boys.'

'You have? Who was it? Where did he get them from? . . . how did he . . . ?'

'He worked for the insurance company, Mr Harton.'

For a moment I just sat there, trying to assimilate what I had just been told.

'You mean,' I began, eventually, 'that it was the same insurance company in each case.'

'That's right, Sir. There was just the two common threads running through these cases – the insurance company and the valuer. It really had to be somebody from one or the other company. Once I'd seen how small the operation here is, the odds were on the insurance company all the way. It was much more likely the valuations were being leaked from a place with a lot of staff. The only people who could have done it here were really yourself or Miss . . . Miss . . .'

'Morrison,' Charlotte said, curtly.

'Of course – Miss Morrison. Anyway, it was hardly likely that either of you would have done it. You're both intelligent and it would have been obvious from the outset that it would only be a matter of time before you were caught.'

'So who was it?' I asked.

'It was a junior clerk – though I don't suppose they call them clerks any more. I expect they're all Deputy Assistant Account Supervisors now.' He laughed silently. 'Basically, the lad's got some pretty undesirable friends. I suppose the first time one of your valuations dropped into his filing basket he had a good look at it, then he bragged about it to his mates. Whether he realised its potential or they did I don't know, but the next day he photocopied it at work and put it up for sale to the highest bidder.'

'So he didn't actually commit the burglaries?' I said.

'No, he just sold the information to the ones who did.'

'But surely he must have realised he couldn't get away with it indefinitely,' Charlotte said. 'It was bound to be traced back to him eventually.'

'Yes, but if he hadn't been so greedy it would have taken some time before any link was made. If he'd just copied the valuations then sat on them for a year, say, and if he'd used valuations from other auctioneers, not just yours, the whole business would have been a lot less obvious.'

170

'Why *did* he only use Hampson's valuations?' I asked.

'Pure chance. The first three that came his way were all yours, and he flogged off the lot. Perhaps he thought it would shift suspicion from him to you; perhaps he was just thick and greedy; perhaps he didn't bother to think at all. I don't know. But I do know he made the job easier than it might have been.'

With this he got up and retrieved his raincoat from under my own on the radiator.

'Well, thank you very much for taking the trouble to come in and tell us personally, Sergeant Hill,' I said, feeling as though a great weight had been lifted from my shoulders.

'No trouble, Mr Harton. I was passing by anyway and it was nice to have the opportunity to dry out. One thing though . . .'

'What's that?'

'Would you mind if I kept that catalogue of ivories?'

'Not at all,' I said, picking it up and handing it to him. 'Please have it with my compliments. If you come back later in the week you'll be able to view the sale.'

'I might just do that,' he said as he turned to go. 'Goodbye, Mr Harton . . . Miss Morrison.'

'Goodbye Sergeant Hill,' Charlotte replied with a somewhat sickly smile.

'Well, that was kind of him to come in and tell us what had happened, wasn't it?' I said after the policeman had gone.

'Ha!' was Charlotte's dismissive reply.

'What now?'

'He didn't come in to tell us what had happened: he came in to chat me up. He'd been here for over three-quarters of an hour. If you hadn't arrived when you did it would have been a case for the murder squad, and they would have had me bang to rights, guv.'

'I think you're being a bit unfair,' I ventured.

171

'Rubbish! He was just showing off for my benefit. What about the way he made you sweat before he told you they'd got the people responsible?'

'Well . . .'

'Oh, come on, Richard – all that stuff about the *netsukes* and then the "well, would you have expected a common or garden burglar to have taken the Fabergé box?" stuff. He was just showing off.'

'Perhaps you're right,' I acknowledged.

'I know I am. And if he comes back to view that Japanese sale I shall be out!'

'Well, I'm glad it's all over anyway,' I said, looking out of the window at the rain as it continued to sheet down. 'I found the whole business very unnerving.'

'You needn't really have worried, you know,' Charlotte said. 'You're one of the most transparently honest people I know. Even Detective Sergeant Hill could see that.'

'Then why all the stone-faced questioning and pregnant pauses?'

'I asked him that. He said he was "just shaking the tree to see if any rotten apples dropped out".'

Chapter 15

'Have you got the file?'

'Yes.'

'Have you –'

Charlotte's next question was interrupted by the internal telephone which had barely stopped ringing all morning.

'I can't wait – I'll be late,' I said. 'If it's for me, I'm out.'

'No!' she demanded as I made for the door. 'You know Bob Derby's trying to get hold of you.'

'I don't care . . .'

'Valuations Office,' she said, picking up the receiver and ignoring my protests. 'Yes, Bob, he's right here – I'll transfer you.'

I glared at Charlotte – who returned like for like – threw my briefcase and overcoat onto the table by the door and returned to my desk for at least the fourth time since I had first tried to get away that morning.

'Yes, Bob,' I said, as calmly as possible as I lifted the telephone.

'Ah, Richard, I've been chasing you all round the building all morning. Where have you been?'

'Tying up a lot of loose ends,' I said, being as ambiguous as possible. The last thing I wanted to do was get involved in a long drawn out departmental progress report.

'I see. Well, now I've got you at last, pop over to my

173

office: I want to have a word about Percy Phelps.'

Percy Phelps! What did he want to speak to me about him for?

'I'm afraid I can't at the moment, Bob,' I said, 'I'm going to be late for an appointment as it is if I don't get away now.'

There was an ominous silence at the other end of the line then I heard the Chairman clear his throat.

'Well, you can't keep clients waiting, but call me as soon as you're back, please.'

The line went dead before I could respond.

'Wonderful! That's upset him now.'

'Don't blame me,' Charlotte said. 'I told you at nine o'clock he wanted to see you.'

'Yes, yes, I know. Anyway, I *must* go.'

'Okay, I'll get onto . . .'

Once again she was interrupted by the shrill trilling of the telephone.

'Hampson's Valuations Office,' she announced with all the instant brightness and verve she usually managed to inject into a response to any incoming call on our external line. 'Oh, yes, how are you? . . . good! . . . no . . . well, don't worry because Mr Harton is running late this morning himself . . . yes . . . oh, no, he's leaving at this very moment . . .'

I continued to hover in the doorway.

' . . . yes, I would think he'll be at Greencourt Road in about . . . ' She hesitated and looked at me for assistance.

'Half an hour,' I mouthed.

' . . . in about half an hour . . . yes, that's fine . . . thank you . . . goodbye.'

'That was Mr Wheeler, I take it?' I said, referring to the client I was due to meet in Wandsworth in fifteen minutes.

'Well, sort of, yes,' was Charlotte's enigmatic reply.

'What do you mean – sort of?'

174

'Well,' she said, looking distinctly puzzled, 'when I took down the details of this valuation, when he first called us, I entered his name as *Mr* John Wheeler.'

'Yes.'

'But, just now, he introduced himself as *Sir* John Wheeler.'

'Really?'

'Yes, I don't understand it. I don't usually make mistakes like that.'

'No harm done,' I said. 'I'll alter the file notes and make sure I get it right when we meet. Anyway, what did he want?'

'He just phoned to say he was running late and was concerned that you might get to Greencourt Road before him.'

'Excellent! With a bit of luck we'll arrive at the same moment,' I said. 'I'll see you later, Charlotte. Expect me when you see me.'

Wandsworth Bridge Road was at its worst: serried ranks of parked vehicles on either side of the road with the odd truck or van double parked at regular intervals. The overall effect was one of stalemate: nobody could move anywhere.

I drummed my fingers on the wheel as the car in front of me attempted to edge forward. It gained about a foot, then its driver lost his nerve and its brake lights flashed on again.

It was ridiculous. If I could just manage to advance another six feet or so, then I'd be able to get out of the jam by turning into a side road. From there it would take me no time at all to find an alternative and altogether more fluid route. The problem was travelling those initial six feet.

Again the car in front edged forward, and this time, probably as a result of sheer desperation, the man at the wheel just kept going as he guided it between the stationary delivery van on his left and a large and menacing lorry which was trying to make some forward progress of its own on his right. No doubt realising the motorist in the car had reached a kamikaze psychological state, the lorry driver brought his vehicle to a violent, shuddering halt, accompanied by the standard asthmatic wheeze of its air brakes.

At last that vital six foot strip of road lay open before me like an empty piece of no-man's land on an otherwise overcrowded battlefront. I advanced into it a couple of feet then slammed on the brakes once more: the lorry driver had had enough – he was coming through.

I watched incredulously as he bore down on me. I've always had the greatest of respect for drivers of large vehicles and their driving skills, but on this occasion it was evident that my man's judgement was fatally flawed. However, even as his cab drew alongside me, I still half expected him to stop.

He didn't. At least, not until his rear wing had gouged a three-foot long furrow down the off-side of my car. As the remorselessly slow, ripping and tearing noise continued I put my hand on the horn and held it there. Eventually, in response to the single, loud, continuous blast of distress the lorry shuddered to a halt once more and gave another bronchial, coughing wheeze.

Unable to get out of the driver's door since it was still blocked by the tail-end of the lorry, I clambered over the gear stick with some care and eventually emerged from the passenger door. Even that was a challenge since there was little more than a foot between that side of the car and the double-parked delivery van which had been the root cause of our particular piece of localised congestion.

'What the hell do you think you're doing?' I exploded as the lorry driver hung out of his cab surveying the problem.

'Did I 'it yer, mate?' he asked, with what appeared to be genuine innocence and puzzlement.

'Of course you bloody hit me! I exploded once more, jabbing my finger at the precise point on my vehicle's highly polished bodywork where it was still attached to the lorry like a Siamese twin.

The man scratched his head and looked perplexed.

'I didn't feel nuffin, mate,' he said.

'Well, I bloody well did,' I continued to fume.

'I'll pull forward and clear it,' he said, immediately restarting his leviathan.

Before I could stop him he'd shaken the thing into life once more. Then, with a crash of gears and in a billowing cloud of acrid diesel exhaust smoke he turned the three-foot gash on the side of my car into a four-foot one. Beside myself with rage I stormed up to the lorry as the driver clambered down from his cab.

He had looked quite small sitting in his great big cab, but by the time he'd descended to the ground he'd put on somewhere in the region of six inches in height and approximately three and a half stones in weight. Even by long-distance lorrydriving standards he was a fine figure of several men.

Instantly I felt my anger melting away. I became convinced we could settle this matter like civilised human beings.

'Sorry, guv,' he said, as he bent to examine the damage on my car,' 'but I thought she'd go. I didn't feel a thing. I was paying more attention to the other bleedin' side, see.'

'That's all right,' I said, awash with compassion and understanding. 'It could have happened to anyone.'

'Mmmm,' he said, prodding at a piece of my car's metallic paintwork which promptly detached itself and fluttered to the ground. 'I don't 'spect you was even moving, was yer?'

'No,' I replied, 'no, I was stationary.'

'That's what I thought,' he went on. 'It's my fault, anyway, guv. Let me just grab a pen and paper from me cab and we'll swap details. You won't have no problem wiv our insurers – they're used to payin' out.'

Twenty minutes later, I arrived at last outside number fifteen, Greencourt Road, SW18.

'Ah, Mr Harton – I beat you to it after all,' my client laughed as he ushered me into the large, red-brick house.

He was a tall, rather donnish man but he had a pronounced stoop which reduced his height by several inches. His grey hair was a celebration of self-expression over discipline, and he was dressed comfortably in a shapeless sports jacket, corduroy trousers and old suede shoes. I felt instinctively that Sir John Wheeler was going to be my sort of client.

'I don't know . . . er . . . Mr Harton,' he said, his voice quiet and hesitant 'whether your highly efficient secretary has explained to you what I'm up to here?'

'She said it was a valuation for probate purposes to be followed by disposal of the entire contents.'

'Yes . . . er . . . well, that sounds better than the way I put it,' he chuckled. 'I think I told her that I needed a figure for the legal leeches then you could flog the lot.'

'Amounts to the same thing, I think,' I smiled.

'Yes, now, I expect you'd like to have a good look at the place, wouldn't you?'

'That's right. If you could just quickly show me round, then I'll get started.'

'Right! Good! Now! We may as well start here – this is the entrance hall as you can see; then through here is the drawing room, as my aunt always insisted on calling it. I think it's too grand for it really.'

I wasn't at all sure I agreed with him. It was really quite a grand room: large with French windows leading into the garden at the back of the house, and with some very good furniture to grace it.

178

There was a particularly nice Regency satinwood sofa table of about 1815 with what, at first glance, I took to be a tea caddy standing on it. A second look immediately revealed the box to be not a caddy but a maahogany casket.

'Oh, that was Aunt Eleanor's urn,' her nephew said when he saw what I was looking at. 'She's not still in it, though. She left very precise instructions for her ashes to be scattered on the sea off Lizard Point in Cornwall. I'm not sure why. I can't remember her ever going as far as Bognor let alone Cornwall, but doubtless there was some reason for it. Perhaps it was rooted deep in her childhood or something like that. I suppose we shall never know now.'

He gazed down on the casket for a moment.

'Did you scatter the ashes personally?' I asked.

'Oh, yes, I went down to Eastbourne yesterday and spread them on the waters.'

'Eastbourne? But I thought you said her wishes were that they should be scattered off The Lizard in Cornwall.'

'Oh, yes – those *were* her wishes. But it's a devil of a long way to Cornwall, and since I had an appointment in Eastbourne . . . ' He looked momentarily thoughtful. 'Anyway, I'm sure I read somewhere that the current runs from east to west in the Channel, so she's bound to get there in the end.'

I looked at him to see if he was pulling my leg. I decided he wasn't.

'One thing, though,' he said, dropping his voice to barely a whisper, 'don't mention it to Cousins, she's a stickler for correctness.'

'Cousins?'

'Of course, you haven't met, have you? Cousins was Aunty's cook-housekeeper. She's been with the old girl since the year dot. And looked after her wonderfully I might add.'

'I see.'

'And, I'm glad to say, Aunty's done the decent thing and looked after Cousins.'

'In her will, you mean?'

'Yes, she's pretty well left her everything, apart from a few bequests to charities like the RSPCA and the RNLI. Quite right too, she's worked for peanuts for ages. It's only fair that she gets her nose in the trough now.'

I was beginning to see Sir John Wheeler as an increasingly colourful and eccentric character. Until then I had assumed he was sole beneficiary as well as executor. Now it appeared he had been excluded totally from sharing in his aunt's estate and, rather than being resentful about it, he positively applauded the decision.

'You're not a beneficiary, then,' I checked as we wandered from the drawing room to the less spacious but still fairly impressive dining room.

'No, no,' he replied, shaking his head vigorously. 'I wouldn't know what to do with the money quite frankly, and anyway, Aunt Eleanor never really approved of me. As far as she was concerned there were only four possible professions for a man: medicine, law, the army or the church – though not necessarily in that order of preference.'

'And none of those appealed to you, Sir John?'

'No, not at all. I was never bright enough for medicine; law bored the pants off me; I was in the army during the war and turned down a commission . . .'

'Why?'

He looked puzzled by the question.

'Because I didn't want to be an officer,' he said, shrugging his shoulders as if there could have been no other reply. 'That drove Aunt Eleanor right up the wall when she heard,' he added.

'And what of the Church?'

'Well, I suppose I could have done that and made a

reasonable fist of it,' he conceded, 'but I've never believed in supernatural beings and life hereafter and all that sort of thing, so it didn't really seem right. I know belief in God has never been considered essential for securing a bishopric in the Church of England, but *I* just wouldn't have felt comfortable with it.'

'I can understand that,' I said, as we passed from the dining room into the kitchen.

'I don't suppose there's anything here you can sell,' Sir John went on, looking about the room.

'There may be some china and glass, but, otherwise, no.'

'What am I going to do with it all?' he asked. 'The old refrigerator and washing machine – all that sort of thing?'

'Oh, no need to worry about that,' I assured him. 'I'll get it all cleared for you. It can either go to the small saleroom we use in Twickenham for selling household items or I can get in a second-hand dealer to make an offer for the lot.'

'Ah, good . . . good . . . ' he twittered happily, 'I just want the whole place emptied as soon as possible. It's a big reponsibility for poor Cousins here all on her own . . . this is the morning room . . .'

As the tour of the house continued it became evident that it really was a very worthwhile collection to get hold of. True, there was no single item worth tens of thousands of pounds but there were several pieces each worth well into four figures. Just as important as the overall value of the contents was the fact that Sir John had no intention of putting reserves on any of the lots.

'No, no,' he said. 'I'll leave all of that to you. As long as you think the right prices are being paid then you go ahead and sell the stuff. I certainly don't want any of it back.'

It seemed my original, instinctive feeling that Sir John Wheeler was going to be my sort of client was well founded.

'And this is Aunt Eleanor's room,' he continued, leading the way into a large, bright room with windows overlooking the garden, a mahogany fourposter bed on the opposite wall and a Persian carpet on the floor.

'That's a nice carpet,' I observed, stooping to examine it properly.

'Is it? . . . oh, good . . . ' Sir John replied rather vaguely, 'it used to belong to Aunt Eleanor's brother – Uncle William. I've no idea what it is . . . he went out to Australia in the end, I think . . . '

'Tabriz,' I said.

'No, no . . . I'm pretty certain it was to Australia . . .'

I looked up at my client. His expression suggested deep concentration.

'No, Sir John,' I said gently, 'I mean the carpet – the carpet comes from Tabriz, in Iran.'

He looked blank for a moment then he uttered a single, short, bellow of nasal laughter.

'Ha! I see . . . Tabriz . . . yes!' He laughed again. 'I thought you'd said "*to* Briz". I was trying to work out where on earth Briz is, and why you should know better than I where my Uncle Willy emigrated to.'

I too started to laugh, as much at my client's honking guffaw as anything else.

'Ha! . . . yes . . . to Briz!' He took out his handkerchief and blew his nose loudly.

'Anyway,' I said, 'it should make two to three thousand.'

'Ha! Good old Uncle Willy!'

The next room was Cousins's. She was a rather tall, angular lady who, at a guess, was probably in her late sixties. It must be said she was not exactly quick to smile.

'This is Mr Harton who'll be taking care of selling all the furniture,' my guide said, brightly.

'Hello, Mrs Cousins,' I said.

'Miss,' she retorted.

'I'm sorry . . . *Miss* . . . Cousins.'

She nodded, stood up and walked over to the window, presumably so as not to be in the way of my inspection of her room.

'Are any of the pieces of furniture, or pictures, or ornaments in here your own?' I asked.

'None of the furniture. None of the pictures. All the ornaments.' The reply came back like volleys of rifle shots.

'Fine ... fine ...' I murmured, already backing towards the door. 'I won't have to trouble you any more today, Miss Cousins ... thank you ... thank you very much ...'

'She's pretty harmless really,' Sir John confided as we made our way back to the ground floor, 'but I do admit she has a bit of the Mrs Danvers about her, particularly when her routine is upset.'

As I began the valuation proper I wondered how on earth I could organise the removal and sale of the entire contents of 15 Greencourt Road without upsetting Miss Cousins's routine. The scenario did not look promising.

A little under two hours later I was ready to head back to the office and make arrangements to ship everything saleable into the auction rooms. My client saw me off at the gate.

'I've got your home number, Sir John,' I confirmed, briefly checking the details on file, 'but is there an office one as well, just in case I need to contact you urgently?'

'No, I'm one of those people who works at home – not that I do very much now really.'

My curiosity about what he did for a living had been aroused much earlier when he had catalogued his aunt's approved list of professions and then rejected them one by one. He was apparently far from hard up. After all, he didn't seem at all upset at being excluded from the will, but I couldn't even begin to place him in any sort of career.

'You're retired then?' I probed.

'Sort of . . . yes . . . well, no . . . well, yes, I suppose I am really . . . as retired as I am ever likely to be, anyway.'

'Oh?'

'Yes, the thing is, people like me *never* really retire, you see.'

'Why? What is it you do?' I asked finally, unable to support the suspense any longer.

'Well, I suppose I'm what is commonly referred to as an inventor, although I prefer to think of myself as a problem solver.'

'I see.'

'Yes, not that I've ever invented anything that has forced me to flee to a tax haven or anything vulgar like that. But I have come up with one or two gizmos which have helped to make the lives of a few people a little easier.'

'How interesting. What sort of things?'

'The sort of things you will never have heard of,' he replied with a smile. 'Almost everything I've devised has been for a specialist branch of the engineering industry. I was fortunate enough to have a sort of unofficial consultancy with what was once my father's company – it was mainly defence work. They used to bring me some of their more intractable problems and I would try to sort them out, sometimes with some modest degree of success.'

'You must be very clever.'

'Not really. Most of it is just common sense you know . . . that and mathematics . . . I've always been quite good at mathematics.'

'Fascinating,' I said. 'Have you always made your living by inventing.'

'No, very rarely in fact,' he laughed. 'I've done lots of things: I've been a school teacher, a writer, a crossword compiler, and I inherited a deep-sea fishing trawler which I ran for a while.'

He made it sound a perfectly logical career pattern.

'A deep-sea fishing trawler?'

'Yes, it was left to me by an uncle – not Willy, another one. I was advised to sack the crew and put the boat up for sale immediately, but that seemed all wrong to me. After all, it was the crew's livelihood I'd inherited. I'd never met any of them, and for all I knew they had wives and children and mortgages as most people do.'

'So what did you do?'

'I signed on as an unpaid member of the crew and went out with them three or four times to see what their lives were like.'

Looking at the stooped lanky figure of my client with its unruly mane of flowing grey hair, I found it hard to picture him striding across the pitching, slippery, fish-scale-covered deck of a deep-sea trawler.

'How did the crew take your signing on for the voyages?' I asked.

'I must admit they were less than euphoric. To begin with I believe they regarded me as a spy – which I was, I suppose. Then they made it quite clear they thought I was a madman – which may also have been right. Then they just accepted me as a bloody nuisance . . . which was fine.'

'So you won them over in the end?'

'Oh, yes,' he said, as though it had only ever been a matter of time anyway, 'and I believe I did so as a result of using a simple linguistic device.'

'And what was that?' I asked.

'Well, I noticed they prefaced everything they said with one particular word.'

'And what was that?'

He beamed at me benignly.

'Have you ever read George Orwell's *Politics and the English Language*?' he asked.

I confessed I hadn't.

'You should, you should. It's most interesting and informative. In it he sets down six elementary rules for the use of English. One of them is never use a long word when a short one will do. He's quite right of course. Long words tend to be Latin in origin and are often difficult to understand, whereas short words are much more likely to come from good old Anglo-Saxon and are usually quite easy to comprehend.'

'Really,' I said, wondering just where this was leading.

'My crew's preferred word was certainly short, extremely pithy, and probably derived from the German – *ficken* – to strike.'

'Ah, I see. But how did that help?'

'Oh, very simply: it shocked them into accepting me as a normal human being rather than some sort of old freak. I just walked into the galley one day within earshot of two or three of them and said, "where the dot-dot-dot-dot-'s my tea?'. The effect was electrifying. I never looked back.'

I laughed again.

'And do you still own the trawler?' I asked.

'A bit of it,' he replied. 'But not for much longer. We put together a deal whereby they could buy me out over a number of years. I just regard my investment in the boat as an interest-free loan.'

'That's very generous of you.'

'Not really. I wouldn't want to live with my conscience if I was responsible for those chaps being thrown on the scrap heap. Their lives are quite hard enough as it is.'

I nodded in agreement, opened the old wrought-iron gate and prepared to go.

'I'll be in contact within the next couple of days,' I said, shaking his hand. 'It's been a great pleasure meeting you, Sir John.'

'And you, Mr Harton,' he said, 'I shall look forward to hearing from you . . . but before you go there is one small thing . . .'

'What's that?'

'I'm not a knight.'

'You're *not*!'

'No . . . nor a baronet . . . nor in any way ennobled I'm afraid . . . although I must confess I could get used to it . . . Sir John Wheeler does have rather a nice ring to it . . . don't you think?'

'Well, I don't know,' Charlotte said. 'All I can tell you is that he introduced himself as *Sir* John over the telephone this morning.'

'But he couldn't have,' I insisted. 'Why would he lay claim to a title he doesn't have? He's not an idiot; a trifle eccentric possibly, but certainly not an idiot.'

'Whereas I am?' Charlotte enquired, with a cool sarcasm which contrasted vividly with the overheating of her complexion.

'I didn't say that,' I replied quickly, having long since learnt that flashpoint was unlikely to be far off once the colour of Charlotte's face began to approach that of her long, flame-red hair. 'All I am saying is that I spent the entire morning addressing the man as *Sir* when he's just plain *Mr*; and that makes me look an idiot.'

'Well, it's not *my* fault. He said . . .'

'No, no, just forget it,' I interrupted sharply. 'I'm quite sure you're right. Mr Wheeler obviously did exactly what you said – he telephoned you this morning and told you he had a title. I expect he does it all the time.'

'But . . .'

'No! Just *forget* it. I'm going to see Bob Derby. I don't know how long I'll be.'

Although to some extent a man of moods, Hampson's Chairman was always the same in one respect: he had a seemingly inexhaustible reservoir of energy. This gave him an unfair advantage over our competitors which

187

was fine but it also provided him with a head start on his own staff, which was not so good.

As long as he was busy it wasn't too bad. He could consume huge amounts of work, run his secretaries off their feet and generally keep himself amused without getting on the backs or under the feet of his departmental directors and managers. If, however, a hiatus occurred in his workload, as seemed to have happened that very day, then he could be serious trouble.

Like a powerful machine, racing out of gear, he would become a wholly destructive force until a specific project or problem came along. Then, as long as it took his fancy, the rest of us could breathe easy again. As I sat across his desk from him that afternoon it was evident no such diversion had presented itself.

Sitting forward in his chair he drummed the desk with the fingers of his left hand.

'You say he gave you his name and address without any fuss,' he checked once more.

'Yes, he accepted liability,' I assured him.

'I shouldn't set too much store by that,' he sniffed. 'Doubtless it will all be your fault once his insurers get hold of it.'

'But he signed the diagram I drew of the accident acknowledging that my vehicle was stationary.'

He thrust out his chin like a petulent child.

'We'll see, we'll see,' he recited, doubtfully. 'Anyway, what I really wanted to talk to you about was Percy Phelps.'

'Yes?'

'Yes,' he said. 'Percy popped in to view the furniture sale yesterday afternoon and I had a chat with him.'

I said nothing.

'You're not exactly his flavour of the month.'

'Why's that?'

'Because, according to him, since you arrived here

188

he's been slowly frozen out of any work from Hampson's.'

'That's not quite true,' I protested, albeit a little lamely.

'But very nearly?' the Chairman suggested.

'There just haven't been many house clearances that would have suited Percy.'

'Now, how can that be true, Richard? Percy will handle anything and everything. You know that.'

It was true: Percy was prepared to handle anything and everything. In the dealers' Debrett's he was just one rung up from the totters – the old rag and bone men who still plied their trade in the streets of London from horse-drawn carts.

A big, strong man, still fit and active although he was now in his early seventies, he had indeed had a lot of work from Hampson's in the past. But times had changed, and now, rather than seeking cash offers from the likes of Percy Phelps I tended to send most household items for auction at Bailey's in Twickenham. They would dump the unsaleable pieces free of charge and offer the rest in their next weekly sale. Keeping an eye on it all meant more work for me but I was satisfied that the owners generally got a far better return than they would if somebody like Percy made an offer for the lot.

I explained my thinking to the Chairman.

'That may well have been the case in the past, Richard,' he agreed, 'but I think you'll find Percy's become a little more generous with his tenders these days. He assures me he's prepared to stand toe to toe with the best of them now.'

'Well . . .'

'The long and the short of it is I want you to give him a chance on the next house clearance you get, Richard.'

'All right, Bob,' I agreed, knowing there was no point in arguing.

'And I understand from Charlotte you're handling one at the moment for some titled chap.'

'Er . . .'

'Well, you are, aren't you?'

'Not exactly, no.'

'What do you mean? Either you are or you aren't.'

'Well, yes, I'm handling a house clearance, and no, it's not for a titled chap.'

'But Charlotte said . . .'

'There was a misunderstanding.'

'How could anybody misunderstand whether somebody had a title or not?' he asked impatiently. 'Was his Christian name "Duke" or "Earl" or something like that?'

'No, Bob,' I said quietly. 'There was just some sort of misunderstanding over a telephone call. There's no problem. It's all been straightened out, and title or no title he's an ideal client.'

'Good, then it's an ideal opportunity for you to give Percy the chance to quote to clear the residue of the contents.'

'Well, I'd rather . . .'

'I want Percy to quote!' he interrupted.

'Okay, Bob. Whatever you say.'

'Thought I might find you here,' Philip Lawrence said as he elbowed his way through the happy hour crowd at the bar.

'Why was that?'

'I've just seen your car in Russell Mews. What happened? Looks as though you ran into a bus. Mine's a pint by the way.'

I recounted the morning's events in the Wandsworth Bridge Road.

'Just one of those days I suppose,' he said as I passed him his drink. 'Cheers!'

'Cheers,' I replied, sipping at my own beer. 'In fact, as days go this one has been rather mixed; certainly not all bad, but I have to agree, not all good either.'

Philip listened to my account of my experiences with John Wheeler and Robert Derby.

'Unlike Charlotte to start dispensing titles so freely,' he remarked. 'I don't think I've ever heard her address anybody as "Sir".'

'Oh, she does if it's a client,' I assured him, 'but that's as far as it goes.'

'Yes, that's what I thought . . . Hello! Here comes your beautiful better half.'

'I turned to see Sarah who, with liberal use of her elbows, was fighting her way through the crush.

'Hi,' she said, finally making it to the bar. 'Sorry I'm late – the traffic was diabolical. I suppose we should make tracks right away.'

I looked at my watch.

'We should really,' I said. 'By the time we've dropped off my car at your flat we'll just have time to get to the cinema.'

'This complicated life you two lead,' Philip said, finishing his pint. 'I shall go straight home to my baked beans on toast.'

'You poor old thing,' Sarah teased. 'Why don't you come with us?'

'Heaven forfend that I should ever play gooseberry to such a loving couple. Anyway, Richard will want to tell you all about his day, and I'm not strong enough to listen to it all again.'

'I take it your day was not so good,' Sarah said, smiling, after Philip had disappeared into the crowd around the door.

'It could have been better,' I said. 'Didn't you see the car?'

'No, what's wrong with it?'

'I'll show you,' I said, checking the time once more. 'Come on, we'd better go.'

Sarah had also parked in Russell Mews, a narrow

cul-de-sac off Vanbrugh Street, and like my own car, hers was pointing in the wrong direction.

'You turn first,' I said, as we entered the mews, 'and I'll catch up with you.'

I jumped into my battered vehicle, started it and sat waiting for Sarah to complete her manoeuvre. A moment later she drew up alongside. As she slowed to pass through the narrow gap left between my car and another parked on the opposite side of the street I wound down my window.

'Look at that,' I shouted, hanging out of the window and pointing down at the damage.

Sarah shook her head in disbelief, then drove off down Vanbrugh Street at her usual fiery pace.

A minute later I too had turned around at the bottom of the mews. I was just about to enter Vanbrugh Street when a well-dressed, bespectacled man of medium height spread-eagled himself on the bonnet of my car. He seemed to be waving a business card at me.

Too surprised to do or say anything I just sat and waited as he clambered off the bonnet and sidled his way along to the driver's door.

'Good evening to you, Sir,' he said.

For a moment I thought he might be pioneering a new recruitment technique for the Jehovah's Witnesses.

'I think I might be of some assistance to you,' he went on, slightly out of breath. 'You have just been involved in an automobile accident – I saw it all.'

'You did?'

'Yes indeed. What is more, you should go straight to hospital and get checked out – you may well be suffering from whiplash.'

It was then that I realised he was American. His accent was so soft that I hadn't detected it immediately. It was the word 'whiplash' which gave him away – at that time, that particular injury hadn't crossed the Atlantic, although it had already reached epidemic proportions in the States.

'Well, actually . . .' I began.

'Don't worry, Sir,' he went on, talking quietly but quickly. 'I saw exactly what happened and I will be only too happy to give an account of it, and swear it before a notary if that should prove necessary.'

'That's very kind, but . . .'

'She drove up this street very fast,' he continued, removing his gold-rimmed spectacles and polishing them energetically with a white cotton handkerchief. 'But when she saw there was no room she stamped on the brake. It was too late, however.'

I sat spellbound, listening to this vivid account of an accident which had never happened.

'You wound down your window and remonstrated with her about the damage done to your car, but she took no notice at all.'

I shook my head in amazement.

'Then she sped off in that direction,' he said, pointing down Vanbrugh Street. 'And you were about to set off in pursuit when I managed to stop you.'

'Er . . . yes . . .' I said.

'Here is my card, Sir.'

'Thank you very much,' I replied, taking it from him.

'You will see that on the back I have written both the address of my London hotel and the number on the licence plate of the young lady's vehicle.'

'Yes . . . I see that . . .' I said, turning over the crisp, white card in my hands.

'And on the other side, of course, you have my name and my office address in Boston.'

'Yes . . . yes . . . indeed,' I muttered, looking at the face of the card. 'Well, what can I say but . . . thank you Mr . . . er . . . Tewson . . . thank you very much indeed for being so public-spirited in a foreign country.'

'Not at all, Sir,' he replied. 'Good evening to you.'

As the neat, dapper figure strode off down Vanbrugh Street I realised that my close encounter with Mr William Tewson of Boston had taught me two lessons I would never forget. The first was how seriously one should always take one's public duty. The second was how sceptically one should receive any eye-witness account of anything.

Chapter 16

Miss Cousins was not happy. But that was perfectly understandable really. After the number of years she had worked for John Wheeler's aunt, she was bound to find the selling of 15 Greencourt Road a bit of a wrench. Nevertheless, I was beginning to feel that she held me solely responsible for each and every one of the changes which were presently taking place.

Sitting rigidly upright on the edge of one of the woodseat kitchen chairs, she stared straight ahead. Then she looked at her watch for the second time in as many minutes.

'I'm sure Mr Phelps won't be long,' I said. 'I expect he's caught up in the traffic. It was particularly bad this morning and . . .'

'*I* got here on time,' Miss Cousins pointed out, 'and *I* had to come over from my sister's place in Eltham.'

'Did you?'

'Yes, I did, and that's a fair old trek in the rush hour, I can tell you.'

'Yes, I'm sure it is,' I replied, silently cursing Percy Phelps and shifting uncomfortably on my own hard little chair.

It was a quarter to ten. Percy was already fifteen minutes late.

'I mean, I don't have to do this,' she went on.

'No, I'm . . .'

'I'm only doing it for Madam's sake.'

'Yes, well . . .'

'But if I left it all to Mr John this place would still have furniture in it this time next year.'

I smiled. Miss Cousins didn't.

'Why it just couldn't all have been taken at the same time I don't know. He just has no idea how to organise things. Madam always said that of course.'

'Well, it's not really Mr Wheeler's fault,' I offered in his defence. 'What we took away yesterday was for our Belgravia rooms. What we have left here now . . .'

'Is all perfectly good stuff if you ask me. Just look at that cooker. You can't get cookers like that any more.'

She was right – you couldn't. But that was chiefly because nobody wanted cookers like that any more.

'Oh, I agree – it's been beautifully looked after. Unfortunately it's not of any sale value.'

'That's silly!' Miss Cousins snapped. 'I know plenty of people who . . .'

I heaved a deep sigh of relief as she was stopped by a heavy rapping on the front door.

'Ah, that must be Mr Phelps now,' I said, leaping to my feet and getting to the kitchen door before the housekeeper could get up. 'You stay where you are, Miss Cousins, I'll let him in.'

I am not sure when Percy first started dying his hair but he had been doing it as long as I had known him. Sometimes he would permit just a little distinguished greying around the temples but on other occasions it would be a uniform, unbroken, unbelievable, jet black. That morning was one of those occasions.

'Good morning to you, Mr Harton,' he said in his remarkable, booming bass voice, at the same time raising his old tweed hat to reveal the full glory of his latest session with the tincture bottle. 'It's been a long time. You won't mind if we get started right away – only I have several other visits this morning . . . so this is the hall . . .'

I had to admit as he lumbered past me into the house, Percy Phelps did have a certain style. Here he was, nearly twenty-five minutes late; not a word of apology, just the suggestion that I was likely to delay him further.

'Hold on a minute, Percy,' I whispered, catching him by the sleeve. 'There are a couple of things I want to explain to you.'

'Explain?' he boomed, whilst somehow managing to make the word sound conspiratorial.

'Yes,' I said, raising a finger to my lips and nodding over my shoulder towards the kitchen. 'The house-keeper, Miss Cousins, is here.'

'Is that bad?' he asked, dropping his voice to a cavernous rumble.

'She might be a little difficult.'

'Ah!' he nodded, 'I see.'

'But, although she is the chief beneficiary of the will, she has no say in what happens to the contents – that's between me and the executor.'

'Good, good,' he said.

'But it's worth trying to keep her sweet if we can,' I concluded.

'I shall be the epitome of charm,' he assured me, tapping the side of his large, hooked nose. 'You can rely on me, Mr Harton, you know that . . . sitting room through here is it?'

The distinctly Dickensian figure of Percy Phelps stumped off into the late Aunt Eleanor's drawing room without waiting for a reply.

Everything about him was larger than life, from his deep, booming voice and huge nose, down to his size twelve feet, or to be strictly accurate, down to his size twelve *foot*. I never established how Percy had lost the lower part of his left leg but lost it he had. I had heard it rumoured it was the result of enemy action in Italy during the Second World War, but I had also heard it suggested it was the result of turning over a supplies lorry whilst blind drunk on newly liberated Chianti. Whatever the cause, Percy Phelps was equipped with an artificial left leg from the knee down; although I would defy anybody to spot it had they not been told. True, he walked with a very slight limp but even that was hardly noticeable.

'Not a lot in here,' he said, gazing around the near empty room.

'No, just the old armchairs and the fitted carpet,' I confirmed.

'All right. Next room, then,' he said, knitting his brows into the frown I remembered of old.

From the drawing room we went to the dining room, then the morning room, then upstairs to the bedrooms. Fortunately, Miss Cousins had stayed put in the kitchen rather than dogging our footsteps around the house, but eventually we arrived at the lion's den.

'Just get in and out as fast as you can, Percy,' I said as we paused for a moment outside the door. 'And don't discuss values in front of her. She's got strange ideas about what everything should be worth.'

'I know the sort, Mr Harton,' he replied. 'You can rely on me.'

Miss Cousins, who was standing by the sink, looking out of the window, turned as we entered the kitchen.

'Ah, Miss Cousins,' I said, 'this is Mr Phelps.'

The housekeeper regarded Percy very coolly. Undaunted, he brushed me aside, advanced across the linoleum towards her with his hand thrust out in greeting.

'How do you do, Madam,' he thundered, gripping hold of her own limp hand before she could take evasive action. He shook it vigorously then released it. I felt a surge of relief. For one awful moment I had thought he was going to kiss it.

'Miss!' retorted the recoiling lady.

'I'm so sorry – *Miss*,' Percy corrected himself. 'It must

be a great blow for you to leave such a beautiful house.'

'Not really – I'm buying a bungalow.'

'A bungalow!' he said, like some latterday Lady Bracknell.

'Yes, a bungalow,' Miss Cousins repeated forcefully, as if Percy had in some way impugned her good name.

'An excellent idea,' he countered, immediately. 'Very useful buildings, bungalows – especially if one suffers from vertigo.'

'Everything in here is to go, Mr Phelps,' I interrupted.

'Of course, Mr Harton, of course,' he replied.

He strode across the kitchen and yanked open one of the cupboard doors.

'A quick look in here . . .'

Next a drawer was subjected to a rapid inspection.

'. . . and in here . . .'

He closed the drawer with a bang, frowned again and said, 'Two hundred and fifty-five pounds, Mr Harton and I'll be lucky to see twenty-five pounds profit at the end of the day.'

'What did he say?' Miss Cousins asked, looking at me.

'Nothing to concern yourself with, dear lady,' Percy assured her. 'Mr Harton and I will . . .'

'May I have a word with you outside, Mr Phelps?' I asked.

'Did he say two hundred and fifty-five pounds?' demanded the housekeeper.

'I'll be back in one moment, Miss Cousins,' I said, ushering Percy out of the room.

'But, he said . . .' she began, trailing along behind us, 'that he was offering two hundred and . . .'

She was interrupted by a startled cry from Percy.

I looked round to see him lurching across the entrance hall. Plainly, he had stumbled but now he seemed unable to regain his balance. In a bizarre series of hops he was bouncing towards the front door. Then I saw his left foot. It was twisted at a grotesque angle,

199

pointing backwards with the sole of its brown brogue shoe uppermost. Its grey, woollen sock was corkscrewed and stretched as though there was nothing in it from the ankle up.

As Percy hopped away, the foot remained in the middle of the hall while the sock got longer and longer, finally detaching itself from its owner completely. As I stared down at the abandoned shoe and hosiery, Percy succeeded in halting his progress towards the front door by grasping hold of the bannister rail as he was passing the staircase. He turned and looked back at his discarded prosthetic.

'Oh, dammit!' he said. 'My blasted foot's fallen off again.'

A moment later, in the kitchen doorway, Miss Cousins collapsed to the floor like a crumpled flower.

She was still looking pale a quarter of an hour later as I urged her to take another sip of the cooking brandy I had located in one of the cupboards.

'No, no,' she insisted, screwing up her face at the smell, 'I'm, better now, thank you. I just need to get up and moving again . . . oh, dear. . .!' Once again her knees gave way beneath her and she sank back onto her chair.

'You just take it easy,' I said. 'I've rung for a taxi. It'll be here any minute.'

'But I can't afford a taxi all the way to Eltham . . .' she protested.

'Hampson's will take care of that,' I said. 'You had quite a shock out there. You're certainly not going back to your sister's by public transport.'

'Well . . . yes . . . I do still feel a bit wobbly I suppose,' she agreed. 'It did give me an awful turn.'

'I'm sure it did. After all, you weren't to know it was an artificial foot.'

'No,' she said, shaking her head and overcoming her natural revulsion for the smell of brandy. 'It was awful –

like something out of one of those terrible horror films you see on the television.'

'Yes, Mr Phelps was very upset at the distress he'd caused you.'

She took another sip of the brandy then stood the glass on the table next to her elbow.

'Well, he was very kind in the end,' she said. 'Offering to drive me back to Eltham in his van. Did he find the missing bolt for his leg, by the way?'

'Yes, it was on the stairs.'

'Oh, good – I'm glad he found it.'

I checked my watch once more, wondering how long the taxi was likely to be. Miss Cousins was beginning to show signs of making a complete recovery and it would only be a matter of time before she recalled Percy's opening offer for what remained of the contents of 15 Greencourt Road. At last there was another rap on the front door.

'Ah, that'll be the cab,' I said. 'Are you feeling strong enough to stand up now?'

'Oh, yes, I'm all right now,' she replied, slowly rising. 'The only silly thing is I can't remember what we'd been talking about before I fainted – my mind's a complete blank.'

'Never mind,' I said, steering her across the room by her elbow, 'I'm sure it will all come back in time.'

'Yes, but I know your Mr Phelps had said something . . .'

'Bungalows,' I interrupted as we headed across the hall. 'He was talking about bungalows. I think you were just about to tell us where you intended to live.'

'Was I?'

'Oh, I think so. Where had you in mind, Miss Cousins?' I asked, reaching for the door handle.

'Well, I had thought about Cornwall – near the sea, where Madam's ashes were scattered. I'd like to be close to her, but . . .' she paused thoughtfully, 'It's such a long way from my sister in Eltham.'

'Yes,' I agreed, opening the door to the cab driver. 'Perhaps you should think about somewhere nearer.'

'You're probably right,' she agreed, as the driver took her arm and steadied her down the front step, 'but it's difficult to know where.'

'Had you considered Eastbourne?' I suggested.

'Hampson's Valuations Office,' I said, picking up the telephone.

'Ah . . . hello, Mr Harton,' replied the now familiar, hesitant voice. 'It's . . . er . . . John Wheeler here . . . er . . . I was just calling to tell you to go ahead and accept Mr Phelps's offer for the stuff at . . .'

'That's it!' I said.

'. . . er . . . sorry . . . what?'

'That's it!' I repeated. 'What you just said – it's how it happened!'

'How what happened? I'm afraid I'm not with you, my dear chap.'

'It's how you became ennobled.'

'Er . . . how? Not by accepting Mr Phelps's offer, surely?'

'No, no – what you said before that.'

There was a long silence.

'What *did* I say before that?'

'You said: "It's . . . er . . . John Wheeler here . . ." '

'Y-e-es,' he said doubtfully.

'Well, that was how it happened: "It's . . . er . . . John Wheeler here"; "It . . . ser . . . John Wheeler here"; "It's . . . Sir . . . John Wheeler here".'

There was another silence at the other end of the line, then a loud hoot of laughter.

Chapter 17

As a boy I had been an enthusiastic model aircraft maker. Although my natural favourites had been Spitfires, Hurricanes, Stukas and the like, I'd also had a soft spot for a large, silver and white Viscount airliner. There had been something about its solid, fat toothpaste tube body which I had liked and found both friendly and comforting.

For some reason, as Bernard Thornton and I approached the real thing on the tarmac at Gatwick Airport, the same warm emotions were not being engendered.

'That is one very old aircraft,' Bernard observed.

'I must say,' I replied, 'I had no idea they were still in the air.'

'This one isn't yet,' he said, crossing himself. 'God, how I hate flying.'

Bernard had mentioned this particular phobia several times since I had persuaded him to accompany me on my trip to the Channel Islands. He had been so opposed to the idea of taking to the air that I had not really been confident of his meeting me at the station that morning. Fortunately, the lure of our main valuation had proved too much for him. It was a sizable collection of eighteenth-century English glass and porcelain in a private house on Guernsey. However, before he could get his teeth into that I had some more prosaic fare for him, and before we could get started on that, we had to put the flight behind us.

Slowly making our way up the boarding steps I looked at the slim, silver wings and the old four-bladed propellers and wondered how many thousands of miles they had travelled.

'I never understand why the damned things stay up anyway,' Bernard said, 'and looking at this piece of aviation history, I'm not at all convinced it will.'

'Safe as houses,' I replied.

'Having just discovered my place has extensive dry rot, I find your analogy less than reassuring.'

'Sorry,' I said, 'but you really are worrying about nothing, Bernard. These old buses could go on flying for ever.'

'I don't want this particular old bus to go on flying for ever,' he replied. 'I just want it to get us to Jersey.'

'It will,' I assured him. 'It will.'

Of course, I was right. Apart from a few minor bumps due to turbulence it was a very smooth and relatively fast flight. Certainly, my companion barely had time to recover from the white knuckle tension of the take off before he was bracing himself for the descent on Jersey. Mintues later we were out in the clean Channel Islands air.

'Thank goodness that's over with,' Bernard said, mopping his brow. 'When do we next have to take to the air?'

'Tomorrow,' I replied, 'But that's just between the islands – not too serious.'

'Huh! They'll probably try to pack us into a Sopwith Camel,' he moaned. 'I can assure you, Richard, if it's anything smaller than a jumbo jet, you're on your own.'

Less than an hour later we were sitting in our hire car outside the substantial home of Rick Freeman, lead guitarist for one of the 1970s' most successful heavy metal groups.

'And what is it you say he does for a living?' Bernard

asked, leaning forward in his seat and looking up at the house.

'He's a guitarist with Malice.'

'What?'

'He plays with Malice.'

'Why?'

'Why, what?'

'Why is he so vicious about it?'

'About what?'

'The way he plays.'

'I didn't know he was.'

'Then why did you say so?'

'I didn't.'

'Yes, you did. You said he plays with malice.'

'No, no, Bernard – I said he plays with *Malice*. They're a pop group – heavy metal.'

'Heavy what?'

'Metal, Bernard. Have you never heard of heavy metal?'

He thought for a moment.

'I've heard of heavy water,' he said eventually, 'though I've never really been clear what that is.'

'Well, it's nothing to do with heavy metal,' I said. 'Heavy metal is a type of very loud pop music much favoured by bikers and headbangers.'

'Headbangers?'

'Yes.'

'What in God's name are headbangers?'

'They're people who work themselves into a sort of trance when listening to heavy metal music.'

'How?'

'Well . . . by banging their heads.'

Bernard looked at me sideways and raised an eyebrow.

'By banging their heads?' he said.

'Yes . . . well . . . more by swinging them round violently, I suppose.'

'You don't say.'

'Afraid so,' I confirmed.

'Oh, brave new world . . .' he said, looking up at the front of Rick Freeman's house once more.

The instructions to make the valuation had come out of the blue. Mr Freeman's accountant had telephoned my office a couple of weeks earlier and asked me if we could make an insurance valuation for his client, and what it would cost. I gave him a quote on the spot, he offered me half that amount and we settled at three-quarters plus expenses. I had then arranged a lightning piece of advertising in the local papers which had resulted in two more valuations, and the trip was thereby guaranteed to be financially successful.

'I suppose they let him live on the island because he's terribly wealthy,' Bernard said, still looking at the house.

'No, I understand he's actually a native of Jersey, so he could live here anyway.'

'Well, looking at this place, I suspect your Mr Freeman is still a very rich boy.'

'Oh, no doubt about that, Bernard.' I agreed. 'It's just that as a native he can buy a house like this for his three-quarters of a million, whereas a non-native would get a medium-sized bungalow for the same price.'

'Yes, it's a great idea – the two-tier price system. I think they should do it everywhere – especially in Kensington, where I was born.'

The large, panelled front door of the house was painted in such a high gloss that Bernard and I were able to adjust our ties and tidy our hair in the reflection as we waited for our knock to be answered. When the door was opened it was by a woman with looks best described as devestating. Her brown hair was long and wavy and her eyes were so dark as to be almost black. With no make-up that I could detect, and dressed in a man's baggy white shirt and a pair of faded blue jeans, she appeared the archetypal gipsy beauty.

'Hello, you must be from Hampson's,' she said in an accent more reminiscent of Roedean than Romany.

'Yes,' I said, 'I'm Richard Harton and this is my colleague . . .'

'Bernard Thornton,' Bernard said.

'Hi! Come in. Make yourselves comfortable in the drawing room.' She pointed to a pair of double doors. 'I'll find Richard – he's playing cricket with the children in the garden.'

Bernard and I watched spellbound as Cherry Freeman left us and went in search of her husband – one of the wild men of rock – who was apparently currently engaged in an orgy of cricket with his two small children. Once she had disappeared from sight, Bernard turned to me, blew out his cheeks and shook his head. He'd said it all.

The drawing room was large and untidy. Furnished with expensive modern leather and suede covered chairs and sofas, it was littered with newspapers, magazines and children's toys. Here and there a piece of some value would rear up out of the contemporary chaos – an art deco bronze, a Lalique glass vase and, at the far end of the room, what looked to be a Tiffany table-lamp. Drawn to it irresistibly, Bernard lurched over to examine the piece.

'Is it right?' I asked after a while.

'As rain,' he replied, still poring over the piece. 'Tiffany Favrile, dating some time beween 1899 and 1920. It's a . . .'

Bernard stopped in mid-sentence as the doors opened and our client entered the room. He was of medium height, slightly built, with blond hair, which although quite long was carefully styled. Dressed in a cream silk shirt, white cotton trousers and yachting shoes, he failed to conform in any way with his perspiring, tortured stage image.

I found myself staring at a long, smeared grass stain on his left knee. He glanced down at it too.

'I fell over in the garden,' he said by way of explanation, 'diving for a slip catch.'

'Did you hold it?' I asked.

'Hold it?' he grinned. 'I didn't get within a foot of it. I never could catch.'

His voice was quiet and a little husky, probably as a result of many years of screaming himself hoarse for his fans.

'That's supposed to be quite good isn't it?' he asked, pointing to the lamp.

'Yes, indeed,' Bernard replied. 'It's by Louis Comfort Tiffany – Favrile glass and gilt bronze. It dates from sometime between the turn of the century and 1920. Have you had it long?'

Mr Freeman paused and thought for a moment.

'Must be about five years,' he said, eventually. 'I bought it in some glitzy Manhattan gallery because Cherry said she liked it. I expect I was ripped off. My New York agent was supposed to be advising me but I think she was on commission from the gallery owner.'

'What did you pay?'

'Twenty thousand dollars, I think.'

Bernard winced and appeared to do a rapid, mental calculation.

'Well, that was quite enough for it then,' he said, raising his eyebrows, 'but I suppose it's caught up pretty well – you might even show a profit now.'

'Doesn't really matter,' the quitarist replied. 'We're not likely to sell it – Cherry likes it too much.'

'That's the important thing,' Bernard said, turning his attention to one of the art deco bronze and ivory statues. 'Now, this Valkyrie on horseback – where did that come from?'

'I got that in London. It's got a signature somewhere. "Colinet", I think.'

'That's right. It's by Claire Jeanne Robert Colinet and it's probably circa 1910.'

'Yeah, I think that's what they said,' Rick Freeman confirmed, nodding. 'What's that worth then?'

'About three thousand, I suppose. What did you pay for it?'

'Oh, less than that,' he replied.

'Well, there you are then,' Bernard concluded with a smile, 'it's just a matter of swings and roundabouts. And as long as you like what you buy, and as long as you don't have to sell it to pacify the bank manager, the price is irrelevant.'

'That's how I look at it,' Mr Freeman agreed. 'Shall I show you the rest of the house?'

Just like the drawing room the remainder of the house was first and foremost a home, however, there were plenty of treasures dotted through its rooms and corridors. Every now and then we would come across something which had cost a great deal of money, and more often than not it would be half hidden beneath a pile of children's toys or clothing.

There had been no great theme behind their buying. Obviously, they had simply spent their money on whatever had taken their fancy at the time. Of course, there was nothing wrong with that, although sudden bursts of unrestrained enthusiasm coupled with unlimited funds had resulted in certain excesses in the area of interior decor.

'What d'you think?' our client asked as we entered the huge master bedroom.

'Very striking,' I replied.

'Quite unique,' Bernard added.

'Yeah, it is unusual, isn't it,' Rick Freeman agreed. 'It was done by an American girl. She's really into English landscapes.'

'She certainly is,' Bernard agreed, adding: 'Do you ever manage to get any sleep?'

209

Our client grinned.

'Oh, you get used to it,' he said. 'It takes time, but you do get used to it.'

The 'it' in question was a strikingly bold mural which covered each of the four walls of the room from the dado rail up. It was a depiction of what I assumed to be an imaginary pastoral landscape, with each wall representing a different season. It was really quite clever with one season blending into the next in each corner, and opposing walls contrasting the blistering heat of Summer with the snows of Winter, and the lush grass of Spring with the russets of Autumn. Added to all that, as you worked your way up the walls night fell: the ceiling being a blue-black canopy dotted with a thousand gold and silver stars.

'The idea was that we could lie in bed and light up whichever wall we fancied,' Rick Freeman continued. 'Or just turn on the ceiling lights and contemplate the cosmos.'

'And do you?' I asked.

'No,' he replied, shaking his head, 'we're always too tired. It's the kids you know – they really take it out of you.'

Ten minutes later, at the opposite end of the house, our client shuffled a little uncomfortably as he chose his words with care.

'It's my . . . well, I suppose you could list it as my . . . recreation room?'

He looked doubtful. It was strange that such a characterless room should be causing him such problems. To all effects and purposes it was a small square box, with a large futon on the bare wood floor. There was a single window with a small Oriental chest under it, but by far the most remarkable thing about the room were the four mountainous banks of speakers – one in each corner.

'There must be enough equipment in here to put

this room into orbit,' I said.

'I don't know about that,' Mr Freeman remarked, 'but I reckon you'd blow the end wall out if you ever turned the volume up to full.'

'I can well imagine it,' I replied.

'Why on earth do you need so much power?' Bernard asked. 'After all, it's not a large room.'

'It's not so much power as clarity,' our client explained. 'I can lie there relaxing and pick out every note, just as if I was playing it myself.'

'Relaxing?' Bernard said, incredulously. 'It looks more like a torture chamber than a recreation room to me.'

'No, no,' our client insisted, 'it's definitely a recreation room. Apart from anything else, it's the only place I'm allowed to smoke nowadays. Cherry's got really strict about the kids seeing me with a cigarette, let alone a joint.'

'I take it you mean cannabis rather than the Sunday roast,' Bernard said nonchalantly, still inspecting the room.

'Shhh!' Rick Freeman cautioned, glancing over his shoulder. 'If she as much as hears the word she'll be up here like some avenging angel. She never used to mind, but since we've had the kids she's gone all puritanical about it. If I do ever roll one up now I puff the smoke straight out the window so she can't smell it. Pathetic, isn't it?'

'Probably no bad thing, really,' Bernard replied.

'Perhaps not,' Mr Freeman grinned, 'but think what would happen if some of Malice's fans got hold of it – it'd probably be the end of my career. I'd have to become a concert pianist or something like that.'

Three hours later we were back in the car on our way again.

'Where are we going now?' Bernard asked. 'Somewhere for lunch I hope.'

'Afraid not,' I replied.

'Why not?' he complained. 'I'm famished. I didn't have any breakfast because of that damned flight.'

'We've still got two more valuations to do this afternoon,' I explained.

'Are they likely to be big?'

'Can't tell. One is nineteenth-century English pictures and Renaissance bronzes . . .'

'Well, you can do that,' Bernard interrupted.

'I don't know anything about Renaissance bronzes,' I pointed out.

'So what? I don't know anything about them either. Just take the details and we'll research them later.'

'I don't know,' I said. 'I think it would be better if you actually saw them. You know how many fakes there are about.'

'Yes, and you'll be just as good at spotting them as I would.'

'Well . . .'

'No! No more argument,' he insisted. 'You can do the bronzes and pictures. What's the other valuation all about?'

'It's a collection of pot-lids.'

Bernard made a strange little choking noise.

'A collection of pot-lids?' he said, eventually.

'Yes,' I confirmed.

'You've agreed to value a collection of pot-lids?' he queried again, his voice trembling with disbelief.

'Yes.'

'In that case, I'll do the bronzes and pictures and *you* can do the pot-lids.'

'Hold on,' I said, 'A moment ago you told me you knew nothing about Renaissance bronzes . . .'

'I've changed my mind.'

'. . . and you'll certainly know nothing about the pictures.'

'I can learn.'

'Bernard! Anyone would think I'd just asked you to do a job in a leper colony.'

'Richard! I would have been far happier if you had.'

This was not the first time that I had observed this sort of extreme reaction from a member of Hampson's ceramics team. The last time had been when I'd asked Bernard's normally affable right-hand man, William Baron, to come with me on a valuation. As usual, he had been helpfulness itself and was thumbing through his diary when I mentioned the job included a collection of crested china.

For the uninitiated, crested china was produced from about 1870 to 1935 during which short time over two hundred factories churned out over six thousand different tiny shapes – everything from manically grinning pussy cats to models of cathedrals and military tanks. They would have a town crest slapped on them and would then be sold as souvenirs of whichever town it happened to be. To anyone other than the most dedicated enthusiast they are mind-numbingly boring. I realised immediately that William Baron was no enthusiast.

Initially, on hearing the words, he had frozen, then he'd closed his diary and refused to open it again.

'I'm sorry, Richard,' he'd said. 'I really would like to help, but crested china is beyond the call of duty. Tens, hundreds, perhaps thousands of nasty little presents-from-Blackpool and Margate, and most of them worth a few pounds each.'

'It's no good,' he went on, shaking his head, 'I won't do it . . . can't do it. I'd rather be fired . . . anything but a valuation of crested china!'

Obviously Bernard Thornton felt much the same way about pot-lids.

'It's not just the items themselves,' he said as we drove along. 'Some of them are really quite charming – if you like that sort of thing.'

'So, what is it, then?' I asked.

'Quite frankly, Richard,' he replied, 'it's the bloody people who collect them. They're so earnest. They know all there is to know about them. They know whether what they've got is the first, second or third issue. They know whether a particular design is more valuable with a flat top or a domed top. They know whether the subject should have a purple or a white bodice. And in the end, what are we talking about? Fish paste pots and hair cream jars, that's what. That's all they were, Richard, and these people salivate over them as though they're the treasures of Tutankhamen. It's absurd.'

'But there are lots of other utilitarian objects which are now collected,' I pointed out.

'Yes, but most of them don't attract fanatics.'

'Oh, come on, Bernard. Not all pot-lid collectors are fanatics.'

'No, I agree, Richard – not all of them are. But you've taken sales. You've seen the hardcore collectors – they'd kill for a "Washington Crossing The Delaware" or "The Buffalo Hunt". They're like rabid dogs.'

'They're not that bad . . .'

'Oh, yes they are, and what's more they all think they know all there is to know about it.'

'Well, most of them do know more than I do . . .'

'Exactly!' he shouted, stabbing a finger into the air. 'And most of them know more than I do, and if you think I'm spending the rest of the afternoon being lectured on our client's particular example of "Pegwell Bay" – worth sixty pounds instead of fifty pounds because it's got dark cliffs instead of white cliffs – I must hasten to disabuse you of such an idea.'

We drove on a little further in silence, then I made a suggestion: 'Why don't we do both valuations together, like we did this morning?'

214

'I'm not doing pot-lids,' was Bernard's reply. 'I've never pulled rank on you before, Richard, but if necessary I will this afternoon – I am *not* doing pot-lids.'

'Oh, but I think you are, Bernard,' I replied, swinging the car into the driveway of a small, neat bungalow.

'What? What do you mean? Where are we?'

'This is the place with the pot-lids, Bernard,' I said. Then I waved the ignition keys of the car in front of him. 'And these are the keys of the car which only I am insured to drive.'

For a moment he stared wild-eyed at the car keys, then at the unprepossessing bungalow, then at me.

'You swine!' he said. 'I'll get you for this.'

A short while later we were standing in the sitting room of the bungalow, overlooking a terrace with a large, kidney-shaped swimming pool. The owner, Mr James Simpson, looked out proudly at the limpid blue waters.

'Always kept at eighty degrees,' he announced proudly, 'summer or winter – it makes no difference – I swim every day. That's why I'm so fit. I never get colds. I've never even met my doctor. I bet you two can't say that.'

'Oh, on the contrary,' Bernard replied in his most seriously bored tone, 'I don't think *I've* ever met your doctor either.'

Mr Simpson looked puzzled, then he gave a single, barking laugh.

'Oh, yes, I get it!' he said. 'Yes, yes, I get it.'

Bernard acknowledge his words with a languidly poisonous smile.

'I'll show you the collection now, shall I?' Mr Simpson said. 'Then you can get on. I don't expect you want to hang about.'

Bernard smiled again, nodded to our client but, mercifully, remained silent.

Mr Simpson was probably in his early sixties. Darkly

215

tanned with tightly curled grey hair, he overflowed with
the surplus nervous energy characteristic of so many
self-made men. His accent suggested his formative
years had been spent in south London, but it had
obviously travelled far and wide since then.

One wall of the Simpson sitting room was taken up,
floor to ceiling, with a massive, illuminated display
cabinet which had obviously been custom built to house
our client's collection.

'Designed it and wrote the specification myself,' he
announced proudly. 'And stood over them as they built
it. They were good lads, but they didn't know what it
was to work until they did a job for Jim Simpson . . .'

Bernard muttered something close to my ear. I didn't
hear exactly what he said, but the word 'fanatic'
featured.

'. . . a fair day's work for a fair day's pay – that's
always been my motto,' our client continued as one by
one, he unlocked the four large, glass sliding doors.

I estimated the collection amounted to about a
hundred and fifty pieces. Not all the items were
pot-lids. There were dessert plates, vases, mugs and
comports, but all were printed with the brightly
coloured subjects associated with that particular field of
collecting.

'Some lovely bits in here,' Mr Simpson observed.

'Yes, indeed,' I agreed, while my colleague remained
tight-lipped and silent.

'Of course, you know how they did the printing, don't
you. . . ?'

'Yes,' both Bernard and I replied instantly.

'They used to engrave a copper plate for each colour
they were going to use – anything up to four colours,
plus one more for the outline of the picture.'

'Yes,' Bernard said, 'as you mentioned, we are aware
of . . .'

'Then they'd load the first plate with colour – always

yellow to begin with – then roll a piece of tissue paper onto it by feeding the plate and the paper through a sort of mangle . . .'

'Yes, it's a most interesting . . .' Bernard tried once more, but again to no avail.

'. . . then they'd peel off the tissue paper with the colour stuck to it then press that onto the bisque pot-lid – bisque is when the thing's not been glazed.'

'Oh, really!' Bernard replied with theatrical surprise.

'Then they'd wash away the tissue paper, and the coloured impression would be left on the pot-lid.'

I couldn't bring myself to look at my companion. I knew the agony he was suffering.

'Then they'd leave it to dry out for a couple of days, then begin all over again with the next colour . . .'

'Blue,' Bernard said, looking pointedly at his watch.

'What's that?' Mr Simpson asked.

'Blue,' Bernard replied abruptly. 'The next colour was always blue.'

'That's right,' Mr Simpson agreed, quite unper-turbed, 'then red, then green, then the black or brown outline. Once that had been put on they'd dip it in glaze and fire it. And did you know . . .'

'That it wasn't until then that they could actually see the finished picture,' Bernard interrupted once again, this time exhibiting some real signs of stress.

'That's right! That's right!' our client said. 'All that work, every time for each . . .'

'Fish paste pot.' Bernard spat out the words as though they were hemlock on his tongue.

'Well, not always, of course,' the collector continued enthusiastically. 'They packaged all sorts of things in pots like these, but you're quite right in saying that fish products were sold in them. For instance, that one at the back there – "Pegwell Bay, S. Banger, Shrimp Sauce Manufacturer" – that's worth a hundred and seventy at today's prices and that would have contained . . .'

217

While having no choice but to listen to Mr Simpson, I hadn't been looking at him, instead I'd been watching my colleague carefully. I now judged he was close to leaping on the man, clutching him by the throat and choking the life out of him. I thought it would be as well to avoid such an event.

'It's certainly a most interesting collection,' I began, 'but since we've got another appointment after this one we should probably make a start on the valuation now. It was for insurance purposes I believe?'

'Yes, yes,' Mr Simpson confirmed. 'That's right.'

He hovered beside the display cabinet apparently uncertain of whether to remain or go.

'Don't feel you have to stay with us, Mr Simpson,' I said. 'We'll give you a call when we've finished here.'

'Okay,' he replied, 'I'll be out by the pool then. Just shout when you're done.'

'Well, that wasn't too bad,' I remarked to Bernard, once Mr Simpson had left us. 'I had thought he'd be the type who'd breathe down our necks all afternoon.'

Bernard snorted, took off his jacket and tossed it over a chair.

'This is going to be the fastest valuation you've ever been involved in, Richard,' he said. 'You start at that end and I'll start at this and we'll be out of here in half an hour.'

'But there must be a hundred and fifty pieces in here, Bernard,' I protested.

'So what? Stand aside boy,' he muttered. 'I'll show you how to make an inventory and valuation.'

Just over thirty-five minutes later the valuation was complete. Bernard, who had done 80 per cent to my 20 per cent, picked up his jacket and threw his notebook over to me.

'Here, catch!' he said. 'You can get Charlotte to type that lot up when we get back.'

I looked at the pages of indecipherable hieroglyphics.

'She'll never be able to understand this lot.'

'Of course she will.'

'And there are no prices here.'

'No – you can get those from the latest price guide.'

'I've got a better idea,' I said. 'You get *your* secretary to type up this lot and *you* check the latest price guide.'

'Why don't we compromise?' he suggested. 'I'll get my girl to type a draft copy, but you go through the price guide.'

'It's a deal,' I said, handing back his notes. 'I'll give Mr Simpson a shout, then we can get going.'

Moments later our client had joined us again.

'All done then?' he asked, smiling brightly.

'Yes, all finished,' I confirmed.

'All right, I'll show you the rest of the place.'

'The rest of the place?' I said.

It was a surprising invitation. After all it was only the pot-lid collection we were valuing, not the entire contents.

'Yes – well just the dining room and bedroom really.'

'The dining room and bedroom?' Bernard whimpered. 'Why?'

'Because that's where the rest of the collection is of course,' Mr Simpson replied, already leading the way out of the sitting room. 'I only keep the best pieces in there under lock and key. Everything else is on display in the dining room and bedroom. Here we are look . . .'

As he opened the door Bernard and I hung back.

'Come on,' Mr Simpson said, full of enthusiasm. 'What do you think of that lot, eh? I bet you've never seen a collection like this before.'

Reluctantly, we shuffled miserably into the room, eyes cast down, afraid of what we were about to encounter. I looked up: it was worse than I had imagined.

A narrow shelf ran the whole way round the room about a foot below ceiling height. It was packed to capacity with pot-lids. Added to that, larger pieces were on display all around the room. For pot-lid enthusiasts it was Nirvana; for Bernard Thornton and myself it was Purgatory.

I looked at my colleague. He appeared to be in shock. His jaw hung open as he tried to absorb the scale of the disaster which had just overtaken us. Then, his jaw snapped closed and he cleared his throat.

'And how many pieces do you have in here?' he asked, hoarsely.

'Oh, about two hundred and fifty pot-lids,' Mr Simpson replied.

'Two hundred and fifty?' I groaned, beginning to feel a little weak myself.

'Yes, plus the other pieces, of course.'

'And how many more are there in the bedroom?' Bernard asked, in a lifeless monotone.

'About another hundred and fifty,' Simpson replied proudly.

'But that's over five hundred pieces in all!' Bernard exploded.

'Yes.'

'But . . .' my colleague spluttered, '. . . you must damned nearly have an example of every piece ever produced.'

'Not quite, but I'm getting there,' Mr Simpson said, seemingly not at all ruffled by Bernard's sudden ranting.

'But . . . but. . .,' my colleague ground to a halt and just stood there, open-mouthed again.

'Of course,' James Simpson continued, 'I've got lots of duplicates which I'll sell off one day, but I'm in no hurry. They're all worth more than I paid for them, and they're so interesting aren't they?'

'Er . . . yes . . .' I mumbled, not even trying to sound convincing.

'Just take that one up there . . . second from the right

220

in the corner – the one with the cows on . . . see it?'

'Er . . .'

'Now a normal one of those would set you back, say, thirty-five quid, but not that one.'

'No. . .?'

'No, because that one's got a seaweed rim, hasn't it?'

'Has it?'

'Yes, and that means I could probably get a hundred if I held out for it.'

'You don't say.'

'Oh, yes. And that one up there . . .' He stopped and looked at me with a faintly contented smile. '. . . I hope you don't mind me going on,' he said, 'but it's not often I get the chance to have a chat with real enthusiasts like yourselves.'

Chapter 18

Bernard and I breakfasted and drove to the airport in silence. The previous evening we had eventually got back to our hotel at a little after half past seven, by which time he had claimed to be light-headed with hunger. It was also obvious that he held me personally responsible for the débâcle with the pot-lids. I had hoped he would be in a happier frame of mind come the morning but, obviously, he was not.

'You're still brooding over that valuation yesterday aren't you?' I asked.

'No,' he replied, 'although I can assure you you'll never be forgiven.'

'Then what's the problem?'

'You know quite well what the problem is.'

'I don't, Bernard,' I protested. Then it struck me: 'Of course – it's the flight, isn't it?'

'Yes, it's the flight,' he confirmed through gritted teeth.

'You really shouldn't worry about it,' I said. 'It's just a little hop from one island to the next. It's all over in a matter of minutes.'

'Telling me not to worry about flying is about as much use as telling a turkey not to worry about Christmas,' he insisted. 'And I don't care how *short* the *flight* is going to be, I want to know how *big* the *aircraft* is going to be.'

As we entered the airport building I attempted, once

more, to put his mind at rest: 'Bernard, you really are worrying about nothing. It'll probably turn out to be huge . . . an old Hercules transport plane, I expect.'

Ten minutes later Bernard stood rooted to the spot on the airfield.

'Come on – it'll be all right,' I assured him.

'No,' he said.

'There really is nothing to worry about,' I insisted.

'That's what you said before,' he snarled. 'It'll probably be a Hercules – that's what you said. It just goes to show how much you know.'

'It's obviously perfectly safe,' I maintained.

'There's nothing obvious about it.'

'They've never had an accident.'

'Then they're probably due for one.'

'Bernard!' I said sharply. 'We have to get on that plane.'

'You can do what you want,' he replied. 'But you are not getting *me* up in that.'

'We have to cross over to Guernsey . . .'

'Come along, please, gentlemen,' interrupted a man who had just strolled up behind us. 'We need you all before we can board.'

'Who's that?' Bernard asked, as the man walked on ahead of us towards the small group of people waiting by our aircraft.

'I'm not sure,' I replied, 'but I've got a feeling he might be the pilot.'

My colleague looked at me incredulously, but nevertheless began, once again, to walk in the direction of the aeroplane. Without saying another word I fell into step beside him. It was imperative I got him on that aircraft.

What I couldn't possibly tell Bernard was that I shared some of his concern, not least his fears about the size of the machine. It really did appear to be very small – like a minibus with wings. As we joined the group of a dozen or so people waiting patiently next to the plane I had my first opportunity to examine it closely.

There was no cockpit as such. The pilot, who had now boarded, just sat in one of the two front seats. The one next to him was still empty. Behind the pilot, as far as I could see, there were banks of double seats, some of which folded forward like those in a two-door car. The aircraft was far too small for a central aisle. Instead, boarding was achieved by each passenger climbing through one of three separate doorways – one near the pilot, one near the tail and the other amidships – and then, if necessary, scrambling over the front seats to those behind. For most people it was neither an easy nor elegant manoeuvre to complete. To make matters worse it seemed that the weight of the passengers needed to be distributed carefully.

'The young lady, there, next to me I think,' said the pilot pointing to a very slim teenage girl who looked more than a little startled at being picked out from the crowd.

'It's all right. There's no ulterior motive, Miss,' the pilot went on, smiling. 'It's just that you're almost certainly the lightest, and I need as little weight as possible in the front here. Now, those two ladies in first, behind us, I think,' he continued. His instructions were being given to two burly looking men, in starched white shirts, who had been standing a little apart from the group. On the pilot's selection of the ladies the men stepped forward, ushered them from the crowd and helped them up the steps into the plane.

'Those two gentlemen in the back I think . . .' the pilot went on issuing his directions from where he sat, swivelled round in his front seat.

The two gentlemen he referred to were both on the lightweight side.

'. . . and the lady and gentleman there, in front of them, please . . .'

Within a few minutes Bernard and I were the only

ones left waiting to board. Our seats, the only two remaining, were almost exactly in the middle of the aircraft, just behind and below the wings.

I assumed we had been chosen for that particular position because we were the tallest and, in Bernard's case at least, the weightiest of the passengers.

'Which one of you gents is going to get in first?' one of the burly helpers enquired.

'I will,' I volunteered.

The interior of the aeroplane did look rather cramped now, and the last thing I wanted was to give Bernard an excuse for high-tailing it back to the departures building.

'Okay,' the helper said. 'In you jump, Sir.'

I found that by clutching hold of the edge of the wing with one hand and the door frame with the other, getting into the plane was not too difficult. True, I had to go in sideways to get my shoulders through the narrow opening, and I needed to be bent double, almost in a foetal position, to succeed even then. But once in it was fine. As I settled down and fastened my seat belt I glanced out of the door at my colleague. Once again he appeared to be rooted to the spot, his eyes wide and staring.

'Come on, Bernard,' I urged softly.

'I can't,' he replied, shaking his head.

'Yes, you can,' I said. 'It's perfectly safe.'

'I don't mean that,' Bernard protested. 'I mean I *can't* get in – it's too small.'

'No,' I assured him, 'It's much bigger than it looks once you're inside.'

'That's got nothing to do with it,' he went on, his voice rising a little. 'It doesn't matter how big it is once I'm inside. I can't actually get inside – the door's too bloody small!'

Framed in the narrow entrance, Bernard's bulk did suddenly seem quite colossal. I weighed in at about thirteen stones while he must have been a good three stones heavier. Added to which, he was a little over six feet three inches tall. Allowing for the difficulty I had experienced boarding, I was forced to accept that what he said might just be correct.

'What's the problem, Sir?' asked one of the helpers.

'I can't get in,' Bernard replied.

'I'll give you a hand . . .'

'No! Why won't anybody listen to me?' Bernard shouted. 'I can't get in because the door's too small.'

Both burly helpers peered at the door, then at Bernard, then at the door again.

'I reckon you'll make it, Sir,' the first one opined.

'Yes,' the other agreed. 'It'll be a bit tight but you'll make it. You'll just have to keep your head down.'

'What's wrong back there?' the pilot enquired.

'My colleague doesn't think he'll fit through the doorway,' I explained, much to the amusement of my fellow passengers.

'I suppose he could be right,' the pilot said, craning his neck to look at Bernard, 'but we've never had to turn anybody away yet. What do you think, boys?'

'We'll get him in,' was the confident reply from the more senior helper. 'Now, just put your foot up there, Sir.'

With a look of resigned frustration, Bernard complied, putting his right foot on the lowest of the steps.

'And just grab hold there . . . and there . . . now, up you go . . . and in!'

Bernard's head appeared in the cabin but nothing else followed.

'It's no good,' he growled. 'I told you the door's just not big enough.'

'Turn sideways, Sir,' shouted one of the helpers, now lost from sight. 'Turn sideways, then you'll go.'

Bernard struggled to get his left shoulder forward, but to no avail.

'It's no good, I tell you . . .'

226

'Okay, Sir, okay,' the helper called. 'Get down and we'll try it another way.'

Puce in the face my colleague reversed out of the plane again.

'Got to be feet first I reckon,' confided the first of the burly helpers to the other.

'I reckon you're right, Doug,' his companion agreed. 'I'd better get Andy.'

'Yeah – better safe than sorry.'

Throughout this brief exchange Bernard had looked uncomprehendingly from one helper to the other. It was only when the more junior of them dashed off towards the airport buildings, presumably in search of 'Andy', that my colleague asked if he was to be privy to their master plan.

'We're going to pop you in feet first, Sir,' the senior helper explained brightly.

'*Pop* me in! How?'

'Oh, it's easy enough – we'll just pick you up and slide you in feet first . . .'

'Pick me up?' Bernard squeaked, incredulously. 'You must be joking – I weigh over sixteen stone!'

'Yeah, I thought so,' replied the unmoved helper. 'That's why my mate's gone to get Andy – he's a big lad.'

'But this is . . .'

'Ah, here they come. Won't be long now, Sir.'

Normally, when the departure of any form of transport is delayed the passengers become restless and annoyed. Not so on this occasion. I think everybody was enthralled, and intrigued as to whether it was really possible to get Bernard Thornton's six-feet-three-inch, sixteen-stone frame through the tiny door of that increasingly claustrophobic little aircraft. I, for one, felt that if they did it would be a triumph of optimism over the laws of physics.

Andy, as his colleague had assured Bernard, was indeed a big lad. His arrival on the scene made the whole operation look much more viable. Not just because he was obviously strong enough to snap off Bernard's arms and legs should they get in the way, but because he made my companion suddenly *look* much smaller, thereby reducing the scale of the problem accordingly.

'You just relax, Sir,' the senior helper said to Bernard, who was now rigid with fear, 'and Andy and Tony will pick you up and just slide you in.'

'Just slide me in . . . ?'

'That's it, Sir – it's the height of the door that's the problem you see, not the width. You'll go through it, sitting down, with no trouble.'

'No trouble . . . ?' Bernard repeated.

'None at all. Just trust us, Sir. We've got bigger ones than you in there before now. Now, just sit back . . .'

The man gave Bernard a gentle prod in the chest. Taken by surprise and unable to keep his balance, my colleague staggered back and sat down abruptly on the improvised cradle seat made for him by Tony's and Andy's linked hands. For a moment their knees wobbled under his weight, then they straightened up, and whisking Bernard's feet clear of the ground they began a rather erratic advance on the open door of the aircraft.

'Just relax, Sir,' the mountainous Andy instructed.

'Hold onto our shoulders, Sir,' advised Tony.

Bernard promptly put a vice-like grip about the throat of each man.

'No, no . . . our shoulders, Sir . . . our shoulders . . .' Tony managed to choke in a hoarse, strangulated whisper, 'just hold on to our shoulders . . .'

Partly due to the throat-hold Bernard maintained on each man and partly due to the fact that Andy was much taller than Tony, the bizarre little troika seemed, at that point, to lose all sense of direction. Veering away from the aircraft altogether, they began to describe a wide and somewhat irregular circle on the airfield. My fellow travellers observed the proceedings with a sort of

228

hushed awe as Bernard, legs struck out ramrod-straight in front of him, was carted around the tarmac like some decadent Eastern potentate.

'No, no! Back this way! Back this way!' cried the senior helper, catching hold of Andy's arm and pointing the rogue group at the aircraft once more. 'Go on . . . go on . . . that's it . . .'

They were barely two feet from the door when Bernard released his hold on Tony's throat and, instead, grabbed him around the top of the head, placing his sizable hands over the unfortunate man's eyes.

'I can't see . . . I can't see . . .' Tony howled.

'Doesn't matter,' Andy assured him. 'We're there . . . we're there . . .'

'Right a bit!' shouted the senior helper. 'That's it!'

Bernard's feet and legs arrived in the cabin like some unstoppable medieval battering ram. He snatched at the doorframe to stop himself from being propelled straight past me and through the other side of the aeroplane.

'Whoa!' shouted the senior helper.

'Let go of the door . . . let go of the door . . .' hollered Tony, who could at least see, now that Bernard was no longer blinding him.

'Just slide round onto the seat, Sir,' Andy advised calmly.

Still, Bernard clutched the aircraft's superstructure, although there was now no sign of panic in his eyes, just grim determination.

It was then that the similarity between getting Bernard into that aeroplane and getting a racehorse into the stalls struck me: the two men heaving and straining from behind while the nervous, thoroughbred creature bucked and shied and resisted. It was a near-perfect simile. As he finally crashed into the seat next to me I wondered if the whole operation would not have gone a lot more smoothly if either Bernard had worn blinkers or the helpers had just put a sack over his

229

head. There was no way of telling of course.

'Okay?' I asked as the pilot gunned the engines.

My companion chose not to reply.

A moment later we were bouncing down the runway on our way to Guernsey. Faster and faster we went. I glanced to my right. Bernard's eyes were closed tight, his face and knuckles drained of blood. Obviously he was in his normal take-off condition – terror-induced stupefaction. I looked to my left at the runway markers as they sped past. I looked to my right, again, at the runway markers as they sped past on Bernard's side of the plane. Then I looked out of my window again: more runway markers. I began to wonder if it usually took this long to get this particular type of aircraft airborne. Then, for the first time, I peered past the pilot at the view ahead. To my horror I saw the end of the runway advancing towards us. Beyond that, only the distant, cold sea.

Instantly, my palms were moist with perspiration. I looked round at my companion once more; he appeared to be comatose. Still, incredibly, I could feel the undercarriage bouncing along the tarmac. I saw a white sign immediately ahead of us, then suddenly we were wonderfully, gloriously, stomach-churningly airborne. We soared up above the tarmac and grass for a moment, then plunged headlong over the steep, high cliffs which marked the ultimate end of the runway. For another moment a watery grave beckoned, then, climbing and banking, the pilot pointed the aeroplane towards the island of Guernsey. Within seconds, everybody was talking at once, even Bernard Thornton.

I had given our hotel in St Peter Port as an alternative contact point to our London number in all our advertising on the island. This was just in case anybody decided at the last minute to fix up an appointment with us. It was something I had done as a sort of long-stop. I had certainly not expected the file of enquiries and telephone messages the receptionist handed me on our arrival.

'And the lady seated in the corner over there is waiting for you, Mr Harton,' the receptionist concluded after Bernard and I had completed the formalities.

The lady concerned was probably in her early seventies. She had close-cropped, silver grey hair and was wearing a tweed sports jacket, cavalry twill trousers and highly polished brown brogues. She didn't look up, and appeared to be deeply engrossed in a copy of the *Daily Telegraph*. Every now and then she would read something which would animate her into frowning, shaking her head or nodding vigorously. Whatever her views were she was obviously passionate about them.

'What are you going to do?' Bernard asked. 'It looks as though there's a fair number of calls there.'

'I know,' I agreed, flicking through them. 'Never mind I'll sort them out while you do the main valuation – the collection of glass.'

'Suits me,' he said. 'I'll grab a cab. You have the hire car.'

I left Bernard at the reception desk sorting out his transport and went over to the elderly *Telegraph* reader. She was still deeply engrossed.

'Good morning,' I said. 'I'm Richard Harton of Hampson's. I believe you wanted to see me.'

She raised her head and looked at me over a pair of heavy-framed, half-moon reading glasses, and smiled.

'Ah, morning,' she said, jumping to her feet and tossing the newspaper aside. 'Good to meet you. My name's Graham – Miss Graham. How d'you do.'

'It's very nice to meet you,' I replied. 'How can I help you?'

'I've a few pieces of silver that need valuing for insurance purposes. I've always understood them to be worth a bit, but I've never done anything about finding out how much. I read your advertisement in the paper and thought this would be a good opportunity – yours being a London firm and all that. Not that there's anything wrong with the local chaps of course. Just that I prefer to keep myself to myself. You get so much gossip in a small community like this. Of course, several of my friends say I'm a fool to even contemplate insuring the things. They say they've heard of no end of cases where no sooner has a piece been valued than it's been stolen. What d'you think, Mr Harton? Have you ever heard of that sort of thing happening?'

'Well . . . I . . . er . . .'

'Sounds pretty far-fetched if you ask me. I always think it's better to be safe than sorry. Don't you?'

'Certainly, if the choice is between being insured or uninsured, then . . .'

'Absolutely – and there's so much more crime about these days, isn't there?'

'Indeed, our experience at Hampson's suggests . . .'

'I know, I know – even on this island nothing's safe any more. You know – until reently I'd not even lock my door when I went out, but not now, not now. Now you just can't be too careful – that's what I say.'

'Very wise,' I said quickly, in an attempt to avoid what appeared to be the inevitable interruption. However, it seemed that Miss Graham had said her piece. The floor was mine.

'I'll just have a look in here,' I said, opening my diary, 'and we can arrange an appointment for later in the day when I can come and see your silver. How about . . .'

'Not necessary!'

'Sorry?'

'Not necessary, Mr Harton – I've got it with me. It's all in here.' She pointed to the floor beside her chair where an old khaki pack had lain unnoticed by me.

'You brought it in your car?' I said, wondering just how valuable this silver really was.

'No, no! Heaven forbid, Mr Harton. I don't own one

of those dreadful machines. Never have and I never
will. Though I dare say I'll have to take a ride in one
eventually – when I'm in my box. But until then my bike
will see me through perfectly adequately, thank you.'

'*A bike?* You brought your silver here in a backpack on
a bike?'

'Of course. What's wrong with that? I go everywhere
on my bike.'

'But what about security?' I asked.

'What about it?' Miss Graham replied.

'Well it's not a very secure way of transporting it, is it?
I mean, what if you were robbed?'

'Robbed? Robbed?'

The suggestion obviously filled Miss Graham with
incredulity.

'Who's going to bother to bash a batty old bird on a
bicycle over the head?'

'But if it is valuable . . . ?'

'Well, that's what I'm here to find out,' she said
decisively. 'D'you want to have a look? I don't know
what your charges are but I expect they're reasonable.'

'Let's have a look,' I agreed, 'then we can discuss the
fee.'

Miss Graham sat down again and, leaning sideways in
her chair, scooped up the haversack and dumped it
down on the low, glass coffee table in front of her.
There was a dull, metallic rattling sound.

'Won't be a minute,' she said as she unbuckled the
covering flap and folded it back. 'Now,' she went on,
diving down into the pack, 'there's this – I don't know if
that's any good . . .'

She had pulled out a small two-handled cup. It was
absolutely plain, but quite charming.

Taking it from her I examined it carefully.

'It was my Father's,' Miss Graham explained. 'He
always said it was Irish. Is it?'

'No,' I said. 'I don't think this particular piece has

travelled very far at all in the last two hundred and fifty years.'

My client looked puzzled.

'I think it's a Channel Islands piece,' I explained, 'and I suspect it dates from about 1720.'

'But, surely that's a harp on it isn't it. Just there – look.' Miss Grham pointed at the heavily rubbed set of marks on the cup.

It was true, the middle one of the three marks did look like a harp – the chief mark on Irish silver. The other two were so badly effaced it was impossible to tell what they were.

'It does look like the Irish harp,' I agreed. 'And until relatively recently there was a lot of silver with that mark in museums up and down the land, all catalogued as Irish, but now it's known that it originated in these islands. That particular mark was used between about 1690 and 1730.'

'Fascinating,' Miss Graham said, staring at the piece through her half-moon spectacles with renewed interest. 'Is it worth much?'

'Yes,' I replied, 'but in all honesty I don't know how much. I'd have to check it with our silver department when I get back to London.'

'Not thousands, surely?'

'No, but at a guess – and don't quote me – somewhere between five hundred and a thousand.'

'Good Lord!' Miss Graham shook her head vigorously in disbelief. 'You do surprise me. I thought it would be two or three hundred at the most. Let's see what else we've got in here . . .' She delved deep into the khaki pack once more. 'Ah, yes – what about this?'

I placed the cup on the coffee table and reached out greedily for the new offering. It was a plain, shallow bowl about six inches in diameter with a single, pierced, flat handle. Just below the rim were four fairly well defined marks: the lion passant to show it was silver; the crowned leopard's head to indicate it was made in London; a capital 'E' for 1662; and the maker's mark 'RF'.

'Do you know what this is?' I asked.

'No, can't say I do,' Miss Graham replied brightly, 'but Father used to use it as an ashtray sometimes.'

I suppressed a shudder at the thought of such sacrilege.

'It's a Charles II bleeding bowl,' I said.

'Crumbs!' Miss Graham exclaimed, staring at the item suspiciously. 'You mean leeches and all that sort of stuff?'

'That's right,' I confirmed. 'Once the surgeon had opened the blood vessel the blood would be collected in a bowl like this. The maker's mark doesn't mean anything to me offhand but it's almost certainly recorded.'

'Amazing,' Miss Graham said. 'And do people want this sort of thing these days?'

'It would make between two and three thousand at auction.'

'Oh, my goodness!' Miss Graham gasped, still staring at the bowl in my hands.

'Anything else?' I asked.

'Well, there are some beakers and some spoons . . .'

Ten minutes later I was able to calculate mentally the total value of the silver on the table in the hotel foyer to be in the region of £25,000. It had all been stashed away in the old khaki haversack where it had rattled about without even the luxury of a sheet or two of newspaper as wrapping. The beakers Miss Graham had mentioned had turned out to be a pair, which, like the bleeding bowl, dated from the reign of Charles II. The spoons had been a little earlier. They had ranged from Henry VIII to James I.

I quickly scribbled down descriptions, took measurements and weighed each item. Then I helped her as each piece was hastily bundled back into the pack.

'I'm sure I could get some old newspapers from the hotel receptionist,' I said.

'No, no, Mr Harton, they'll be fine,' insisted Miss Graham.

'Well . . . it really won't do them any good . . .'

'Nonsense,' she scolded. 'They've all survived pretty well so far, I don't suppose the ride back to my cottage will do for them – not unless I'm flattened by a lorry, that is. I agree that probably wouldn't do them any good.'

'You're not seriously contemplating taking that lot home on your bike, are you?' I asked.

'Of course,' Miss Graham replied, as if such a course of action had never been in doubt.

'But, now you know what it's all worth . . .'

'It's worth exactly what it was when I cycled in with it this morning,' she replied, yanking at the straps to tighten them.

'Yes, but you wouldn't have brought them in on your back if you'd known this morning that they were worth twenty-five thousand pounds, would you?'

Miss Graham looked thoughtful.

'Well, would you?' I repeated.

'If I'd known what they were worth I wouldn't have needed a valuation, of course,' she said eventually, 'but otherwise, I think so – yes.'

With that, she hauled the pack onto her back, tightened the straps once more, shook me roughly by the hand and strode out of the hotel, negotiating the revolving door wth consummate ease. The last sight I had of Miss Graham was through the window, as, with bicycle clips firmly in place, she rattled off down the street on her big, black, pre-war bike.

'Please fasten your seatbelts and extinguish all cigarettes,' the stewardess's voice crackled over the intercom. 'We are about to begin our descent into London Gatwick.'

'Here we go,' I said. 'Well, all in all, I think it was a worthwhile trip.'

Fortified by several gins and tonics Bernard had not withdrawn into his normal moribund state as landing approached. In response to my comment he arched an eyebrow, then said; 'Richard, you are talking to a man who has been forced to fly hundreds of miles in an elderly aircraft which is held together only by sealing wax and willpower; a man who has been forced to value the largest collection of pot-lids in private hands; a man who has undergone the humiliation of being man-handled feet first into an aircraft endowed with all the aerodynamic streamlining of a crane-fly; a man who –'

'Yes, yes, Bernard,' I cut in. 'But the Renaissance bronzes were good. And you've got some of them for sale.'

'Yes . . .' he conceded.

'And the glass valuation was good, and you got some of that for sale.'

'Yes . . .'

'And you've made a worthwhile contact with a collector of art nouveau and art deco.'

'The pop chappy, you mean. . .?'

'Yes – and several of my calls yesterday brought in reasonable ceramics for sale.'

'Yes . . .'

'So, next time I arrange a trip to the Channel Islands and I need a ceramics specialist . . .'

'Yes, yes – all right, I guarantee you'll get one, Richard,' he said. 'And I promise you won't have to put up with the bitching and moaning you've had this time.'

'Well, that's good news,' I said. 'I'll hold you to that.'

'You won't have to,' my companion replied as he gazed out of his window at the neat green fields below us. 'Because it won't be me who'll be with you. It'll be William Baron – I guarantee it.'

Chapter 19

Patrick Faulkner's office was deserted. A cigarette was still burning in his secretary's ashtray but otherwise there was no sign of life. As I leant over to stub out the butt the telephone on Patrick's desk rang. I picked it up.

'Hampson's Furniture Department,' I said, still screwing the cigarette end against the bottom of the heavy glass ashtray.

'Mr Faulkner. . . ?' said the voice at the other end of the line rather doubtfully.

'No, I'm afraid he's out of his office at the moment,' I replied. 'Can I help?'

There was a pause.

'. . . is Helen there?'

'No, I'm afraid she's not at her desk either, Harry.'

This time there was silence at the other end.

'Who is that?' asked the voice eventually.

'It's Richard Harton, Harry. What can I do for you?'

'Oh . . . Mr H!' Harry Sutton sounded at once relieved and cagey. 'I didn't recognise your voice, Sir.'

'Never mind, I recognised yours, Harry. What can I do for you?'

There was another long silence. Whatever it was Harry wanted to tell Patrick, it was clearly not for my ears.

'Come on, Harry,' I teased, 'don't be shy – you can tell me.'

'Well . . . I . . .'

'Don't tell me you and Patrick have gone into partnership.'

Another long silence.

'. . . course not, Mr H,' he protested. 'It's just that I've got this couple down here with a clock . . .'

'Yes.'

'Well . . . the thing is, they want to sell it . . .'

'Excuse me for saying so, Harry,' I said, 'but this is hardly front page news, is it? I mean, most people who take things to auction rooms tend to want to sell them . . .'

'I know, I know, Mr H. What I mean is they want to sell it quick.'

'So what's the problem? You have weekly sales.'

There was another pause as Harry arranged his reply.

'Well . . . the thing is,' he said again, 'it's too good for Bailey's, Mr H. Just too good for one of our sales.'

I sank slowly and gently into Patrick Faulkner's large, creaking chair.

'Now hold on a second, Harry,' I said. 'I just want to get this straight. You are telling me that you intend to send a clock to Hampson's for sale because you're concerned it wouldn't make enough money at Bailey's. That is what you're telling me, isn't it?'

'Yes, sir.'

I was unable to stop myself from giving a bellow of laughter.

'What's so funny, Mr H?' asked the aggrieved sounding voice on the telephone.

'Nothing, nothing, Harry,' I assured him. 'And how *was* Damascus?'

Another silence, then: 'Damascus? I've never been to Damascus. I was in Cairo once, but . . .'

True, it was unlikely that Harry Sutton had received a divine revelation on the road to anywhere. But, if what he had just told me was true, some sort of spiritual change had taken place. After all, although it would be putting it too strongly to suggest the entire staff at Bailey's were crooks, they were most definitely opportunists. To a man they watched like vultures for anything going through their saleroom on which they could make a turn. Now, Harry Sutton, the Godfather of it all, would have me believe he was referring a client to Hampson's because he was concerned the said client's clock would sell for less in Twickenham than it would in Belgravia. It was too good to be true. There had to be more to it.

'What sort of clock is it?' I asked.

'It's a longcase, Mr H. With a really nice marquetry case.'

'Is there a maker's name.'

'Yes, it's signed "Charles Gretton in Fleety Streety".'

'Fleety Streety?'

'Yes, you know – with an "e" at the end of everything, like Ye Oldy Sweety Shoppy.'

'Oh, I see what you mean,' I said, swivelling round in Patrick's chair to grab a reference book from the shelves behind me. 'Hold on, Harry. I'll just see what Mr Gretton's dates were.'

I thumbed through the book looking for the name of Harry's maker.

'Ah, here we are,' I said. ' "Gretton. Chas., The Ship, Fleet St., apprenticed to Lionel Wythe in 1662; admitted to the Company of Clockmakers in 1672; master in 1700; an eminent maker . . ." It sounds good – as long as it's right, Harry.'

'I reckon it's okay, Sir,' he replied.

'Have you talked money with the owners yet?'

'No, Mr H. That's why I was ringing Mr Faulkner.'

'Right. Are they happy to bring the clock into Belgravia or should we come down to you?'

'No problem at all – they're raring to go.'

'All right then, Harry, send them along.'

'Okay, Mr H, but what about Mr Faulkner – is he going to be there when they arrive?'

'I'm sure he's around somewhere. But if he's still missing when they arrive, I'll deal with it.'

This time there was a particularly pregnant pause at the other end of the line.

'Lesser men might be offended by your lack of faith in my ability to handle this consignment, Harry,' I said.

'Gawd bless you, no, Sir,' Harry insisted. 'There was nothing further from my mind . . . it's just that I've been cracking Mr Faulkner up, you know – to the owners. Like he's the only person to talk to in London.'

'Yes, Harry. Don't worry, I'll try to find him.'

'If you would, Sir. And ask him to give me a ring – if it's not too much trouble. I would appreciate it.'

I had hardly put down the telephone when Patrick stormed back into the office. He was rather red in the face and perspiring slightly as if he'd been taking exercise. Although, knowing Patrick as I did, I realised such an explanation was unlikely.

'What the hell are you doing here, Richard?' he asked abruptly, taking off his jacket and tossing it onto the hook behind the door. 'Haven't you got any nice, fat, fee-earning valuations to do?'

'What's put you in such a filthy mood?' I asked.

He hesitated, shook his head and gave a very weak smile.

'I'm sorry, dear boy,' he said, 'but it's bloody Derby. I've just had an hour's grilling about why my departments aren't meeting their projected turnover figures.'

'Oh, I see.'

'The reason is a simple one of course: the projections were complete bloody rubbish. Every year I put in a set of figures based on the previous year's turnover plus a bit for inflation. Every year our Chairman says they're pathetic and unrealistic and adds thirty or forty per cent to them. Then he belly aches to *me* when we fall short of *his* totally groundless expectations. It's the same every damned year . . .'

'Well, I've got some good news,' I interrupted.

'As long as it's not that you've just landed some vast valuation, dear boy. Because if it is you know what you can do with it. I've got to spend the next week oiling round my trade contacts trying to get some decent pieces for our next good sale . . .'

'No, no, Patrick. It's just what you need . . .'

I explained about the telephone call from Harry Sutton, and the imminent arrival of what purported to be a fairly valuable clock.

To my surprise Patrick didn't seem to find it at all unusual that Harry Sutton was sending clients to him.

'No, no,' he said, 'Sutton and I have a very good working relationship. He often refers vendors to me.'

'Well, that's good to know, I replied. 'I'd always assumed that Harry and his merry band considered the unknowledgeable client as fair game.'

'Not really, dear boy. They're a bit fly of course, but not bad really. Anyway, if you'll excuse me I'd better get on to Sutton before these people get here.'

'Of course,' I said. 'But I wonder if you could give me a call when the clock arrives – I would like to see it.'

'Sure,' he replied as he picked up the telephone and began dialling. 'Sure.'

It was nearly an hour later when I realised Patrick had not been in contact.

'Perhaps the people have taken the clock somewhere else after all,' Charlotte commented without looking up from her typewriter.

'That's exactly what I'm worried about,' I replied. 'I knew either Patrick or I should have gone down to Bailey's and seen it there.'

'Well, there's no point in worrying about it. Why don't

242

you give Fatty Faulkner a ring and see what's happened?'

'No,' I said, 'I think I'll actually go round to the Furniture Department.'

A few minutes later, as I walked the short distance from my office to Hampson's main entrance, I saw a strikingly tall, good-looking woman sweep down the front steps of the salerooms. She was probably in her mid to late forties and was elegantly and expensively dressed. Behind her came a short, balding man with a pot belly and bad complexion.

I don't suppose I would have given him a second glance had he not climbed into the same car as the woman. It was a new Volvo with a roof rack – the approved dealers' wagon – and it was parked on the double yellow lines immediately outside Hampson's.

The rather repellent little man got into the passenger seat while his attractive companion walked round to the driver's door. As she did so she took a parking ticket from under the windscreen wiper and tossed it, flamboyantly, high over her shoulder. With that she climbed into the car and they drove off.

Patrick Faulkner was standing with his Head Porter, John Adams, poring over a fine, tall, marquetry longcase clock which was standing against the wall just outside the office. I did not need to be told it was the Gretton.

'I thought you were going to telephone me when it arrived,' I complained.

'What?' Patrick looked up. 'Oh yes, so I was. I'm so sorry, dear boy. It completely slipped my mind. Never mind – here it is. What a beauty, eh!'

'Is it right?' I asked, beginning to look it over.

'Yes,' he replied. 'It's been reduced in height by an inch or two but they've not damaged the marquetry so that can easily be restored. Unfortunately the hood seems to have been altered rather a lot. It was probably broken at some stage and rebuilt. Of course, that will detract from the sale price a bit.'

I nodded as I inspected the finely inlaid walnut case.

'But, it is the original case?' I asked.

'I've no doubt about that at all,' Patrick confirmed, standing back and looking the piece up and down once more.

'What's it going to make?' I asked.

'After restoration . . .' he began.

'You're going to have it restored?' I said, surprised that Patrick was intending to take such a step. The general rule of thumb being to leave any restoration to the eventual buyer.

The last thing one wanted was to incur a big repair bill and end up with a piece so clean and shiny that it looked as though it had come out of a dealer's showroom. When it came to auctions it was best for the items to have a 'lived in' look about them.

'Yes, just a little work here and there,' Patrick confirmed. 'I have a first-class chap who knows exactly how far to go. He'll give his eye teeth to get stuck into this one.'

As he spoke he ran the back of his hand gently over the heavily decorated door of the case. It was obvious he was in love with the piece.

'So how much will it make?' I asked again.

'I shall probably estimate it in the catalogue at five to seven thousand, although it could make more.'

'Not bad,' I replied. 'What were the owners like?'

Patrick smiled.

'As it happens, they were a really odd couple. She was all *Tatler* and *Horse and Hound* and he was very definitely *News of the World* and *Racing Times*. I suspect she'd been an absolute knockout in her youth. Not that she'd have to do a lot to make me sit up and take an interest now . . .'

'But they're dealers,' I said.

'What?'

244

'They're dealers,' I repeated. 'I saw them leaving – brand new Volvo, roof rack, everything.'

Patrick Faulkner laughed.

'Volvo or not,' he said, 'I can assure you those two are not in the trade, dear boy. I have no idea what they, or more importantly, she does for money but I do know it isn't dealing.'

'Well, I'd put money on it that they are,' I insisted.

'Then you'd lose, dear boy.'

'How can you be so sure?' I asked.

Patrick hesitated, looked at John Adams for a moment, then at me. 'I'll tell you what, old thing,' he said. 'I'll treat you to a Chinese tonight and explain it all then. It's very entertaining stuff.'

I was absolutely dumbfounded. I could hardly believe it: Patrick Faulkner, openly known as one of the meanest men in Hampson's – second only to Charles Morrison-Whyte – had just offered to buy me dinner. It was unprecedented. I had never known him as much as offer round a packet of wine gums, and now he was waving a Chinese meal under my nose. And, as luck would have it, I couldn't accept.

'I can't I'm afraid, Patrick,' I said. 'Sarah's meeting me here after work. We've arranged to have a bite somewhere this evening.'

'Ah, the delicious Miss Bishop – my favourite blonde ice maiden. The solution is simple: she must come too.'

It was *a* solution, certainly. But whether it was the correct one or not I wasn't at all sure. Patrick's comment about Sarah being an 'ice maiden' was reasonably well founded when it came to her relationship with him. She did tend to freeze him out whenever they met, chiefly because – and in complete agreement with Charlotte – she found him just a trifle too friendly. However, I suspected she would be prepared to grit her teeth and suffer the inevitable under-the-table kneesy-kneesy just to be able to say afterwards that she had eaten a meal paid for by Patrick Faulkner. At least, I hoped she would.

'Patrick,' I said, 'we'll look forward to it.'

'You must be joking!' Sarah said, eyes wide with disbelief. 'Patrick is going to buy us both dinner? You must have misheard what he said.'

'No, no,' I assured her. 'It's true: we're both invited and Patrick's paying. The question is: can you endure an evening of being mentally undressed by him?'

'Richard, just for the sheer joy of being able to say that I have had a meal at Patrick Faulkner's expense, I would seriously consider being actually undressed by him.'

'That's what I said,' Charlotte added as she covered her typewriter and turned off her desk light.

'I'm surprised he didn't ask you too,' Sarah said.

'Oh, he did,' Charlotte confirmed. 'About half an hour after he'd invited you and Richard. But, unfortunately, I've got a date I can't break tonight. It's a shame. I could have given you moral support.'

Sarah smiled.

'Well, there'll certainly be plenty of immoral support. Never mind. I'll cope. I wouldn't miss it for the world.'

The Tao Tao Restaurant, just off Chelsea's King's Road had been an important haunt of London's beautiful people. It was one of the places visiting American film stars were always being photographed going into or coming out of. A couple of years earlier, to get a good table at Tao Tao meant you had arrived.

But that was all in the past. The darlings of the gossip columnists had moved on to discover and make chic other eating establishments, and the only throwback to those halcyon days in the Tao Tao were the outrageously high prices it still charged.

Not that this meant it was short of trade. The food was undeniably good, and there were still plenty of people who were unaware that it had ceased to be the place to be seen. Indeed, it still attracted the odd second-division film or television star, but none of the big names anymore.

'Let's have a drink, shall we?' Patrick said, undaunted by the danger of being perceived as being passé. 'I do like this place, don't you? I used to come here a lot in the good old days. Where's that damned waiter?' He raised his hand high above his head and clicked his fingers noisily.

Despite it still being early evening, the large, low-ceilinged restaurant was filling up fast. The rush seemed to have taken the staff a little by surprise.

'What will you have, my dear?' Patrick asked, reaching out and cupping his own pink, pudgy hand over Sarah's. 'A gin and tonic, perhaps?'

'That would be lovely, Patrick,' she said, sliding her hand out from below his and picking up the menu which had been lying on the table in front of her. 'I'm absolutely famished. I hope you've brought lots of money with you.'

'No trouble there, Sarah – American Express will see us through. Where is that damned waiter? Little sods are never around when you want them. Waiter! Waiter!' he shouted, snapping his fingers once more.

When the waiter did eventually arrive he took our drinks order impassively and hurried away. It was a full ten minutes before he returned with the drinks. The delay did not have a good effect on Patrick.

'What's going on here tonight?' he asked the stone-faced man as he set down our glasses on the table.

'Very busy,' the waiter replied tersely, then turned to hurry off again.

'Hold on, hold on!' Patrick said, his stentorian tones stopping the man in his tracks. 'You can take our food order now. Otherwise, I've no doubt, it'll be another half an hour before we as much as see you again.'

The waiter took out his pad and pen without saying a word.

'Now,' Patrick continued, 'what would you like? I can thoroughly recommend the Szechuan dishes . . .'

It was sometime after the man had trotted away with our order that I broached the subject of our clients with the clock. I did this partly because I was dying to know the full story; partly because I thought it would take Patrick's mind off what was obviously going to be a very long delay before we actually got anything to eat; and partly because it would divert his attention from Sarah's cleavage which seemed to have taken on mesmeric qualities as far as he was concerned.

'So what's the story behind those two this morning?' I asked. 'How come you're so certain they're not dealers?'

'Because,' he began, looking up at last, 'no dealer would have done the deal they did this morning. That's why.'

'What deal was that?' Sarah asked.

'A deal, my dear, where they parted with seven thousand pounds' worth of clock for three thousand – that's what.'

I had no idea what Patrick was talking about and said so.

'It's perfectly straightforward, Richard,' he said. 'Beauty and the beast are leaving these shores *tout de suite*. They didn't actually explain why, but I got the impression that our friends in the Customs and Excise, not to mention their colleagues in the Inland Revenue have a few anomalies they would like to discuss with them.'

Patrick paused in his story and looked over his shoulder towards the doors to the kitchens.

'Isn't there any sign of our blasted food yet?' he asked. 'This is really getting beyond a joke.'

I shook my head.

'So what happened?' I asked.

'The woman said they were liquidating everything,' he continued. 'They're completing on the sale of their house tomorrow but the buyer they'd lined up for the clock had let them down.'

'So they decided to put it in an auction – right?' Sarah said.

'Wrong,' Patrick replied. 'An auction was no good. They needed to get rid of it instantly. They went to Bailey's to see if Harry Sutton and his little band of helpers would buy the clock from them.'

'But why on earth did they choose Bailey's?' I asked. 'Why didn't they go straight to a West End dealer? Any one of them would have snapped it up.'

'Pure chance and ignorance,' he replied. 'They were driving into London to cart it around the trade when they saw Bailey's and decided to give them a try . . . I say, if we don't get some bloody food soon there's going to be trouble.'

'I still don't understand why they didn't want to auction it,' Sarah said. 'They could leave it at any auction room immediately. They wouldn't have to cart it around any more. And when it was eventually sold the money could be sent on to them – wherever they might be planning to go.'

'Exactly!' Patrick said, grasping her hand again. 'They would have to leave a forwarding address, and that is something those two have no intention of doing. When they leave the country tomorrow they are going to vanish without trace.'

'Well, in that case,' I said, 'I don't understand why we've still got their clock.'

'Simple,' Patrick replied, smiling indulgently. 'It's not their clock any more – it's mine . . . ah, there's the manager . . . hey! . . . you! . . . yes, you! . . . come here!'

The manager was a dimunitive, unsmiling, grey-haired man with a rather imperious look. Slowly, he crossed the room to our table.

249

'You have a problem, Sir?' he asked.

'Yes, and so will you if we don't see some service here soon,' Patrick snorted. 'We've been sitting here for forty-five minutes and haven't seen hide nor hair of any food yet. Perhaps you'd be good enough to galvanise your staff into some sort of action.'

The manager listened carefully then, slowly pointing around at the full room, said: 'Very busy.'

For a moment I thought Patrick Faulkner was going to explode. 'Well, let me tell you, my friend,' he hissed, drawing closer to the clearly unmoved manager, 'you're going to be less busy very soon if you don't get some food on this table – savvy?'

The manager gazed at Patrick as though my colleague had just crawled out from under a rock. Then he nodded stiffly and set off towards the kitchen where the two swing doors were now opening and closing rhythmically as the small army of waiters hurried in and out.

'Absolutely bloody ridiculous!' Patrick cursed. 'I do apologise . . .'

'Never mind that,' I said. 'What do you mean about the clock being yours now?'

'What? Oh, that – exactly what I say. I bought it from them for three grand.'

'But that's completely against company policy . . .' I began.

'I don't know if you've ever noticed, my dear,' Patrick said, turning to Sarah, 'but your consort has a nasty puritanical streak.'

'I think it's called honesty, Patrick,' she replied, smiling.

'Oh, not you as well!' he said, holding up his hands in mock despair. 'To be in such saintly company.'

'But Bob Derby would go through the roof if he knew,' I said.

'As far as I'm concerned our beloved Chairman can

go wherever he pleases, just as long as it's a long way from me . . . ah! At last!'

With very little style our original waiter dumped a dishwarmer in the middle of our table and deposited a number of bowls on it. A second waiter followed suit. They were about to make good their escape when Patrick caught one of them by the arm.

'Where's the wine?' he asked.

'Coming,' replied the pinioned waiter.

'So's Christmas my little man,' Patrick growled. 'Get it – now!'

He momentarily released his grip on the man's arm then tightened it again.

'Hold on,' he said. 'What's that?' He was pointing to a gently bubbling bowl over one of the burners.

The waiter peered into it.

'Squid,' the man replied.

'Anybody order squid?' Patrick asked.

Sarah and I both shook our heads.

'Nobody ordered squid,' Patrick informed the waiter through tightly clenched teeth. 'And where are my Szechuan king prawns?'

The waiter shrugged.

'You not order prawns – you order squid,' he said sullenly.

I closed my eyes and waited for the outburst. To my surprise it didn't come. When I looked again I saw Patrick had caught the waiter by his shirt front and had drawn him very close.

'Don't tell me what I did or did not order,' he was saying very quietly. 'Just take that dish away and bring me my Szechuan prawns within the next five minutes or I will make the opium wars look like a tea party. Do you understand?'

The waiter nodded.

'Say: "Yes Sir",' Patrick insisted.

'Yes Sir,' the waiter complied, with no sign of sincerity.

251

Patrick released his hold on the man's shirt front and watched him as he returned to the kitchen with the unwanted squid. This time, as he passed through the swing doors, there was a sudden explosion of sound as, behind the scenes, people began to scream at one another.

'The message seems to have got through at last,' Patrick said, turning back to Sarah with a smile. Then he pointed at the food. 'Please don't wait for me – do start.'

Minutes later, with wine in our glasses and even Szechuan king prawns on the table, Patrick seemed his old, laid-back self again.

'You're very quiet all of a sudden,' he said to me as he topped up Sarah's glass.

'Well . . . it's the clock . . .' I began.

'Richard, for God's sake don't be such an old woman,' he said.

Then, after a moment's pause he went on: 'You know Derby's talking of offering you and Lawrence directorships, don't you?'

I sat there open-mouthed. I had no idea any such proposal was even being considered.

'No,' I said.

'If he wants to he can just push it through of course,' he went on, 'but for the sake of appearances, unity and all that rubbish he's asked for the agreement of the existing directors.'

'When?' I asked.

'He sprang it on us yesterday. Of course, Charles is against it on principle – he's not wildly flattering about either of you. Bernard thinks it's an excellent idea, and I . . . well . . . I don't have any major objection. Philip Lawrence can be a bit bloody-minded on occasions but he certainly knows his stuff.'

'And me?'

'You've got a good record,' he said. 'You've built up your department well . . .'

'But?' Sarah said.

'But, sometimes I get the impression you've not altogether joined the real world – as with this clock.'

'What exactly do you mean, Patrick?' I asked.

'Well, fair enough, buying goods from clients is against the rules – conflict of interest, all that sort of stuff.'

'Yes,' I agreed.

'But, just take today's case . . .'

'What about it?'

'Those two were not going to sell that clock at auction at any price. I told them exactly what it was worth. I told them it could make seven thousand or more in the right sale but they didn't want to know.'

He took a large slug of wine.

'Now,' he went on. 'If I'd followed Derby's house rules, that would have been it. They would have packed it back in their Volvo and ended up knocking it out to some trader just down the road. Does that make any sense? The dealer makes a fat profit and Hampson's make sod all – brilliant! Just what we're in business for.'

'But to buy it for three thousand when you know it to be worth so much more . . .' I began.

'But you forget,' Patrick interrupted, 'I'd also *told* them it was worth a lot more. The decision was theirs: they could offer it under the hammer, pay the commission and other charges, and get a cheque for six thousand or so in two or three months' time; they could continue trotting round the trade until every clock dealer in London had seen it; or alternatively they could take three grand in lovely, crisp, crinkly notes from me with no questions asked. Now you tell me what's wrong with that, Richard. They're happy. I'm happy. Hampson's should be happy. What's *your* objection?'

'I know, I know,' I said. 'Put like that . . .'

'There is no other way to put it,' he replied, 'because that's exactly how it happened.'

We continued our meal in silence for a while. I had to admit that Patrick could hardly be accused of pulling the wool over anybody's eyes. And yet, I still felt uncomfortable about it. Perhaps he was right – perhaps I hadn't joined the real world.

It was Sarah who broke the silence. And it was with a question I should have thought of.

'How did you manage to lay your hands on three thousand in cash just like that, Patrick?'

'Ah, now that's something I did want to discuss with Richard . . . would you like some pudding by the way? . . . or just coffee? . . . where's that blasted waiter gone this time?'

'What did you want to discuss?' I asked.

'Well, I drew the money as payment in advance to a vendor,' Patrick replied nonchalantly.

'You mean it was Hampson's money?' I said.

'Yes, and there's no need to sound so shocked,' he went on. 'It's all perfectly above board, like any other pre-sale advance to a vendor. Hampson's have simply advanced three thousand pounds to me against an item valued at five to seven thousand pounds. You can hardly say they're over-exposed, can you? . . . where is that bloody waiter?'

'Sounds safe enough to me,' Sarah agreed.

'But advances have to be sanctioned by a second director,' I observed. 'Are you saying Bob Derby signed it off?'

'No, of course not,' Patrick replied. 'Charles Morrison-Whyte always okays advances to my clients and I okay advances to his. That way neither of us has to keep justifying our every move to Derby. As a system it works very well.'

'And you'd prefer it if this particular transaction wasn't brought to the Chairman's atention?' Sarah smiled.

'In a nutshell, my sweet. I mean, why burden the man

with trivial details? He carries such a heavy load as it is . . . WAITER!'

'By the way,' Patrick said, when the coffee had at last arrived, 'I'd prefer it if you didn't disclose the purchase price of the clock to Harry Sutton.'

'Why not?' I asked.

'Because he's currently under the impression that it cost me a little more than three thousand.'

'Oh, so Harry Sutton gets a cut of the action too,' Sarah said.

'Of course – you've got to give the man some incentive,' Patrick replied.

'What's he on?' I asked. 'Fifty per cent?'

'No, no, no, no,' Patrick said, screwing up his face in disgust. '*I'm* the organ grinder. *He's* just the monkey. But he is in for a cut.'

'How much have you told him you paid for the clock?' Sarah asked.

'Er . . . five thousand.'

I laughed out loud. 'Talk about honour among . . .'

'No!' Patrick cautioned. 'Don't say it, Richard – don't say it.'

It took another twenty minutes to get hold of the bill. Patrick scrutinised it as thoroughly as he would a suspect piece of furniture.

'Typical – they've included the squid,' he snorted. Then, glaring about him, he raised his arm high in the air, and snapping his fingers loudly, bellowed, 'MANAGER!'

This time the grey-haired major-domo was at his side in an instant.

'You have more problems?' he enquired in a flat monotone.

'Yes, I do,' Patrick replied. 'In fact my friends and I have had nothing but problems ever since we arrived. Your staff have been surly and slow. When the food did arrive, it was wrong, and now the bill has turned out to

255

be a work of pure fiction.'

'What do you mean?'

'I have been charged for a dish we did not order.'

'Take off then.'

'Oh, I will, don't worry. And I'll take something else off as well . . .'

'What's that?'

'The service charge, old son. Because as far as I'm concerned we've not had any bloody service.'

For the first time I thought I detected a flicker of emotion on the features of the manager.

'You can take off if you want,' he said, with some dignity, 'but remember, my waiters depend upon service charge for living.'

Patrick summoned up a smile as poisonous as cyanide.

'Quite frankly, old boy,' he sneered, 'we couldn't give a toss whether your waiters live or not.'

As he spoke he removed his American Express card from his wallet and threw it down on top of the bill. The manager picked it up and handed it back to him.

'No take,' he said.

'What?' barked Patrick.

'No take American Express.'

'You always used to,' Patrick complained. 'What about Diners Club?'

'No! No take any card any more.'

'What!' gasped Patrick, who was beginning to look perplexed. 'Since when? You always used to take cards.'

'Since almost one year,' replied the manager, a malevolent glint appearing in his eyes. 'You pay please.'

'I *can't* damned well pay,' Patrick blustered, 'I haven't brought my chequebook with me.'

'Cash! You pay cash, please,' the manager suggested.

'Don't be damned silly – I don't carry that sort of cash around with me.'

'Pay now, please,' the manager said with annoying insistence.

'How much is it?' I asked.

'Seventy-two pounds, twenty-four pence,' Patrick said, 'excluding the service charge.'

'What!' Sarah almost choked. 'For a Chinese meal! I don't believe it!'

'Always was pretty pricey in here,' Patrick said, mopping his glistening brow with his handkerchief.

'You pay – now!' the manager shouted.

It had not escaped my notice that he was becoming less and less polite as his confrontation with Patrick continued. What was more, he was no longer alone. He was now supported by six of the waiters who were slowly moving to encircle our table. As they did so one accidentally brushed against Patrick.

'Get off!' my colleague shouted, jumping up and pushing the man away. 'Typical! We couldn't attract the attention of one of them all evening, now we've got six of the little sods.'

His outburst was countered by a stream of rapid and spirited Chinese. It seemed to me the whole situation was getting out of hand.

'I've got my chequebook with me,' I admitted reluctantly. 'Give me the bill, Patrick – I'll pay.'

'You pay – now!' the manager said, turning his attention to me.

'Ah, well done, old thing,' Patrick said, handing over the bill with obvious relief. 'Make sure you deduct the service charge, won't you.'

There was a fresh outpouring of what I assumed to be Oriental abuse.

'You got banker's card?' the manager enquired suspiciously.

'Yes,' I said, beginning to write the cheque.

'You write two cheques,' he insisted. 'One for . . .'

'Yes, yes, I know,' I said, wearily. 'One for fifty pounds and one for the balance.'

'Yes, you write – now!'

'Well, since everything seems to be under control now, I'll leave you two to it,' Patrick said pushing his chair aside.

'What?' I gasped, hardly able to believe what I was hearing.

'I'll be off, old thing. We'll sort this lot out tomorrow. Goodbye, my sweet.'

He stooped and kissed Sarah's hand, then strode off towards the door.

'And don't let that bunch of toss-pots give you any trouble,' he called as he vanished into the night.

The reaction to his final comment was extreme: one of the waiters tore the cloth from the table spilling chequebook, wallet and pen onto the floor. As I stooped to pick them up I was pushed and trodden on. The situation had most definitely got out of hand.

I stood up and caught the manager by the collar.

'Tell these monkeys to back off,' I said, 'or no cheques.'

He said something in Chinese and the men slowly backed away from our table and grouped behind him.

Releasing my hold on the manager, I sat down again, completed the cheques and set them down with my banker's card on the table. Without saying a word the manager noted down the number on the back of both cheques then threw the card on the floor. This was really too much.

'Pick it up!' I thundered.

Seven pairs of black, gimlet eyes stared at me in silence.

'Pick it up!' I repeated, not sure what to do if he didn't.

Fortunately, he snapped an incomprehensible order to one of the waiters who picked up the card and handed it to me.

Sarah had remained quiet and calm throughout. As I put my chequebook and pen back in my pocket, she rose and we began to walk, slowly, towards the door.

Suddenly all hell broke loose again. Both manager and waiters began to push and jostle us, shouting and screaming all the way. Then, out of the corner of my eye I saw what I thought was the glint of steel. Sarah saw it too.

'Just hold on!' she shouted, turning on the mob. 'That is enough! I'm a solicitor and if you don't permit us to leave this establishment without further let or hindrance, I'll make sure the lot of you are up in front of the local magistrate first thing tomorrow. Now back off!'

There was an electric moment of hesitation then the manager muttered something and the waiters melted back into the restaurant.

'Well, that was a very impressive performance,' I said, as we walked back, arm in arm, to my car. 'I'd no idea you were so well connected in magistrates' courts.'

'I've never actually set foot in one in my life,' she laughed, 'but fortunately that lot didn't know it. Anyway, it was more exciting than the average Chinese nosh.'

'Yes,' I agreed. 'Although it's probably par for the course, when you dine with Patrick, to end up paying for the meal and having your throat cut as well.'

'And that would be a pity, especially since you're about to be invited to become a director of Hampson's.'

'Oh, that hasn't happened yet,' I said. 'You heard what Patrick said about Morrison-Whyte. I think he only mentioned it to buy my silence over this clock business.'

'And will you keep mum?'

'I think so. It's not really anything to do with me. Two directors are fully in the picture, and it would seem that the client's quite happy, but . . .'

'But what?' Sarah asked, squeezing my hand gently.

'But I'm still uncomfortable about it. Something just doesn't feel right – not right at all.'

Chapter 20

'Somebody's in a hurry,' Charlotte said as she got up to answer the frantically buzzing entryphone. 'Yes . . . hello . . . okay, hold on.'

She pressed the button to open our office door below.

'It's Fatty Faulkner,' she said, 'and he appears to be in some distress.'

'Probably feels guilty about not having repaid the seventy-two pounds he owes me,' I said.

'Not forgetting the twenty-four pence,' added Charlotte.

Patrick Faulkner's continued non-payment of his restaurant bill debt had become a standing, if not very good, office joke. Three and a half weeks had passed since the débâcle at the Tao Tao and Patrick continued to be evasive about clearing his account.

Up until now he had been going to great lengths to avoid me, so this sudden and unheralded visit to the Valuations Office amounted to a radical change of tactics on his part.

Charlotte and I sat and listened as he thundered up the stairs. A moment later he burst into the office. Red in the face and perspiring more than usual, his hair was windblown, his shirt was open at the neck while his tie hung halfway down his chest. The exertion involved in ascending our stairs had also left him seriously short of breath. This was a Patrick Faulkner I'd not seen before. This was indeed a Patrick Faulkner in some distress.

260

'Thank God you're in, Richard,' he blurted, in between breathless gasps. 'I'm in trouble . . . big trouble . . . you've got to help me.'

'How much did you want to borrow?' Charlotte asked unsympathetically.

Patrick appeared not to hear her.

'What I'm going to tell you now . . . must not get outside these four walls . . .' he said, looking urgently first at me then at Charlotte. 'Do you understand?' he asked. 'Do you both understand?'

'I think you'd better sit down, Patrick,' I said. 'You don't look too good.'

He nodded and dropped into the chair on the other side of my desk. For a moment he sat there with his head in his hands, then he looked up, seemingly more composed.

'Now, whatever has happened?' I asked.

'It's a disaster,' he began. 'A complete bloody disaster. I just don't know what I'm going to do, Richard. I don't know what to do.'

Charlotte and I said nothing. After a long pause, Patrick continued.

'It's that bloody clock – the Charles Gretton,' he said. 'I think it's done for me at Hampson's, Richard.'

'But how, Patrick?' I asked.

'That pair that brought it in – they absolutely screwed me. And I walked straight into it, all starry-eyed.'

'But, what exactly's happened?' I asked.

'I sent the clock off to my restorer the day after it arrived here.'

'Yes,' I said.

'He did his usual first-class job on it, and had it ready for collection the middle of last week.' Patrick stopped, took out his handkerchief and wiped his palms. 'We were quite busy,' he continued, 'so I arranged to collect it at the end of this week, and he asked if he could display it in his window until then. I had no objection so that's what he did.'

'Don't say it was stolen from his shop,' Charlotte said.

'Oh, if only it had been,' Patrick replied, shaking his head. 'If only it had been.'

'So what did happen?' I asked.

'This morning, about two hours ago, a girl went into the shop and asked my restorer where he'd got the clock from. My chap explained it wasn't his and that it belonged to a client. She then said she was ninety per cent certain it had in fact been stolen from her father's house in Berkshire a month ago.'

'Oh, hell!' I said.

'You can imagine my reaction was a little stronger than that,' Patrick said. 'Anyway, she telephoned Daddy at his city office, he whizzed over to the restorer's, positively identified the bloody clock – produced photographs and everything – and duly summoned the Met.'

'What are you going to do?' Charlotte asked.

'Well, one thing's for certain: I've got to tell Bob Derby what's happened before he hears it from the boys in blue. If he gets it from them first I'm dead. But, then, I may be dead anyway. I have a terrible feeling this may be the last straw as far as he's concerned.'

He leaned forward, his elbows on his knees, and stared at the floor.

'What do you want me to do?' I asked.

'Just don't mention that Harry Sutton was lined up for a share in the profits,' he replied. 'Derby would read all sorts of things into it.'

'All right,' I agreed. 'As far as I'm concerned, I know nothing about that angle.'

'Good man,' he said, rising to his feet. 'Right, I'm off to see the Chairman. I may not be a director of Hampson's when you next see me.'

'Good luck, anyway,' I said. Then I thought of something else. 'Patrick . . .'

'Yes,' he said, turning in the doorway.

'. . . what about Charles Morrison-Whyte?'

'What about him?'

'Well, he sanctioned your three thousand advance. What's he going to say?'

'Oh, you know Charles,' Patrick said. 'First in, first out. If asked, he'll simply claim he was unaware the advance was for me personally and that he'd no idea I'd bought the clock.'

'What a pal!' Charlotte observed.

'We're both grown-ups,' Patrick replied, shrugging his shoulders. 'He knows I'd do the same for him.'

It was a little over an hour later that the internal telephone rang. Charlotte answered it.

'Valuations Office . . . yes, Bob . . . I'll tell him . . . goodbye.'

'I take it that was the summons to the Chairman's office,' I said.

'It was,' Charlotte confirmed. 'Right away if you please.'

'Well, wish me luck,' I said, crossing myself.

Charlotte grinned.

'Just don't let him make you head of Furniture and Clocks – I'd miss you.'

Robert Derby was standing behind his desk looking out of the window onto Vanbrugh Street when I arrived in his office.

'Hello, Richard,' he said, turning round with a smile. 'Take a seat. You've heard about this cock-up with the longcase clock no doubt.'

'It has been brought to my attention' I replied, risking a grin.

The Chairman laughed.

'Yes, I have no doubt Patrick's been knitting his alibi together this morning. I must say, he didn't get much support from Charles. And Harry Sutton was apparently innocent as a new-born babe.'

'You know all about it, then.'

'Yes, Patrick was a gibbering wreck within five minutes

so he spilled the lot anyway. I ask you – what a bloody fool: he tells somebody, who doesn't give her name and address, that her clock's worth seven thousand. Then when he offers her three for it, and she accepts, it doesn't even cross his mind that it might be hot. The problem with Patrick is that he's both greedy *and* lazy. We can but hope that this has taught him a lesson.'

'You're not . . . not . . . er . . .'

'Asking for his resignation? No, I'm not doing that, Richard,' he laughed again. 'Although I know that's what he expected, and probably what I should have done. However, I'm giving him another chance.'

'Good.'

'What I have told him – and I wanted you to hear this from me since I know Patrick's version will vary from the original – is that this is his last chance. If it hits the press, he's on his own. If the police prosecute, he's out. He has to repay the three thousand in full. He has to pay the restoration bill personally. And I, and nobody but I, will sanction all further advances to furniture department clients.'

'Is there any chance that the police will prosecute?' I asked.

'No,' he said. 'I've already spoken to them and they say not. Now are you going anywhere near the Furniture Department in the next few minutes?'

'I was intending to pop in there, yes.'

'Good, drop that on Patrick's desk, please, and inform him we are not a registered charity.'

I picked up the sheaf of papers he pushed across the desk towards me.

'Expenses claim?' I enquired.

He nodded.

'There's a Chinese meal there, for Patrick and two supposed overseas clients, which comes to eighty pounds with the service charge,' he said, shaking his head. 'It would have been cheaper if he'd flown them to Hong

Kong. If he thinks we're standing that he can forget it.'

'Quite right,' I said, and slipped quietly from the room.

Patrick was sitting at his desk, looking morose when I bowled into his office, but he managed to conjure up quite a convincing smile.

'How did it go?' I asked.

'What? Oh, with Derby you mean. Fine, fine. I just laid my cards on the table and said if he didn't like it, he'd better get himself a new Director of Furniture.'

'And you had no trouble with him?'

'No – I'm used to dealing with Bob. His bark's a lot worse than his bite.'

'Good,' I said, 'I'm so glad.'

I turned to leave, then stopped.

'Oh, by the way, Patrick,' I said, 'is there any chance of a cheque for that Chinese meal?'

'I'd be happy to oblige, old boy,' he said, leaning back in his chair. 'Just let me have the bill sometime.'

'I did let you have the bill, Patrick – the morning after.'

'Did you really?' he said looking surprised. 'I must have mislaid it somewhere. I'll try to remember to look it out, old thing.'

'No need, Patrick. I've got it here,' I said, producing his rejected expenses claim with a flourish. 'It somehow got included in your last month's expenses – including the service charge I didn't pay, I see.'

For a split second he looked perturbed, then the old silky-smooth veneer was back in place.

'So that's what happened to it,' he said. 'My girl must have included it accidentally . . . but, what are you doing with *my* expenses claim, Richard?'

'Oh, Bob Derby just asked me to drop it in to you, and to tell you that Hampson's isn't a registered charity. I'm not sure what he meant.'

'Nor me, old thing. Nor me.'

Chapter 21

'Are you sure it's not hay-fever?' Sarah asked.

'I'm positive id's nod hay-feber . . . a-shoo! . . . I've neber suffered from hay-feber . . . a-shoo! . . . and I'm nod suffering from id now . . . a-shoo! . . .'

'Well, you're certainly suffering from something,' she said.

'Id's de smoke . . . a-shoo! . . . in here,' I struggled on, pointing to the dense pall of cigarette smoke which invariably hung at head height in the bar of the Marlborough Arms, the pub at the end of Vanbrugh street. 'Id's de smoke . . . a-shoo! . . . I'm allergic to.'

'But it doesn't usually take you this badly.'

'A-shoo!'

It did sometimes seem that my allergy was getting worse, and yet I could often go for weeks without an attack. Something had obviously set it off.

'Led's ged oudside,' I sniffed, dabbing at my streaming nose with my very damp handkerchief. 'I'll be bedder owd der.'

'Can't wait,' Sarah replied. 'You know I hate pubs anyway.'

'I know . . . a-shoo! . . . id's just dad id's a convenient place to meed . . . a-shoo!'

The cool air of the early evening met us as we stepped out onto the pavement. All the tables and chairs were aready taken so we moved a few yards down the street and leaned against the railings of the private house next door to the Marlborough. A gentle breeze, the first of the day, stirred the empty crisp packets on the pub tables.

'Ah, dad's bedder,' I said, still sniffing. 'All I needed was a liddle air.'

'I'm sure some of it must be psychosomatic, you know,' Sarah said, sipping at her white wine and soda. 'After all, all we've done is exchange the cigarette smoke in there for the carbon monoxide out here, and suddenly you're better . . . well, almost, anyway.'

'Id's god nudding to do wid psychology,' I insisted. 'Id's just dad wretched cigared smoke in der.'

'Then why don't you sneeze and get all adenoidal *every time* you set foot in a pub?'

'Because somedimes, like today, id's worse dan odders.'

One more sniff and suddenly I could breathe again.

'Ah, that's better,' I said.

'So what made it worse today?'

'The fans in the marquee this afternoon, I think . . . hold on, how many times did I sneeze?'

'I don't know,' Sarah said. 'I can't say I was actually counting.'

'I think it was only eleven.'

'So?'

'So I always sneeze a dozen times. You know that.'

'Yes, and that really is psychosomatic,' she said.

'I don't care what it is – I always sneeze twelve times,' I insisted. 'Mind you, perhaps I did. Perhaps I just lost count.'

'Perhaps you did, but what's all this about fans in the marquee this afternoon – what fans?'

'Patrick got hold of some electric fans to move the air around,' I replied. 'Unfortunately they moved the dust around quite efficiently as well.'

It had been quite a good idea really. The temperature

inside the marquee had risen steadily over each of the two viewing days as the sun had burned down on the canvas, so it was a sensible move to get some sort of air conditioning system for the actual sale day. In the end, however, the red faces in the tent had not been due to the ambient temperature.

The marquee had been set up in the garden of a pleasant house not far from Windsor. The contents were not particularly spectacular but were interesting enough to be just viable as a sale on the premises. We reckoned the increased prices which are always paid at house sales would more than compensate for the additional costs incurred.

We were right. The sale had ticked along nicely with some very respectable prices being paid for what was on offer. By the time I reached the penultimate lot, Patrick Faulkner, installed in his usual place next to the rostrum, was looking very satisfied with himself.

I covered the microphone with one hand and leant over to speak to him.

'I don't have any reserve on this lot,' I said.

The piece concerned was, in my opinion, the nicest thing in the house. It was a little Regency rosewood bookcase, with four open shelves above a cupboard. It only stood about our feet high, but it was exquisitely inlaid. Not with other woods, but as was the fashion during part of the Regency era, with brass. The metal had been cut into thin strips, scrolls and complex arabesques. It was some of the finest craftsmanship I had ever seen. That little bookcase was worthy of a home in the Brighton pavilion. and I knew Patrick had high hopes for it.

'No, it's going without reserve, old thing,' he whispered, 'but I'm holding a fistful of bids on it and I still think it'll be bought by somebody out there.' He pointed to the crowd in front of me in the marquee.

I glanced round briefly to look at the lot as the

porters lifted it onto the showing table.

'How much do you reckon?' I asked, looking down at Patrick again.

'Oh, five to seven thou . . .'

He didn't finish the sentence. Instead his face froze, mouth open, eyes goggling. I had no idea what had paralysed him in that way but whatever it was was clearly in the vicinity of the showing table. I decided I did not want to see it.

As I studied Patrick's features, his expression changed from one of pure horror to one of deep, agonising pain. For a split second he looked as though he might just burst into tears. He threw out his arms in a futile flailing gesture, then he too turned away, unable to watch any more.

It was not a particularly loud crash. It was more of an abrupt 'crump' noise. As 'crumps' went, however, it sounded like an expensive one. Taking my courage in both hands, I swivelled round in the rostrum and looked towards the showing table away on my left.

The two young porters who had lifted up the bookcase to display it were still standing on either side of the table clutching hold of the cupboard section. Unfortunately, there was no sign of the delicate, fragile, beautifully inlaid open shelves which should have been sitting on top of it. Following their dumb-struck gaze I half stood up and, leaning forward, peered over the rostrum at the floor in front of the table. There, face down on the hard, dry ground was the mangled corpse of the missing piece of the bookcase. Unknown to anybody, including the owner, the top of the bookcase had never been screwed to the cupboard base. The whole thing had been moved from room to room, tipped upside down, displayed, viewed and generally mauled. But it had held together without demur. It had waited until the actual moment of sale before its top had decided to part company with its bottom.

John Adams, the head porter, rushed forward to raise the wreckage from the floor gently. With the help of one of his colleagues, the shattered remains were temporarily laid to rest on the showing table. Looking at it, one thing was certain: it wasn't going to find a buyer that afternoon.

'I'm afraid, ladies and gentlemen,' I began, 'that for obvious reasons . . .'

There was a loud 'boing!' as a piece of brass inlay sprang out of the woodwork and vibrated noisily in the otherwise silent tent. It made a sound curiously like that of a Jew's Harp.

'. . . for obvious reasons,' I continued, 'I have no choice but to . . .'

'Twang!' Another scroll of brasswork twisted free of the rosewood veneer and noisily reverberated around the marquee.

'. . . but to withdraw this . . .'

'Boing! . . . Twang! . . . Twang. . .!'

'. . . lot.'

'. . . Twang!'

'So you think it was dust from the marquee that really brought on that sneezing fit, then,' Sarah said.

'Probably, or perhaps I'm allergic to Regency bookcase fragments – I don't know. I just wish I could remember whether I've sneezed eleven or twelve times.'

'Well, I'm absolutely convinced it's ninety per cent psychosomatic,' she insisted. 'What you need to do is take your mind off it. Have you heard any more about this impending directorship?'

'Shhh!' I said. 'Walls have ears around here.'

'That's as may be, but have your ears heard any more about it?'

'Not a word. You know as much as I do. The only time it's been mentioned to me was by Patrick Faulkner at the Tao Tao.'

'Why don't you ask *him* what's happening?'

'After this afternoon's débâcle I don't think I'd find him hugely receptive.'

'What about Philip?' she asked. 'Has he heard anything about it?'

'I shouldn't think so.'

'Well, haven't you asked him?'

'No – you know Faulkner told me it was all hush-hush.'

'Yes, but Philip and you are friends. Surely it wouldn't hurt just to ask him if he's heard any rumours.'

'If he had, he would have told me.'

'Not necessarily. You haven't told him.'

'I know but that's different.'

'No, it's not,' Sarah protested. 'You've probably both been fed the same rumour and neither of you is telling the other.'

'That's as may be. As far as I'm concerned, I was told to keep it confidential and that's what I'm doing.'

'But . . .'

'Anyway, there's a Board Meeting next week and if I don't hear anything following that, I'll speak to Patrick and find out what's going on.'

'How's your nose?' she enquired suddenly.

'My nose? Fine. Why?'

'There you are – ninety per cent psychosomatic. Once you take your mind off it you feel better – oh, look, here comes Philip now.'

He was easing his way through the crowd which was now spilling off the pavement into the road. He looked tired and hot. His tie was undone, his jacket was thrown over his shoulder and his shirt sleeves were rolled up.

'Hello, you two,' he said. 'Whose round is it?'

'Mine,' I volunteered. 'What are you having?'

'A pint of the coldest lager you can get, please.'

'Okay,' I said, and set off for the bar.

It was the better part of ten minutes before I re-emerged into the evening air.

'What happened?' Philip asked, reaching for the long-awaited pint. 'Did they have to send to Denmark for it?'

'No,' I replied. 'Der's quite a crowd in der now, and de barrel wend off so dey had do change id.'

He looked at me strangely.

'Here,' he said, 'you sound pretty blocked up all of a sudden. Are you all right?'

'Yes – id's jus' de smoke in der,' I explained.

It was precisely that moment that I knew I had only sneezed eleven times. There was no doubt about it, because once I'd sneezed twelve times I could guarantee I would not sneeze again that day. And suddenly I knew I was about to sneeze – at least once more.

Unable to get to my handkerchief in time I hurriedly turned away from Sarah and Philip.

'A-SHOO!'

'Ah, that's better,' I said, mopping up after the event, and putting my handkerchief back in my pocket. 'I just knew I hadn't . . .'

The expression on the faces of Sarah and Philip stopped me. A strong feeling of déjà vu swept over me. I had definitely been there before, and it had not been many hours earlier. They both looked now as Patrick Faulkner had looked earlier in the day. Some appalling disaster had occurred to which I was not yet privy, and just like the incident with the Regency bookcase, half of me would have been quite happy leaving it that way.

Their eyes were focused on some point somewhere behind me. I knew I would eventually *have* to turn and look but I saw no reason for not putting it off as long as I could. In the event, that was not to be very long at all.

'Oh! How disgusting!!'

The voice was that of an upper-class male, but rather high pitched, almost strangulated.

The 'how' was pronounced 'hi', and the 'disgusting' as if the first 's' were a 'z'. Yes, it was a terribly upper-crust

272

voice but its owner sounded emotionally disturbed.

Sarah's and Philip's eyes opened even wider in their horror. Still I stared at them. I just did not want to look round.

'Hi dizgusting!' the voice repeated, rising, improbably, another octave.

I turned and looked.

Standing about ten yards behind me were a couple. She was probably in her late teens and very pretty. He was older, perhaps mid-thirties, and was wearing a double-breasted blazer with a brightly coloured hand-kerchief in the breast pocket. She was looking at him in the same way Sarah and Philip had been looking over my shoulder. He simply looked shocked – as though he'd been mugged, or shot, or something.

At first glance I could see nothing amiss. Then I saw it – smack in the middle of his forehead. It was a huge lump of gunk. As I looked at it in disbelief it started slowly, almost imperceptibly, to slide down towards the brdge of his nose.

I turned back to Sarah and Philip for some reassurance that my sneeze and the unspeakable mess on the man's forehead were in no way linked. I was wasting my time. They, along with several other of the people gathered nearby, had just collapsed into crazed laughter.

'I . . . I . . .' I stuttered, turning back to my victim. 'I'm *terribly* sorry.'

He started to change colour as rage began to supersede shock.

'I really am *terribly* sorry,' I repeated.

What more could I say? What on earth could I do? I didn't know the etiquette of the situation. Should I offer to remove the offending material? If he accepted my offer, should I do it with my handkerchief or should I just whisk out his silk job from his top pocket and clean him up with that? Or, should I just hit him before he hit me?

Fortunately the matter was taken out of my hands by his companion. Producing a tissue she wiped his forehead, looked serious for a moment, then, just like most of the other spectators, she burst out laughing. As she clung to the lapels of his blazer, almost unable to stand, even he managed a sort of twisted grin.

'I've never been so embarrassed in my life,' I told Sarah as we drove off. 'I thought he was even going to try to hit me at one stage.'

'How could he? He couldn't get near you. You were lethal at anything up to twenty yards.'

'Ha, ha,' I said. 'And thank you so much for your support.'

'It wasn't my fault. I was laughing so much I could hardly breathe. Never mind, as far as I'm concerned, it's definitely proved one thing.'

'What's that?'

'You really are allergic.'

Chapter 22

Philip Lawrence and I stood at the open door of the tent looking out on the sodden showground. It had now been raining for almost seventy-two hours and the whole place was awash.

Hastily laid duckboards floated on the sea of mud in the main walkways, and spurs from these treacherously slippery paths led off into the more important, official show marquees. No such aids were provided for those with a mind to visit the ordinary commercial exhibitor. Anybody wishing to get to these tents or stands had, in the majority of cases, to wade across a six-foot strip of oozing mire. Nor was the sludge passive: it was greedy. It gripped hold of wellingtons, removed sensible shoes and devoured children's footwear like some great insatiable beast. It was very clear that its close proximity to the entrance to Hampson's tent was not conducive to doing business.

'How much longer have we got?' Philip asked.

'About fifteen minutes less than the last time you asked,' I replied.

'How long is that?'

'It's a quarter to four now,' I said, looking at my watch, 'and we can pack up and go home at five o'clock on the dot.'

'God! Another hour and a quarter of this,' he moaned. Then he stretched, yawned, and ambled over to one of the rather comfortable garden chairs arranged around the table in the centre of the tent. 'This is so *boring!*' he said, slumping into the chair.

'I know,' I said, joining him at the table, 'I've got so much going on back at the office at the moment.'

'I'm the same,' he sympathised. 'The catalogue for next month's good silver sale should go to press on Monday.'

'Not going to make it?'

'Not unless I catalogue a hundred and fifty lots before lunch it won't.'

We sat in silence for a few minutes.

'Whose idea was this anyway?' he asked eventually. 'Yours or Bob Derbys?'

'I think the official line is we're jointly responsible,' I replied, flicking through one of our publicity handouts.

'Then you should both be shot.'

'That's a bit harsh,' I protested. 'It would have been a different matter if the weather had been good.'

'I'm not so sure. People visiting County Shows don't want to carry baskets full of antiques around with them.'

'No, I know they don't, but it's easy enough for them to bring photographs.'

'So then we end up giving wildly inaccurate valuations on the strength of which they take their stuff along to their local auctioneer and sell it there. All we're doing is touting for business on behalf of our competitors.'

I didn't reply. It was an argument we'd had before, and I was beginning to believe Philip was right. It was true that most of the people who did bring items in for valuation took them away again. That, of course, was their prerogative but there was the nagging doubt that if they decided a few days later to sell them, then it was probably the local auctioneer who would benefit, not Hampson's.

'A free information service, that's all we are,' Philip concluded with a disgruntled sniff.

'Well, here's a chance,' I said, rising to my feet as a large lady, encased in a semi-transparent, green plastic raincoat and matching hat began the uncertain journey from the duckboards to the entrance of our tent. She was carrying two bulging carrier bags.

'It's bound to be for you,' Philip said. 'She's not a silver person. She's a Staffordshire pottery person.'

'I'll bet you a pint it's silver,' I said, as I set out to rescue her from the morass.

'You're on – and I can already taste it.'

Wellington boots had become our usual footwear over the three day show so I had no trouble in reaching the woman. Relieving her of one of the bags, I took her by the arm and led her, high stepping through the sludge, to the gently oozing coconut matting inside our tent.

'Now Madam, how can we help you?' I asked once I had escorted the dripping figure to the table.

'I've got some silver for you to see,' she replied, as droplets of water ran off her rain-hat and down her nose, plummeting from there to the floor.

'Excellent!' I said. 'Mr Lawrence here will be only too pleased to help you.'

'Right,' she said, turning to Philip, 'an' d'you do china stuff as well? 'Cos I got some of that an' all.'

A slow smile crept across my colleague's formerly grim features.

'Ah, no, that will be Mr Harton's department,' he said, gesturing to me.

'Oh, right,' the woman said, delving down into the first bag. 'Well, all this stuff in here's china, so it'll be best to do that first.'

By any standard it was an awful collection. The majority of pieces were without any sale value at all, and there was no single piece worth more than five pounds. Eventually, however, the relentless unwrapping and re-wrapping of bits and pieces came to an end. We had finished the first carrier bag. The woman stood up, straightened her back for a moment, then sat down again.

'Everything in this bag's silver,' she announced, still peering out from below her plastic rain-hood.

With a deep and abiding sense of relief I gestured silently to my colleague who had been deep in the sports pages of the *Daily Telegraph*. He lowered the newspaper and regarded the lady with a cold stare. Then, tossing the paper aside, he got up and came to the table.

'Let's see what we've got here, shall we,' he murmured, giving the woman a synthetic smile.

The performance with the china was repeated with the silver, or to put it more accurately, the electro-plated nickel silver. Dozens of individually wrapped items were individually unwrapped, then individually wrapped up again.

Throughout Philip remained stone-faced, his voice flat and expressionless, as he recited the litany of values: 'Three to five pounds . . . no sale value . . . five pounds . . . no sale value . . . five pounds . . . no sale value . . . no sale value . . .'

I began to feel uncomfortable. I had never before seen Philip so patient with such a load of junk. It seemed inevitable that he would snap at some stage. He did, but not until the very last items to be pulled from the bag had been produced from their newspaper and stood on the table in all their glory. They were a perfectly ordinary, and perfectly horrible, pair of plated 'steeple' salt and pepper pots – the sort of thing you'll see on any table in any seaside hotel or boarding house.

Philip leant forward on the table, closed his eyes for a moment, then said: 'Very fine . . . early English . . . thirty to forty thousand.'

Without any evident flicker of surprise the woman simply nodded and started to re-wrap the worthless pair of items in their newspaper.

'Er ... I said thirty to forty thousand,' Philip repeated, as nonplussed as I at her reaction.

'Yes,' she said, putting the little parcels back in her bag.

'Well ... I ... er ... wouldn't you want to sell them if they were worth that much?' he blurted.

'No,' she replied. 'Leastways, not without 'aving a word with me 'usband first.'

My colleague's mouth opened but he seemed to reconsider what he was going to say.

'Madam,' he began, 'I'm terribly sorry. What I said was quite wrong. I'm afraid those items are really of no value at all. Please accept my apologies. I don't know what came over me.'

Apparently as unmoved by Philip's grovelling apology as she was by his bogus valuation, the woman simply nodded and set off for the door. I escorted her out to the relative safety of the slimy duckboards.

'That was appalling,' I said, when I returned to the tent. 'You could have given the poor old dear a heart attack.'

'I know, I know,' Philip confessed. 'I must be cracking up – it's the sort of thing I'd expect from Bernard Thornton. It's time I got out of this business, Richard. I think it's beginning to get to me.'

'What's beginning to get to you?' asked a voice behind us.

We both stood rock still for a moment frantically trying to remember if we had just said anything the Chairman of Hampson's might have found offensive. My mind was a blank.

'Hello, Bob,' I said. 'What are you doing here? We weren't expecting you.'

'No,' he said, shaking the water from his Macintosh. 'I was a few miles up the road so I thought I'd just pop in and see how you two chaps were getting on.'

'Oh, we're just fine – enjoying every nail-biting

'minute of it,' Philip said, as well aware as I that Bob Derby's 'surprise' visit had probably been planned for weeks.

'You sound a touch disenchanted, Philip. What's the problem?'

'Well, people aren't really that keen on bringing their family heirlooms to a County Show, Bob. That's what the problem is,' Philip explained.

'What? Haven't you had much brought in, then?' he said, throwing his coat over a chair.

'Having two feet of mud outside hasn't helped,' I pointed out.

'I know. I had to buy these,' the Chairman replied, pointing down to a pair of near pristine green wellies. 'I got them from a stand over there. Otherwise I would have ruined a perfectly good pair of brogues.'

As we stood looking out at the never ending deluge, a small, bald man staggered towards the tent, his knees buckling under the weight of the large box he was carrying.

'Is this Hampson's tent?' he enquired, breathlessly.

'Yes, let me help you with that,' Bob answered, stepping forward to take the box.

'Careful, careful,' the little man warned. 'It'll fall straight through the bottom. I've only got it in the box to keep it dry.'

Whatever it was, from the expression on Bob Derby's face when he took hold of it, it clearly weighed a great deal. He and the man set it down on the creaking table.

'Oh, this is very nice,' the Chairman said as he stripped away the cardboard to reveal a large, Japanese, bronze tiger. It was over two feet long and exceptionally good quality.

'It's Meiji period – late nineteenth century,' he went on. 'I'm not sure about the signature but we can research that later. How long have you owned it?'

'It was my father's,' replied the man, polishing his

rain-spotted glasses. 'He travelled a great deal in the East.'

'Had you any idea what it's worth?' Bob asked.

'None.'

'Well . . . I would expect it to make between fifteen hundred and two thousand were it to be offered in our Belgravia salerooms.'

'Goodness me!' the little man said, very nearly dropping his spectacles in his surprise. 'I had no idea – I was expecting a few hundred.'

'Would you like us to offer it for you?' Bob continued, smiling reassuringly.

'Well . . . er . . . yes . . . yes, I think I would.'

'Fine, I'll just take a note of your name and address . . .'

Relieved of his weighty burden, the small bald figure moved quite nimbly through the swamp on his way back to the boardwalk. In our tent, Bob Derby, Philip and I sat staring at the £2,000 bronze.

'Now, what were you two moaning about?' Bob asked, smiling in a way which I for one found particularly annoying. 'Ah, yes – people don't bring family heirlooms to County Shows . . .'

'All right, all right!' Philip said. 'But if you'd been sitting here for the past two days . . .'

'Yes, yes, I know,' the Chairman interrupted. 'Life can be so unfair, can't it. Never mind.' He drew two envelopes from the inside pocket of his jacket and handed us one each. 'Perhaps this will cheer you up.'

'What is it?' I asked. 'Recall to Belgravia?'

'Very droll,' he replied, shaking his raincoat prior to putting it on again. 'Actually, they're invitations for you both to join the Hampson's board – no, don't say anything now. Read them; think about them over what's left of the weekend, and give me your decisions on Monday.'

He stepped out into the rain, turned and looked back into the tent.

'And by the way,' he said. 'I hope you both decide to accept.'

By two minutes past five, Philip Lawrence, the tiger and I were all in the Guinness tent.

'Well, that was out of the blue,' Philip said.

'What, the tiger or the directorship?'

'The directorship of course. It was always a foregone conclusion that somebody would bring in something good within thirty seconds of Robert's arrival.'

'I suppose you're right,' I replied. 'Had you had any warning about the directorship being in the offing?'

'None . . . well, that is . . . oh hell! I can't keep this up – Patrick Faulkner told me about it a month ago and swore me to secrecy, otherwise I would have told you.'

'Don't worry – he did the same to me,' I grinned. 'Are you going to accept?'

'Well, it's against all my principles to take life too seriously . . . but . . . yes, I think so. What about you?'

'Oh, I think so,' I said, patting the snarling tiger on the head. 'At least, then I'll be in a position to send somebody else to attend the County Shows.'

2/2021